IDEOLOGICAL PERSPECTIVES ON CANADA

T H I R D   E D I T I O N

McGraw-Hill Ryerson Series in Canadian Sociology
General Editor – Lorne Tepperman

SOCIAL MOBILITY IN CANADA
Lorne Tepperman

UNDERSTANDING DATA
B.H. Erickson & T.A. Nosanchuk

THE NEW URBAN POOR
S.D. Clark

SOCIOLOGICAL THEORIES OF EDUCATION
Raymond Murphy with the collaboration of Ann Denis

DEMOGRAPHIC BASES OF CANADIAN SOCIETY, 2/e
Warren Kalback & Wayne McVey

THE SURVIVAL OF ETHNIC GROUPS
Jeffrey G. Reitz

THE URBAN KALEIDOSCOPE: Canadian Perspectives
Leslie W. Kennedy

RELIGION: Classic Sociological Approaches
Roger O'Toole

THE DISREPUTABLE PLEASURES, 2/e
John Hagan

THE CANADIAN CLASS STRUCTURE, 3/e
Dennis Forcese

WOMEN, THE FAMILY AND THE ECONOMY, 2/e
S.J. Wilson

IDEOLOGICAL PERSPECTIVES ON CANADA, 3/e
M. Patricia Marchak

Forthcoming
THE SOCIOLOGY OF MASS COMMUNICATIONS IN CANADA
Arthur Siegel

DEVIANCE: Tolerable Differences
Robert Stebbins

AGING IN CANADIAN SOCIETY
Maureen Baker

IDEOLOGICAL PERSPECTIVES ON CANADA
T H I R D   E D I T I O N

M. PATRICIA MARCHAK
University of British Columbia

McGRAW-HILL RYERSON LIMITED
Toronto Montreal New York Auckland Bogotá Caracas Cairo
Hamburg Lisbon London Madrid Mexico Milan New Delhi Panama
Paris San Juan São Paulo Singapore Sydney Tokyo

This much revised third edition is dedicated to the Canadian Sociology
and Anthropology Association.

IDEOLOGICAL PERSPECTIVES ON CANADA
T H I R D E D I T I O N

ISBN 0-07-549505-8

1 2 3 4 5 6 7 8 9 10 W 7 6 5 4 3 2 1 0 9 8

Printed and bound in Canada

Care has been taken to trace ownership of copyright material contained
in this text. The publishers will gladly take any information that will
enable them to rectify any reference or credit in subsequent editions.

CANADIAN CATALOGUING IN PUBLICATION DATA

Marchak, M. Patricia, date –
   Ideological perspectives on Canada

(McGraw-Hill Ryerson series in Canadian sociology)
3rd ed.
Bibliography: p.
Includes index.
ISBN 0-07-549505-8

1. Ideology.   2. Canada - Social conditions.
3. Canada - Economic conditions - 1945-
I. Title.   II. Series.

HN103.5.M37 1987   320.5'0971   C87-093948-3

CONTENTS

List of Figures

List of Tables

INTRODUCTION

1

The first edition of this book in 1975 was about two versions of the Canadian reality. One describes Canada as a liberal democracy, governed by representatives elected by a majority of adult citizens. The society in this view is maintained by a stable and self-sufficient free-enterprise economy, staffed by reasonably happy and affluent workers. The second describes Canada as a society ruled by an hereditary oligarchy and multinational imperialist corporations, maintained by a large and increasingly impoverished working class. Though these two versions differ fundamentally in their definition of the social structure, they are not greatly dissimilar in their values. Both assume that equality amongst citizens is a rational and just arrangement for a society; that personal freedom should be maintained and cherished; that race, colour, sex, and other conditions of birth should not determine a person's opportunities or status in life. Both value rule by law. Where they differ is in their interpretation of how well these values are achieved by a capitalist system. Following Canadian convention, these two were labelled "liberalism" and "socialism."

Since the first edition was published, the economic outlook has become somewhat less cheerful. The oil-based economy underwent its first serious challenge shortly before the book's publication, and by the turn of the decade even the optimists were suggesting that Canada, along with the United States and Europe, might be entering a prolonged depression. Depressions, as we learned in the 1930s, have a way of altering people's perspectives on society. During that decade, the CCF was born and a social democratic party became a permanent element in Canadian politics. So, too, were Fascist and right-wing parties born: the Arcand Fascist Movement, the Union Nationale in Quebec, and the Social Credit in Alberta. The Fascist movements declined with the onset of war, and the right-wing political parties transformed themselves into conventional liberal parties after the war. Yet in the 1980s, some of the themes which emerged a half-century ago have re-emerged under the label "the new right."

The "new right" has also been called "neo-conservatism" and "libertarianism" and "corporatism." The confusion is caused by the differing messages propounded by various groups associated with this ideology. Some messages are deceptively similar to an ideology that has not been widely held in Anglophone Canada for most of this century, nor in Francophone Canada since the 1930s, and which, in a less diluted form, went into eclipse with the Industrial Revolution. In these earlier forms it was labelled conservatism. It was an important (and possibly dominant) ideology in the feudal period, transported to Canada by a merchant class but here, as elsewhere, it underwent a mutation in association with American and British liberalism. Only in Quebec, upheld by the Catholic Church, did it experience an explicit and richly textured life before Quebec became fully industrialized. As its adherents died, the succeeding generations were too immersed in liberal understandings of the world to grieve for its passing.

Yet the contemporary themes reminiscent of earlier conservative ideology are now put forward together with libertarian views and with fundamentalist religious views. The total "package" has numerous contradictions. It differs radically from both liberalism and socialism in its values and definition of the society. It is opposed to equality, the protection of minorities, and civil rights other than the protection of person and property; it emphasizes the liberty of individuals and freedom from government restraint, and ignores the restraint on freedom of individuals who lack economic power to effectively express their preferences. We need to examine the separate threads of this total package. In the second edition of this book, in 1981, a tentative analysis was offered, but at that stage the "new right" was only in the wings. By 1986, it has become a major ideology in all the industrialized countries, and its adherents include members of governments in Canada. In this edition, we encounter it head on and examine the publications of new right advocates.

The emergence of the "new right" has challenged the previous ideologies. For both liberals and socialists, beliefs and values that had been accepted uncritically for years now came under review. Many people who had not questioned their beliefs for a long time began to rethink what they stood for. This rethinking has also affected intellectuals and their theories of society. This new edition addresses some of the challenges and responses at both the popular and the theoretical levels.

We are in a period of transition. We can describe where we have been, or at least we can interpret where we believe we have been, but we cannot know where we are going. We can identify some, but not all, of the changes that are now occurring, and which affect how we perceive our society. Two phrases have come into our language for these changes: "the new international order" and "the new economic reality." Part of the objective of this new edition of *Ideological Perspectives on Canada* is to examine the meanings of these two phrases, and to consider how the changing material world "out there" is related to our ideological understanding of it.

2

The third edition is organized in this way:

Chapter 1 provides an introduction to the study of ideologies at a general level: what they are, how they relate to social organization, and how contemporary ideologies differ from one another with reference to the values of individualism-collectivism and equality-elitism. It also provides an historical overview of the transition in ideological perspectives between the feudal and contemporary capitalist periods. The central core of this chapter has been completely revised since the last edition.

Chapters 2 and 3 are examinations of the conventional wisdom, the dominant ideology of liberalism. What are the tenets, the values, the explanations given with this ideology, and how well do they describe social conditions? The social conditions under review in Chapter 2 are indicated by statistical distributions on income, occupation, and education. The questions here are about the capacity of the ideology to explain why a quarter of the population lives below the poverty line; why less than 2% of the population receives nearly a third of the total income; why there are systematic differences in wealth and access to social positions between women and men, and between English-speaking and French-speaking Canadians; and why the native population is largely outside the labour force and the educational institutions. This chapter has been completely updated.

In Chapter 3, we examine the case for Canada as an independent nation state and its claims that its economy is characterized by free enterprise and competitive capitalism. Does the liberal framework explain the extent of foreign ownership and control of the economy, the degree of concentration of ownership, the existence and power of multinational corporations, the locus of decision-making, the financing of political parties, and the relationship between political and economic institutions? This chapter has been completely updated and shortened because some of its themes are now taken up in Chapters 7 and 9.

Chapter 4 considers the dying ideology of conservatism as it was expressed in Canada in the first half of the 19th century, as it was maintained in Quebec up to the 1950s, and as it erupted during the 1930s on the prairies. It also discusses corporatism and fascism in the context of the 1930s. This chapter is unchanged from the previous edition.

Chapter 5 provides a discussion of Marxist theory. This is given because the strongest counter-ideology to develop in Canada has a Marxist base, and this can best be understood if some elements of the theory are examined in connection with the more popular interpretations. It is also given because, as theory rather than as either popular ideology or prophecy, the Marxist interpretation has had a profound impact on sociological theory in Canada, especially since 1970. This is followed by a critique of Marxist theory, considerably expanded since the last edition, and a brief discussion of Weberian theory.

Chapter 6 describes and analyzes the development of socialist ideologies in Canada from the turn of the century through to the 1940s. As well, it provides a class analysis of contemporary Canadian society. The class analysis, now somewhat abbreviated, was located in the final chapter of the last edition.

Chapter 7 is concerned with the issue of nationalism and national sovereignty, viewed from both the liberal and socialist perspectives. This is provided first through an analysis of the "cold war" ideology between the late 1940s and the present time. The backdrop of American economic expansion during this period is introduced in this chapter. Nationalist movements in both Quebec and Anglophone Canada during the late 1960s and 1970s are discussed, and the chapter concludes with a brief discussion (added to this edition) of the Mackenzie Valley pipeline debate and the national energy policy.

Chapter 8, new to this edition, describes the new right, first in its libertarian form, then in its corporate form, and finally in its evangelical form. Why has this movement gained popularity during the 1980s? The chapter examines some changes in the international context within which American capitalism operates, and links the new right to these changes. However, the chapter ends with questions about the adequacy of an economic interpretation.

Chapter 9 begins with a discussion of global economic changes which affect North America, and some of the responses Canadians make to the impact of these changes. The concluding section examines the linkages between the ideologies current in Canada of the 1980s and these global changes. This chapter is also new to this edition.

The ideas in Chapters 8 and 9 were originally put forward for discussion in public lectures at the University of British Columbia, February, 1984; at Queen's and at Trent universities in January, 1985; and at Carleton University in July, 1986. I am indebted to members of these audiences for their kind reception and comments.

One small matter: the word "multinational" was in common usage in 1975. Since then, the term "transnational" has gained currency, and most of the global literature now refers to giant, global corporations as transnationals. There are some quibbles about whether the terms should have slightly different meanings, but for our purposes in this book they will be used interchangeably.

Colleagues who have used this text in classes since the mid-1970s will note changes through each edition beyond the updating of factual material. It is a rare opportunity for a scholar to revise a text of this sort because it obliges one to rethink some fundamental ideas from time to time. I have surprised myself by rediscovering thoughts I apparently had in 1975 which still strike me as valid, but of course the greater surprises have been in discovering thoughts I had then, or in 1981, about which I now harbour more doubts.

In simple terms, I seem to have begun with a reformist critique of liberalism in the 1970s, accompanied by a very tentative move toward the only alternative theoretical framework then available: neo-Marxism. By 1980, I was much more inclined to believe that the neo-Marxist paradigm addressed significant questions and provided if not true answers, then at least more helpful answers than other approaches seemed able to provide. By the mid-1980s, I have concluded that much of neo-Marxism has to be discarded before we can move forward to a more powerful explanation of social organization. This is not a regression: I remain convinced that the theories we had in 1970 were hopelessly inadequate; unfortunately, there is no comprehensive paradigm to replace both them and neo-Marxism. I am at this moment unpersuaded by the variety of approaches purporting to go beyond these earlier paradigms. To be frank with readers, I find them verbose and esoteric (as much of neo-Marxism has now become). This impasse need not be seen, however, as a dreadful event — on the contrary, many of us have now travelled this same route, and as we've gained insights and critical understandings we should now be well prepared to venture into new theoretical arenas.

I hope this third edition will provide another generation of sociologists with the chance to travel the same distance, but in much less time, so that they can venture into new areas and help their teachers understand Canada and the world just a bit better.

1 IDEOLOGY AND SOCIAL ORGANIZATION

There is something out there which could be called social reality. It does exist independent of our perceptions of it. Wealth and poverty are real conditions, as are power and the lack of it. There are known institutions such as corporate organizations. There are other means by which the population is organized but which are not formally recognized institutions, such as interest groups, classes, and ethnic groups. There are effects and consequences of social actions. The problem is that all of these realities exist and we know they exist, but human beings do not agree on the nature of their properties and their relationships to one another.

Social reality doesn't appear to us directly. It is revealed to our understanding through a screen of assumptions, beliefs, explanations, values, and unexamined knowledge. Together, these elements of the screen comprise an ideology, and the ideology directs our attention to some realities but not to others; interprets what our senses transmit to our brain; evaluates information not on its own merits but in terms of what is already accepted as truth. An ideology grows with us from childhood. Some parts of it are deliberately transmitted by parents, schools, the media, and the other institutions of our society. Other parts are more casually conveyed through example; the unspoken assumptions and attitudes of those around us. If a complete ideology is subjected to close scrutiny it can seldom meet the test of consistency. It provides explanations which are not logically connected to one another, permits the holding of values which are not congruent. Even so, it provides some dominant themes, some rules of thumb, some central beliefs that guide our actions and our perceptions in our habitual rounds of activity.

Some aspects of an ideology are about the political or public world of events. There is an explanation for the structure of power, for why the public world is ordered in such a fashion, whatever that fashion is perceived to be. Some elements are about a more private world, about what it is appropriate to hope for, how one ought to behave, what it is sensible to believe. These public and private worlds are connected, though many people might hold an ideology, the parts of which do not appear to them to be connected. This is in large part because much of what we think about our private motivations and hopes is perceived by us to be the result of entirely private

1

considerations. We are not inclined to think of ourselves as social-ized beings whose private ambitions are, to a large degree, condi-tioned by the public world in which we grow up and live out our lives.

The child asks the parent, "Why is that family poorer than us?" and receives an answer such as "Because their father is unem-ployed," or "Because sales clerks don't make as much money as sales managers." The accumulation of such responses provides a ready index to the organization of society in occupational terms, and with reference to age and sex roles. The child is informed by such responses that some occupations provide higher material re-wards than others, that an occupation is essential, and that fathers, not mothers, earn family incomes. The child is not provided with an explanation for the differential between sales clerks and sales managers, between the employed and the unemployed, between families in one income group and families in the other, but some children think to ask. There are, then, additional responses such as, "If you work hard at school, you can go to the top," or "Managers are more important than clerks," or "Well, if people don't work, they can't expect to get along in the world."

On the surface, all of these comments are true and they are seen to be true. They do reflect the realities people experience. If one does not get an education, one clearly cannot go to the top. If one doesn't work, one will indeed have problems. Managers generally do earn more than clerks and material wealth does confer status. Ideology is not typically a systematic analysis of society. It does not generally proceed far beyond the descriptive level. For most people, at most times, this is sufficient.

This is sufficient, as well, for societies. The dominant ideology— or conventional wisdom—provides the ready references, the rules of thumb, the directives to the eyes and ears of its members. It is the glue that holds institutions together, the medium that allows mem-bers of the population to interact, predict events, understand their roles, perform adequately, and perhaps above all, strive to achieve the kinds of goals most appropriate to the maintenance of any par-ticular social organization. That the ideology is useful, even socially necessary, does not make it true. There are members of the popu-lation who are dissatisfied with these superficial responses, and who seek explanations that better satisfy their sense of truth. They might ask, for example, why is education related to occupation? What is meant by "the top," and why should people want to go there? Why is status associated with material wealth? What does a sales manager do that makes him important, and to whom is his work important?

Why would anyone not work when the penalties for unemployment are so severe?

These kinds of questions lead to three different positions. One of these is the role of the social critic who points out the inconsistencies, the lack of congruence between empirical evidence and ideological statements. Such critics often seek reforms in the social organization, not so much because they challenge the ideology, as because they find discrepancies between it and their observations of social reality. Another is the role of the social analyst, who strives to understand why people believe what they believe, what relationship those beliefs have to empirical evidence, and how beliefs affect social action. These two, the critic and the analyst, strive to transcend their own ideological perspectives—an undertaking that can never be entirely successful.

There is a third position for those who ask difficult questions. It is the adoption of a counter-ideology: the placing of faith in an alternative version of society, an alternative set of beliefs, assumptions, values, and orientations.

1

Dominant and counter-ideologies grow out of the same social organization. They take the same economic arrangement, the same territorial boundaries, the same population as their units of analysis. But they posit different relationships between these units and different organizations within them. Although the two major ideologies of our time—which we will label liberalism and socialism—claim to explain society in historical and comparative perspective, they both originate in the period of the European Industrial Revolution, and both are unmistakably locked into industrial society as it emerged in Europe at that time.

Because they grow out of the same organization, they have much in common. They are the two sides of a single coin: one describing how the entire structure looks to one who accepts it and expects it to survive; the other, how it looks to one who rejects it and anticipates its demise. Elements of both versions are persuasive when one reviews the empirical data which they use as evidence, and neither is the whole truth.

Ideologies are explanations for the social organization, but they are, as well, evaluations of it. These evaluations tend to be circular: the social organization gives rise to certain beliefs about what is right, appropriate, and desirable, that is, to certain values. These values are then assumed, and the society judges itself by those values. The liberal democracy gave rise to positive evaluations of equality, individualism, material prosperity, and personal freedom. The society is then judged within that framework: does it allow for the realization of these values? The dominant ideology rests on an affirmative answer: yes, this society provides the necessary conditions for equality, material prosperity, and personal freedom. Where there are deficiencies, these are often not recognized. Where the deficiencies are recognized, they are explained not as symptoms of a system that fails but as aberrations or temporary problems in a system that succeeds.

Widespread acceptance of an ideology creates an incapacity for judgement of its truth. There is comfort in believing what so many others appear to believe, in accepting conventional wisdom. There is fear in doing otherwise. Sometimes there are, as well, serious social consequences. To many minds, the person who admits to a deviant perspective is out of bounds, somehow dirty and unacceptable. So successful was liberalism in Canada between the 1950s and 1970s, for example, that the labels "socialist," or "conservative," were widely viewed as repugnant, and this not because those who labelled them this way provided a systematic critique or examination of these other perspectives but because the words themselves were frightening. This occurred even within the liberal perspective which espouses the liberty of the individual to choose beliefs and express them freely.

It is only by contrast that alternative values are considered. Between 1949 and the early 1970s, China appeared to provide an alternative. Such values as community welfare, sharing and public ownership, self-reliance at the community level, and social rather than individual progress were adopted by the ruling Communist Party. These are not the values by which European and North American societies judge themselves, nor do these values grow out of the kind of social organization maintained in Europe and North America. But China, too, has become more industrialized and the values of the 1949 revolution and then of the cultural revolution in the 1960s have undergone rapid change. The "responsibility system" in China of the mid-1980s is not identical to the "free enterprise system" of North America and Europe, but it is, even so, vastly different from the "collectivist" ideology that preceded it. And with the passing of China's revolutionary communism, the world lacks a large-scale alternative social organization. The Soviet organization of Eastern Europe continues to provide an ideological justification of communism, but the social organization appears to be a variant of, rather than a radical alternative to, industrial capitalism. This lack of visible alternatives makes it very difficult for us to imagine and evaluate other ways of arranging social activity; as well, it makes it difficult to remove ourselves mentally from this historical moment and place in order to assess our own society.

Counter-ideologies involve a good deal of imagination. They provide a critique of the present society and a creative vision of an alternative. Both socialism and the "new right" provide these critiques and creative visions, and whether we agree with them or despise them, we are indebted to their proponents for enabling us to imagine other ways of doing things. Like liberalism, these ideologies have grown out of the social organization of industrial capitalism. They are concerned with apparent realities such as mass production technologies, money, wages, markets, industrial property, ownership rights, and distinctions between work and non-work.

Counter-ideologies generally begin with a critical perspective which arises from recognition of inconsistencies between what the dominant ideology portrays as truth and what the senses suggest is reality. They begin, then, as reform movements and their members are social critics. Equality, material prosperity, and personal freedom may be assumed as "right" values, but the society is judged as deficient in providing for their realization. The negative judgement leads to an analysis of social organization which diverges from that propagated by those who hold the dominant ideology and believe it to meet its own objectives. Gradually the analysis turns into a fully developed counter-ideology, an entirely different way of viewing the society.

2

As the introduction makes clear, we are talking about public beliefs. Some people think that ideology is something that happens to others, and generally, to somewhat deranged others. That is not the sense in which the term is used here. We are all immersed in ideological understandings of our world.

The definition of ideology we use in this book is: shared ideas, perceptions, values, and beliefs through which members of a society interpret history and contemporary social events and which shape their expectations and wishes for the future.

A dominant ideology is defined as that particular set of ideas, perceptions, values, and beliefs which is most widely shared and has the greatest impact on social action at any particular time in any particular society.

A counter-ideology is defined as a set of ideas, etc., which is held by a substantial minority and which has noticeable impact on social action. There may be many or few counter-ideologies in any society at any historical period.

There is another definition of ideology (discussed in Chapter 5): the ideas and values of the ruling class, disseminated through agencies controlled by that class in ways that obfuscate class realities for subservient classes. We are not using this definition here, but will examine its utility for an explanation of certain events of recent history in Chapter 6.

Ideology and theory are different entities, though they grow out of the same womb. Theory consists of explicit assumptions, a reasoning by which the assumptions are demonstrated to be linked to conclusions on the one hand, and such material evidence as can be gathered on the other. It is, by definition, open to challenge through the presentation of more complete or contesting evidence, or by a refutation of the logic that links assumptions to conclusions. It is not a faith. It is not unexamined. And it is not expressed by implication and inference. These attributes do not make any theory "right" in any absolute sense; they merely make it open, debatable, and subject to correction when evidence fails to support it.

Growing out of the same womb, ideology and theory are curious fraternal twins. Ideologies are rather like the uterine nutrients which sustain the infant; theories, like the growing spirit of independence manifested after birth. In some ways, theories are rivals and enemies of ideologies because they tend to dissect them. Someone begins by saying, "Hmm, I believe this and that, I think I'll write it all down in some systematic way so that others will think as I do." Then, in the writing of it, the author begins to see some inconsistencies, some flaws in logic, some mismatch between theory and evidence. And the reader, perusing the manuscript, says, "But this isn't good enough." Theories evolve over time, moving further and further away from their ideological base, becoming more sophisticated, more logical, more consistent—but often moving so far from their beginnings that they leave the majority of believers far behind. Sometimes this process destroys the ideology: no one can believe it any more. Sometimes it does quite otherwise: the theory goes off in one direction and believers of the original ideology continue quite undisturbed by theorists because the theorists have forgotten to include them in the universe of discourse.

Ideologies normally attract some people who want to make them public and systematic. In addition to theorists, there are scribes and prophets who define ideologies, trying to demonstrate how their particular beliefs are unique and true. For this reason, we can examine such ideologies through the writings of the scribes and the speeches of the prophets. And, as we begin to see which values they emphasize, which utopian visions they advance, we can label the ideologies and identify them relative to one another with reference to specific values. But for the same reason that we need to distinguish between theory and ideology, we need to recognize the possible differences between what the scribes and prophets say and what a majority of believers accept. At the popular level, ideologies are rarely as consistent as the written versions produced by the scribes and the theorists.

3

Ideologies may be phrased in terms we would recognize as political, that is, they are about the political world and how the public arena should be governed. Other ideologies may also have political implications but may be phrased as religious belief systems. Although the language of discourse may seem very different, there are usually close ties between what people believe about the meaning of human existence or the properties of nature and gods, and what they believe about political governance in the temporal world.

We are concerned here with the major ideologies of our society, the dominant and the counter-ideologies which motivate large numbers of people. And we are concerned primarily, though not exclusively, with how these ideologies link up with economic and political events. There are, in addition to these central ideologies, other versions of the world espoused by smaller numbers of people. Some of these other versions take political forms, some take religious forms. Sometimes these versions are similar to the dominant or counter-ideologies in core values, but they concentrate so much on one value above all others that they appear absurd and extreme to those who fail to share the concern with that single value. When these ideologies are the core of organized group behaviour we label them "sectarian." Sectarian movements sometimes become fanatical in their defence of the cherished values, and are perceived by others as threats to public security or as crazy and paranoid fringe groups. But sometimes these same groups, considered crazy at one historical period, provide leadership in moving the rest of the population away from prevailing ideological understandings toward new perspectives.

All societies make decisions about the importance of the collectivity and the individual: does the society have the right to demand certain actions or forbid other actions for its individual members, or does the individual have the right to do anything he or she pleases, short of physically harming others? As well, societies make decisions about the degree and kind of equality available to their populations. Should all people have equal opportunities, equal rewards for their labour, equal rights, equal power, or should individuals be free to create their own opportunities and gain whatever rewards and power they can on their own? These are vital decisions, though they are rarely made through conscious deliberation in the public arena. They are made, rather, through an accumulation of decisions, ways of doing things, institutional patterns which develop over time and which people tend to take for granted, along with the ideological perspectives that accompany them.

Political ideologies ultimately boil down to these decisions, to the relative emphasis placed on individualism versus collectivism, and on egalitarianism versus elitism. It is in these terms that we can identify the differences between one ideology and another. We have political labels for various positions in our own society, along two continuums: the first, from extreme individualists (society has absolutely no claims on the individual, and there should be no rules, government, or constraints on individual actions) to extreme collectivists (society always has precedence over individuals, and the right to demand conformance with rules for the public good); and the second, from extreme elitism (there should be rulers and the rulers should have complete power) to extreme egalitarianism (all people should be absolutely equal in condition, not just opportunities). The differences between these labelled positions can be noted by referring to the theories, scribes and prophets, but as observed above, we must be wary of assuming that all adherents to labelled positions are consistent in their beliefs. Most people "lean" more toward one position or another, and few have clearly articulated views that fit neatly into any one category.

The political ideologies of our time, relative to individualism and egalitarianism, may be visually plotted as shown in Figure 1.

INDIVIDUALIST AND MARKET-BASED IDEOLOGIES

Individualist anarchism, libertarianism, classical liberalism, and to a lesser degree, contemporary liberalism, treat society as a collection of individuals. Society does not exist in and of itself, it is not an organic whole. Individuals each strive to manufacture the necessary conditions for life, and the market mechanism has emerged as a means of co-ordinating their separate strivings without applying force. The preservation of individual liberty and of the "free market" becomes the major concerns for advocates of these positions.

Individualist Anarchism and Libertarianism

The individualist position is taken to the extreme in anarchist and libertarian ideologies; all other values become subordinate. Anarch-

FIGURE 1

Political Ideologies: Positions Relative to Individualism and Egalitarianism

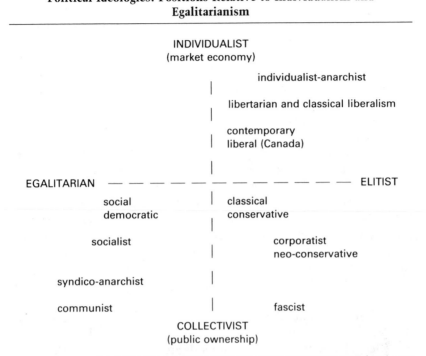

ists would do away with all government and social restrictions on personal liberty; libertarians (though with some differences between various groups) generally accept the necessity of government, but would restrict its functions to the defence of persons and property. Anything which prevents individuals from fully exercising their initiative, entrepreneurial skills, and talents is harshly judged: thus democracy and the welfare state are deemed to be impediments to individual growth. Inequality is viewed as inevitable because people are genetically unequal, and as necessary because the most talented provide the leadership which permits others to survive. Libertarians believe that "pure" capitalism is an ideal social and economic system because it includes a genuinely free market for absolutely all goods and services. In a libertarian society everything would be commodities for sale, including education, all mass media presentations, postal services, drinking water, and the use of highways. This position is central to part of the "new right" ideology. (See Chapter 8.)

Classical and Contemporary Liberalism

Classical (*laissez-faire*) liberalism provides much of the basis for the contemporary libertarian position, the absolutely free market being the key to social development. It has since become modified by concern for the problems of the unregulated market and by greater emphasis on equality of individuals.

Liberalism has a somewhat different meaning in Canada than in the United States. In Canada, it is at the centre of the political spectrum, modified by both social democratic and conservative concerns for the society as a whole. In the United States, the term is used with reference to more extensive reform attitudes, closer to what Canadians would regard as "social democratic," and it is to the left of the political options. In Canada, liberalism differs from the Canadian social democratic view in that while both take equality to be a positive value, the liberal view is that equality of opportunity is sufficient, and that such equality is largely achieved within the present social system. Social democrats argue in favour of greater equality of condition and perceive great inequalities of both opportunity and condition in the present social system.

The free-enterprise market is rarely called "capitalism" in liberal ideology; the word "free enterprise" becomes the euphemism for capitalism. Consonant with the belief that society is made up of individuals, each selling his or her "human capital" (skills and knowledge) on a "free market," liberals are unconcerned with classes and some would deny their existence in capitalist society. A great deal of emphasis is placed on the education system because liberals believe that individuals have equal opportunity in that sphere, each achieving there what their innate talents and hard work permit and thus moving upward or downward in the social system according to ability.

The role of government is to regulate the market-place and ensure that the rules are fair and equitable; government is not itself an economic actor in a truly "free" enterprise system. Further, with class having little importance, government cannot be seen as the agent of any particular class (see Chapters 2 and 3).

Liberalism has been the dominant ideological perspective adopted by Canadians throughout the past 40 years. One political party is called "Liberal" but when we speak of liberalism, we do not refer exclusively to this party. In fact, throughout this period, the two major alternative parties, the Progressive Conservative Party and the New Democratic Party, have shared much of the liberal version of Canadian society.

COLLECTIVIST POSITIONS

Collectivist positions begin with the argument that the society is an organic whole. Society exists independent of the individuals who happen to live in it at any time. But there is an enormous difference in the conclusions and policy positions taken by collectivists of the "left" and of the "right." The basic difference occurs between those who believe that society ought to be more egalitarian (social democratic, socialist, syndico-anarchist, communist) and those who believe it should be more hierarchically ordered (conservative, corporatist, neo-conservative, and fascist). Within each of these general positions, there is considerable difference between the positions closer to the centre and those on the peripheries. Both the social democrat and the traditional conservative positions share many common assumptions with the liberal position. These shared assumptions diminish sharply as we move toward either fascist or communist positions. The diagram suggests a way of seeing the differences between these positions.

Social Democratic

Social democrats accept the basic values of liberalism but place more emphasis on equality. As well, they recognize the existence of classes, of class barriers, and of governments acting in the interests of a dominant or ruling class. They thus share some of the understandings of socialists. They are committed to the gradual and democratic evolution of more egalitarian society where workers participate in management and collective ownership of resources and industries. Canadian social democrats and the parties they have supported have tended to move away from a preference for centralized state ownership of industries, toward a more mixed economy with state planning and markets. (See Chapters 6 and 7.)

Socialist

Socialists perceive capitalism as a system where a ruling class extracts wealth from a subordinate class (or classes), sells products made by labour, and uses the profits to invest in more properties and new technologies which displace or further enslave labour. Classes exist, inequalities are essential to the system, and individual freedom is highly circumscribed by the fundamental requirement that labour must produce goods and services for capital. For the socialist these conditions are unacceptable.

Socialism involves a version of the future which differs markedly from that of liberalism. For liberals, the future is a continuum of the past and present. It is a highly optimistic ideology, assuming eternal progress and gradual elimination of imperfections in the social system. But socialism, identifying capitalism as an oppressive and exploitative system, involves the belief that only through the destruction of capitalism can a more egalitarian and humane system emerge. Capitalism is expected to self-destruct, because its internal contradictions must eventually cause a fatal blockage in the capacities of capitalists to continue accumulating new profits (this is called "a crisis of accumulation" in the socialist literature).

For the liberal, capitalism is a necessary reality and critiques of it are ideology. For the socialist, the liberal version of capitalism is ideology. It is understood by socialists as an essential feature of the capitalist system, because it induces workers to consent to their own exploitation. They are persuaded, rather than forced (though force may on occasion also be necessary), to believe that the system is fair even if it leads to extremely unequal distributions of material wealth and economic power. (See Chapters 5, 6, and 7.)

Syndico-Anarchism (or Socialist Anarchism)

Anarchism as described above rests on a belief in the supremacy of individuals over society. But there is a form of anarchism which rests instead on the belief that small groups should have control of their collective life. One branch of this socialist anarchism emerged within the European trade union movement, espousing the rights of workers' organizations to organize production. A second branch has since appeared, espousing the rights of small communities to govern themselves. Both branches express hostility toward government as well as large capitalist organizations.

Communism

Communism within Canada has been closely associated with an international communist movement. As an ideological position, this is similar to socialism, arguing that capitalism is an avaricious system built on the labour of exploited labour. Although communists anticipate that at some distant stage, centralized governments will become obsolete, they are normally hostile to syndicalist arguments. Their view of the improved society is one in which all production is socialized and all workers, or their direct representatives, have a say in how the society is managed. Communism differs from socialism and even more from social democracy in its argument that capitalism must be destroyed by force, and that a vanguard of advanced thinkers may be required to lead a workers' revolution. Thus, communism is hostile to democratic procedures even though, in reality, communist parties have participated in democratic elections. (See Chapters 5 and 6.)

Traditional Conservatism

Conservatism—like liberalism not to be interpreted as necessarily coincident with a particular political party—shares with socialism a belief that there are classes, that capitalism necessarily involves inequality, and that the market-place should not be the locus of most important social decisions. But unlike socialism, conservatism gives a high positive value to class inequalities: they are necessary because society requires leadership, and well established leaders look after less well established workers. Conservatism thus values a "natural" hierarchy, paternalistic relations between capital and labour. For the conservative, government properly has the right to establish norms for the conduct of social life, though it should have a restrained role in the economy.

The chief difference between conservatism and liberalism is in their respective views of society: conservatives viewing it as an organic whole within which individuals have assigned places; liberals as a collection of individuals each striving for personal goals. Thus true conservatives should be concerned with the collective moral fabric as well as the permanence of a dominant class. Logically, liberals would be less concerned with social and moral issues except where society infringes on individual rights.

This position, tempered by liberalism, characterized pre-Confederation and 19th century Canadian society, gradually diminishing as an effective and popular ideology over the 20th century except in Quebec, where it held sway until the late 1940s. (See Chapter 4.)

Corporatism

Corporatism shares with conservatism the belief in a natural hierarchy of human beings, the importance of planning the economy, and the positive evaluation of social classes. It goes beyond conservatism in arguing that economic units—corporations—should make the decisions about the conduct of economic life. Democratic procedures typical of liberal societies are viewed as unacceptable, because they allow uninformed and unpropertied individuals and groups to choose leaders and policies and thus inhibit social progress.

This position is associated with Italy under Mussolini, and has not had much of a history in Canada though some Canadians flirted with it during the 1930s. At the present time, some Canadians are again flirting with it, and there are curious alliances between some of its advocates and libertarians though the two positions are philosophically very different. The marriage of the two positions has taken the label "neo-conservatism." (See Chapters 4, 8, and 9.)

Neo-Conservatism

This label is now in common usage, together with the label "the new right" to refer to a somewhat contradictory set of beliefs which

combine advocacy of minimal government, establishment of a completely free market, extreme individualism; and strong, centralized
government, controlled markets, and special concern for major economic corporations in the international market-place. The common
core in this position is hostility toward democracy, the welfare state,
unions, and collective bargaining. The label "conservatism" is con-
fusing because unlike traditional conservatives the new right does
not take the view that a ruling class has an obligation to care for its
subjects; but it does share with conservatism the view that there is
a ruling class and that this class is essential for social survival.

Fascism

Fascism is an extreme form of corporatism, going beyond it in
accepting the necessity for force in controlling dissidents. We usually associate it with Nazi Germany in the 1930s and 1940s, but
there was a fascist party in Canada during the 1930s, and a very
small group of followers have persisted throughout this century. (See
Chapters 4, 8, and 9.)

DOMINANT IDEOLOGY

If we identify the dominant ideology as the values and beliefs held
in common by a majority, we would include the liberal, social democratic, and classical conservative positions as falling within its
compass. Although they differ in the degree to which they emphasize
individualism and egalitarianism, they share a number of assumptions we can recognize.

To begin with, proponents of these positions assume the legitimacy of private property rights but at the same time recognize
legitimate constraints on these. They accept (with varying degrees
of approval) the economic drive for profits but again, place limits
on its capacity to drive the entire social system. They accept differential rewards for work associated with numerous social factors
(education, skills, talent, etc.) but reject differences associated with
gender, ethnicity, religion, or other "non-economic" attributes of
individuals. Although both the conservative and social democratic
positions include acknowledgement of the reality of class divisions
in capitalist society, and liberalism does not, all three tend to explain
social events in terms of individuals or non-class groups (for example, men and women, ethnic groups, particular interest groups)
more than in terms of classes. All positions involve notions of social
progress toward a "better" society (with more or with less egalitarianism, depending on the position) to be achieved through gradual
evolution.

The development of the welfare state since 1930 has brought these three positions closer together. Social democrats have pulled governing parties toward greater expenditures on welfare, public education, and public health; conservatives have accepted these reforms as necessary provisions for unpropertied classes, recognizing that the reforms have not threatened property rights for dominant classes and have, in fact, created a stable labour force. In a sense, the welfare state of the post-war era has been a grand compromise, providing enough security to sustain the support of the "left" but never enough to offend the "right."

Political parties wearing these various labels, or political theorists espousing these points of view, make many more distinctions between the positions. It is in their interests to do so, of course, since they have to make their party appear to be the unique champion of individual rights or equal opportunity or whatever. What interests us in this book is not so much the fine distinctions but rather the underlying values to which the parties appeal, and which are apparently important to an electorate. Why would a large proportion of citizens in Canada believe that private property rights and certain kinds of constraints on them are legitimate, appropriate, and fair? Why do people believe that democratic governments are just or unjust; that equality is or is not a reasonable goal for a society? And why do substantial numbers of Canadians move slightly more toward one pole or another in the political spectrum during times of economic change?

4

These two continuums are fundamental to social organization everywhere. All societies arrive, whether through conscious political activity or tacit agreements and traditional activities, at some position between individualism and collectivism, egalitarianism and elitism. There is another set of values which cross-cuts these, providing a third dimension to social organization. It is attitudes toward nature.

Societies dependent on hunting and gathering, and some societies dependent on cultivation of foods, have developed understandings of people as components of nature on the same level with other animate beings. Most such societies also hold the view that there are unseen spirits guiding and judging their activities. Within these perceptions, animals and land are highly valued, and destruction of either is unacceptable behaviour. Thus the hunters must apologize to the beast they have killed, explaining their need for food and their sincere appreciation for the sacrifice made by the animal. Northern native peoples in Canada have frequently expressed their attitudes towards animals in this way, and as well, their reverence and kinship with the land they occupy. Land, for them, is not merely a territory like any other, it is a special space to which they are attached spiritually. To destroy the land is to destroy them.

By contrast, the industrial society treats animals and humans as qualitatively different entities, with humans having the right to kill and conquer all other living things. Land is but a space where human activity takes place: it has no spiritual quality. Rivers may be dammed and diverted, land may be destroyed, even the air may be polluted with impunity, all subordinated to a quest for human survival based on the growth of profits through industrial development.

Within the past decade, new social movements have arisen within industrial societies opposed to the destruction of our environment. Some of these have taken on political aspects, organizing as political parties or as pressure groups. The anti-nuclear movement, the Green Party, and numerous groups devoted to the saving of particular territories are among these. To date, these groups have not developed consistent positions on individualism-collectivism, egalitarianism-elitism. They are, in a sense, outside the mainstream of public discourse, and adherents to environmentalist ideologies could, conceivably, place themselves anywhere within the other political spectrums. These groups challenge all of the existing political organizations. (See Chapter 9.)

Similarly, religious movements sometimes exist outside the main discourse of industrial society. While the major religions in Canada—Christian Catholicism and Protestantism and Judaism—have generally adopted and supported the dominant ideology, smaller and often sectarian groups have challenged these views. Some of these have supported highly individualistic positions (salvationist religions), others more collectivist positions (cultural renewal religions).

Though religions may develop outside the mainstream of political and economic perspectives, they have had significant impact on the development of societies. Max Weber argued that the success of capitalism in Britain compared to other nations in the 18th and 19th centuries was related to the full development there of a "Protestant ethic." In his view, Protestantism, especially in its Calvinist form, created the necessary appetites and justifications for accumulating wealth, reinvesting it in capitalist enterprises, and treating income-bearing activities as primary to human life.[1] Religions, then, can become important components of ideological understandings of society as well as the place of humans in the universe. (See Chapters 4, 6, and 8.)

5

Before we embark on our study of contemporary Canadian ideologies, it might be helpful to recall some history so that we can consider how the ideologies of industrial capitalism emerged in the transition from feudalism. Immediately, however, we are on difficult terrain, because even our versions of history are filtered through our ideological understandings.

In our time, it is generally believed that in the feudal society, each individual knew his or her place. No illusion of potential mobility obscured the class divisions between landed aristocracy and tenant farmers, or between priests and laity, and there was very little room for upward mobility for peasants. This equality was based on deprivation: few had the opportunities to exceed the common condition.

This version of feudalism needs some tempering, first because men and women were certainly not equal, and for both men and women there were numerous distinctions in property rights between tenant farmers, labourers, married and unmarried persons.[2] A town population existed apart from both landed aristocracy and peasantry, and it is not clear whether the ideological premises of the feudal estates were ever fully accepted by townsfolk, or how village understandings of the social world affected the peasantry. Feudal society was certainly more complex than we tend to think it was, but it probably is accurate to say that class and status distinctions were more generally recognized and stable than in contemporary Canadian society.

The major difference in ideology between that social organization and the capitalist organization in Canada, is in an assumption about the legitimacy of inequality. The aristocracy of feudal society assumed that it had the right to dictate conditions of life for others. Of course we do not know whether individual aristocrats acknowledged that this right derived from property and the capacity to starve those without property, or genuinely believed that it derived from God. The official version of rights rested on a religious interpretation of social reality, with God at the apex, a priesthood and the aristocracy next in line sharing responsibility for the salvation and physical survival of the poor. The peasant could not expect to become a lord, but according to the Church, he could expect the lord to provide for him. Collective good was to be achieved not by individual effort, but by knowledgeable leaders guiding obedient subjects to the light, or at least to safety, in an often violent social world. The burden of responsibility of the rich for the poor was often lightly borne, but the belief in that obligation was frequently expressed by the landed aristocracy. Since history is written from the point of view of the literate classes, we have very little knowledge of how much faith the peasantry actually placed in this ideology of *noblesse oblige*.

The agrarian society created more than it consumed, and the surplus was transformed in early market-places into commodities. Some of these commodities were purchased by townsfolk, who in turn sold their skills and products to the landed gentry. Some commodities were purchased by merchants, and eventually some of these commodities were traded beyond the borders of small towns, even on markets far distant from the towns. Gradually, town populations grew, with merchants, skilled and unskilled workers, artists, and professionals. This population did not fit neatly into either of the land-based classes. Their obligations and rights were ambiguous, they were responsible for no one and could look to no one for aid. Over time they developed their own ethos. They were competitive for markets, and competition can flourish only where rivals have equal opportunities. They demanded a new kind of equality: not equality of condition within a class, but equality of opportunity to exceed one's class and to amass wealth. They were inventive of new techniques, and inventiveness flourishes where the inventor profits from his inventions. Thus they sought legal protections on goods other than land. They were mobile and restless and unwilling to have a church censor their ideas. Thus they sought legitimation of a creed they called the rights of the individual: the right of each man (with little acknowledgement of women) to determine for himself his moral obligations. Equality for men, legal protection of property rights, and personal freedom, or individualism, became basic demands. These demands did not grow out of earlier ideologies: they grew out of a changed social context and they reflected the conditions of that urban context.

As the industrial society developed, changes occurred in uses of land. The urban population had to be fed. More food had to be produced on the land and less of it used for the subsistence of the agricultural population. And simultaneously, urban employers began to seek workers in the migrants from rural areas. The *Enclosures Acts* in Britain pushed rural people off land and obliged them to enter urban employment, and various other conditions gradually reduced the number of workers on farms, increased the productivity of rural areas, and undermined the rural culture. As the needs of industrial organizations changed, and as urban populations burgeoned, there arose a need for literate and more specialized workers. This could be achieved by the development of public schools, schools which taught practical skills rather than philosophy, schools which disciplined the workers so that they could contribute their skills to industrial institutions. Equality of opportunity was, in due course, translated as equal chances to compete for higher-paid and higher-status jobs in industry through educational attainment. A labour force for which educational attainment was vital provided the support for an ideology proclaiming the virtues of individualism, private achievement, the pursuit of wealth, and competitive equality.

The leaders of this industrial society had established their personal freedom to determine their own moral obligations: they had dispensed with the belief in reciprocal obligations. They could do this because their own role in that system of reciprocity had been ambiguous from the start. The system of mutual obligations had rested on the open recognition of classes, the legitimation of the class structure, and the common bondage to land and agriculture. The new system of contracts and wages ignored class distinctions and thus left the wealthy free of moral ties to the poor.

One of the pre-conditions for these forms of equality was the development of the nation state. A nation state is a territory larger than a feudal estate which the resident population can effectively defend against outsiders while sustaining their own livelihoods. Such states were not universal organizations. Germany, for example, remained a collection of petty fiefdoms long after Britain and France had become unified under single monarchies. Britain underwent civil strife earlier and concluded these with less bloodshed than France, thereby permitting the British bourgeoisie to expand its markets and organize the British working class while France became embroiled in a prolonged and bitter revolution.

Once unification had occurred, capitalism was more easily advanced. It rests on contracts: the standardization of money and forms of exchange, the relations between employers and workers in which wages rather than personal obligations are the medium, agreements between buyers and sellers, and legally sanctioned guarantees of the right to own private property, including the means of production. These contracts can be maintained through the control of power: where the state has a monopoly of armed power, internal dissent to the forms of contract is quickly extinguished. In the early stages of the industrial state, the control of power shifted from the landed aristocracy and their representatives to the urban bourgeoisie and theirs.

The development of colonies from which raw materials could be extracted gave rise to higher standards of living in the mother countries for the growing middle class as well as the owners of industry, and provided space for the settlement of excess populations. The competition between states, each organized against internal war, provided much of the impetus for the growth of industrialism and the search for colonies. Armies and merchant navies became avenues of mobility. When these avenues and those of the educational institutions were utilized, the arguments of the bourgeoisie for their rights were appropriated by the workers for theirs. The ideology of the urban owners filtered down through the ranks and became the dominant ideology of the capitalist State.

The transition from the feudal aristocracy to bourgeois capitalism is described by Joseph Schumpeter in this way:

Capitalist entrepreneurs fought the former ruling circles for a share in state control, for leadership in the state. The very fact of their success, their position, their resources, their power, raised them in the political and social scale. Their mode of life, their cast of mind became increasingly important elements on the social scene. Their actions, desires, needs, and beliefs emerged more and more sharply within the total picture of the social community. In an historical sense, this applied primarily to the industrial and financial leaders of the movement—the bourgeoisie. But soon it applied also to the working masses which this movement created and placed in an altogether new class situation. This situation was governed by new forms of the working day, of family life, of interests—and these, in turn, corresponded to new orientations toward the social structure as a whole. More and more, in the course of the nineteenth century, the typical modern worker came to determine the overall aspect of society; for competitive capitalism, by its inherent logic, kept on raising the demand for labor and thus the economic level and social power of the workers, until this class too was able to assert itself in a political sense.[3]

The socialist interpretation does not differ in its view that the liberal ideology predominated. It does differ in its interpretation of the role of the working class. For Marx, its early proponent, competitive capitalism, by its inherent logic, raised the power and wealth of the bourgeoisie while condemning the workers to a continual downward spiral. Their political power in the democratic state was, he argued, illusory: none the less, it was an illusion they adopted.

Two events emerged with the development of the capitalist society and liberal democracy. One of these was the breaking away from a land-locked class system and the creation of new channels of mobility; the other was the development of an urban working class and a class of industrial owners. It is to the first of these that the liberal ideology pays attention. It emphasizes the lifting of barriers to personal achievement. It is the second of these that the socialist ideology considers important. It emphasizes the creation of new barriers to collective freedom. Both grow out of the same reality, both begin with the same values. They differ in what they select from that reality to be the paramount feature of the capitalist society.

6

The industrial society is not a static social organization. The processes set in motion by the development of urban populations and competitive capitalism continued. They destroyed the feudal aristocracy and the peasantry. They created new forms of government. They destroyed societies and created new ones in far-off colonies. Change occurred at many levels simultaneously: at the level of the family unit, at the level of education. The liberal ideology explains these changes as cumulative growth. Society is always progressing, always adjusting to new conditions. Its growth is limitless, its perfection is a viable goal. The analogy is to a wheel turning over new territory and adding always to its conquest of distance.

Marx posited quite a different kind of change—cumulative, still, but fraught with internal contradictions. The growth in competitive capitalism would give rise to monopoly capitalism. The growth of wealth at the top would create the growth of poverty at the bottom. The more successful the capitalists were in developing technology and organizing the work-force for their own ends, the faster they brought about their own demise by an organized, efficient proletariat. The wheel in this analogy spins ever faster only to break down from over-use, and its riders are obliged to make a new wheel out of the parts. Marx envisioned the final stages in these words:

One capitalist always kills many. Hand in hand with this centralization, or this expropriation of many capitalists by few, develop, on an ever-extending scale, the co-operative form of the labour process, the conscious technical application of science, the methodical cultivation of the soil, the transformation of the instruments of labour into instruments of labour only usable in common, the economizing of all means of production by their use as the means of production of combined, socialized labour, the entanglement of all peoples in the net of the world-market, and with this, the international character of the capitalistic regime. Along with the constantly diminishing number of the magnates of capital, who usurp and monopolise all advantages of this process of transformation, grows the mass of misery, oppression, slavery, degradation, exploitation; but with this too grows the revolt of the working-class, a class always increasing in numbers, and disciplined, united, organized by the very mechanism of the process of capitalist production itself.[4]

The progression theory assumes a certain consistency to social evolution. The total society is somehow in equilibrium, advancing steadily while keeping its parts intact. We invent the automobile, then we develop new ways of organizing the work process so as to mass-produce it, then we add an arm to government and new taxing procedures so that we can finance the roads it requires, families adjust their life-style to new kinds of mobility and to new workday schedules. The dialectic process identified by Marx and current in socialist literature envisions rather a society in constant crisis, lacking internal consistency, growing unevenly. We invent the automobile which gives us geographical mobility, but to produce it we must enslave labourers to an assembly line; we allow the producer to accumulate profits on the sale of cars, while the society must bear the burden of costs not only for roads but for fuel exhaustion and pollution caused by the invention.

Whether one takes the progressional view of history or the dialectic view, one is struck by the observation that cumulative growth in any aspect of social organization eventually becomes destructive of that organization. Whether we eventually arrive in a different town by riding the wheel from one place to another, or whether the journey itself transforms the travellers, the fact is that the industrial society of the 1980s is not the industrial society of the 1920s or the 1880s. It is qualitatively a different society. The technology has changed dramatically. The social organization has changed. The population balance has changed. The relations between nation states have changed. What has noticeably failed to change is the ideology.

The ideologies at the popular level are very much the same as they were in these other times. Speeches to the Chamber of Commerce reflect the same abiding faith in progress, material prosperity, and general affluence; the same evaluation of private property, individualism, and achievement; the same belief in the existence of equality and opportunity. The slogans of the Left are remarkably similar to those uttered in the trade union struggles of the turn of the century. There is the same belief in massive exploitation by a ruling class, the same faith in the nobility of labour, the same conviction that pervasive equality is both yet to come and highly desirable.

Yet the ideological perspectives of the industrial society are not those of the feudal period. Between the 15th or 16th centuries and the 18th to 20th centuries there was a change. An ideology that had long been embedded dissolved; gradually the new ideologies displaced it, then settled and became stable elements of the new social organization. As suggested in the sketch of the shift from feudalism to industrialism, what occurred was the creation of a new population in the urban centres whose social realities were so different from those of the rural population that it developed new explanations for its actions, new values, and new orientations. Some aspects of these new perspectives did, of course, grow out of the old ideologies. Protestantism emerged from Catholicism, for example. But in large part, they were indigenous developments peculiar to the urban population. It is entirely probable that, long after the urban populations had moved into the industrial era and successfully developed an ideological perspective on industrial society, inhabitants of rural areas remained untouched by both industrial society and industrial ideologies. If they were asked to explain society, they would continue to assume the rural class system, the rights and obligations of feudal lords, the virtues of humility and obedience, and the need for piety. Indeed, some parts of this feudal ideology survived, by transplant, in the colonies of Europe, long after the christening certificates for liberalism had been issued in Europe.

In Canada, for example, some of these values remained into the early 20th century. While these were tinged by the values of liberalism as it was expressed in the United States and Britain, liberalism in its classic form did not emerge as a dominant ideology until very late in history by comparison with these other countries. Nearly a century after the American War of Independence had spawned the notion that individuals should pursue happiness and that this was a legitimate basis for social organization, as long again after the French Revolution had bannered the words "liberty, equality, fraternity," Canada continued to be ruled by a landed aristocracy which gained its wealth through the fur trade, export-import businesses, and banking. Its values were not those of industrial capitalists. It was not engaged in competitive enterprise, and was not generating new wealth out of the production of goods for a market. At the other end of the social scale, the larger part of the population was engaged in farming rather than manufacturing, and Canada was largely a rural country before World War I; indeed, it remained predominantly rural until the 1930s. The slow development of industry and of an industrial urban labour force retarded the development of liberalism as an ideology.

Conservatism, then, has not been absent in Canada, but in the past half-century it has not been a dominant ideology either. The national Conservative political party has been immersed in liberal ideology throughout that period, to such an extent, in fact, that it is indistinguishable from the national Liberal Party at the level of party policies and principles. At the same time, the national New Democratic Party has survived as a liberal reform movement, rather than as a fundamentally different ideological position. In many ways more important than the national political spectrum, the daily life of Canadians is based on liberal premises. To most Canadians, genuinely conservative values appear as anachronisms; genuinely socialist interpretations appear as frightening challenges to what they prefer to believe.

7

Liberalism and socialism can interpret one kind of society, one form of industrial organization. This is the society in transition within the political framework of nation states. Neither is suited to providing a popular interpretation or appropriate set of values for maintenance of a multinational or non-national capitalism in which wage work is not available to many people, surplus is not created out of labour, communications technology becomes more central to political control, and corporations are the chief social as well as economic organizations. Those of us who continue to live in the "old world," like the peasant of the feudal period or the colonials of an imperial empire, are unable to envision or make sense of the developments around us which lead in such a direction. We attempt to interpret them through the ideological perspectives of a society already in decline. Subtly, scarcely intruding on our consciousness, a new set of perceptions and beliefs and their appropriate justifying values will develop around the new technologies and within the corporate empires. Some of this will be transmitted to the generations now living out what may well be the last stage of national states and a social organization which divides the political, economic, and religious realms. These transmissions are phrased clumsily, to fit existing belief systems. Thus we have insights on what might be called "liberal corporatism" and we are puzzled by where the Soviet form of corporatism fits in to our theories of history. But if the past is an indication of the future, it will not be the case that liberalism as an ideology imperceptibly becomes corporatism; nor that socialism becomes totalitarianism; but rather that both are superseded by new ideologies emanating from a new society that has already grown within the old and destroyed its foundations.

2 INDIVIDUALISM AND EQUALITY

It is perhaps unfortunate that one of the major political parties in Canada is called the Liberal Party, since it may appear that a discussion of liberalism is merely a discussion of the practices and policies of Liberals. The party is but one manifestation of an ideological position which goes far beyond party politics and has its origins outside Canada. It still has its strongest expressions and most eloquent defences in other industrial countries, especially the United States.

There is a saying that is no doubt familiar to Canadian ears which catches much of the flavour of liberalism: "I don't care what you do when you grow up, my child, just as long as you are happy." The statement assumes that personal happiness is a legitimate goal and that it can be sought and developed by each individual. It assumes that each child may choose his or her way of life, determine his or her own future, arrange his or her itinerary, and that all are equal in this opportunity. It assumes that there are alternatives available and that a range of equally suitable alternatives exists, to be sampled according to personal taste. It also, but more subtly, assumes that one's happiness is linked with some activity and that the activity in question is a respectable occupation.

This is one of those statements which, because they are so frequently expressed and so widely believed, are not recognized as ideological positions. One may test immersion by noting reactions to a statement that rests on very different assumptions about the world, such as: "You have a duty to perform, my child, and that is to give generously of your talents to the society which has nurtured you," or, "You know your place, my child. Don't try to overstep it." The liberal ideology rests on the premise that the individual is more important than the society and that the society does not have the right to limit his or her freedom to pursue happiness as he or she chooses to define it.

The statement to the child provides the basis for later statements: the individual has the "right" to self-fulfilment, to self-actualization, to the seeking of a personal identity. Individualism may be seldom practised, but it is applauded as a "good thing," and the courage to stand alone is the message of many a childhood romance. The belief that there is equality of opportunity in the educational system lays the burden of proof on the individual. As education becomes ever more the criterion by which status is achieved, individualism and equality of opportunity become ever more the central values of the ideological system. The general belief in the existence of equality and personal freedom enhances the motivation of individuals to utilize the educational opportunities to achieve occupational status and to view their eventual status as the legitimate outcome of their personal and unaided efforts. It is a short step to look back at others who haven't made it and assume that for them, too, the outcome is attributable to personal abilities. It is congruent with these beliefs as well to limit one's charitable donations to the "deserving" since the poor, the unemployed, and the failures must carry the burden of their own short-comings. Their problem is private, not social.

When Canadians are asked why medical doctors earn such high salaries, they explain this in terms of their importance to society and the length of time they spend in educational institutions. When they are asked why managers of firms have decision-making powers while men on the assembly line do not, the answer is again in terms of the greater importance of the decision-maker.

There are reasonable grounds for rejecting these answers as "real" explanations for these events. Doctors may be important to society, but so are many others with and without lengthy educations who receive relatively low wages: sanitation personnel, kindergarten teachers, and nurses, for example. The second response actually provides no explanation at all. It says, in effect, that managers are important because they make decisions and that is why they are allowed to make decisions. There are alternative ways of explaining these inequalities which Canadians, by and large, will not generally offer. It isn't so much that they reject the alternatives, as that the alternatives don't occur to them. Medicine, for example, is organized into private practices from which private profits are extracted. Where it is organized as a community service, as in Austria and Soviet countries, doctors are not especially wealthy members of society, even though their importance to the health of the nation is presumably the same as it is in Canada. Commercial organizations, in the second example, are also organized as private enterprises, and those who own them employ others at the price they think those others are worth to the business, given the supply of workers in those areas. Managers may be no more vital to the enterprise, but they are in better positions to determine their own worth.

1

In order to understand why Canadians give the answers they do to such questions, it is useful to obtain a general picture of the organization of society as described by the liberal democrat.

Think of society as a jigsaw puzzle. The pieces fit together, their jagged edges appearing smooth when linked together. No one piece alone indicates what the total society looks like; the final picture needs all the parts. The pieces of this jigsaw are the institutions of society: the economic, educational, political, legal, communications, military, and religious institutions. If the shape of any one of these institutions is altered, then the other pieces must adjust their own shapes to accommodate that piece. Society, in this view, is always undergoing a process of cumulative change, responding always to slight shifts in population, new forms of technology, altered relations with other societies, or deliberately created changes in the political arena.[1]

Every institutional sector has an occupational hierarchy. Those people who occupy the top positions, that is, the positions with the most authority and responsibility, are specialists: people who have the skills, the knowledge, and the talent to co-ordinate and plan the overall activity within that sector in response to an always changing world. In order to motivate the best people for these important tasks, high rewards are offered: high status, prestige, and income. Beneath these most important positions are a range of professional and technical positions, and for these, too, high rewards are given so there will be the best qualified people filling the posts. As the specialist skills required for jobs decrease, the supply of workers available increases. Then the allocation of workers to jobs is determined by a law of supply and demand. Where the supply falls below the demand, the material rewards are increased. Where the demand falls below the supply, the rewards are decreased. Workers will seek out jobs with the highest rewards, so there will be a tendency toward equilibrium between the jobs that must be filled if the institutional areas are to operate and the supply of workers able and available to fill them. Positions must be filled in accordance with an independent principle, that is, some principle that distinguishes between the most capable and the least capable for certain tasks. In some societies, this principle is blood relationship, or kinship. Chiefs teach their sons or nephews the arts of chieftainship. As societies move into the more complex technological classification, kinship is inadequate as a means of ensuring that the most competent people will perform the most important tasks. Competence depends on the acquisition of technical skills and complex knowledge. The principle that can be utilized to ensure a supply of competent leaders is education. The educational system, then, becomes the means by which the natural leaders and specialists prove their merit, and all people find their levels of entry into the society.

One of the institutional spheres is a co-ordinating body, the function of which is to deliberate on the inconsistencies that naturally arise in such a complex arrangement, to smooth out these wrinkles with legislation, and to adjudicate between the conflicting claims of different sectors of the society. This institution, called government, is the only institution whose leading members at any one time are temporary. All are subject to an electoral vote and may be replaced if unsatisfactory.

2

This view of society provides no recognition of classes. Inequality is recognized, but it is attributed to individual differences, or to imperfections in the system and historical circumstance. The latter can be corrected, and the consequences of the former can be alleviated. When Canadians are asked to which class they belong, they are inclined to answer either that there are no classes in Canada, or to identify the middle class.[2] The great middle, in their opinion, encompasses almost everybody, and the lower and the upper—which must exist if there is a middle—can only be defined in terms of relative wealth. A few may be rich, a few may be poor, but most people, according to this belief, are somewhere between these small groups. This classless society is a pervasive belief and one renewed with the daily reading of the newspaper, the viewing of television, the study of literature, or history, or social science. Canadians may not quite believe that all people have equal opportunity, that birth has no effect on rank, or that anyone may rise to the top. But they see the defects as imperfections in a classless and mobile society, to be reformed or acknowledged perhaps, but not to be interpreted as evidence of a class structure. Golf, appliances, deodorants, and Beethoven are equally available to all, and the lack of class distinctions is nowhere more apparent than in the market-place.

Canadian novels do not entirely reinforce this classless image of Canada, particularly in the period prior to the Second World War. Along with concern for inequalities between ethnic groups and a strong preoccupation with the natural environment, Canadian fiction has implied, if it has not described, the existence of classes. Since the 1950s, however, there has been a growing concern with personal tragedies or private dilemmas of urban characters. A large part of American fiction, to which Canadians may be even more extensively exposed than they are to the work of their compatriots, has been directed toward the exploration of private agonies in an alienating environment. While post-war fiction in both countries identifies the social basis for private traumas, the focus tends to be on the personal rather than the class experience of these conditions.[3] Television dramas are predominantly about private problems, though documentaries occasionally provide acknowledgement of the class context for these problems. Historians, with some notable exceptions, have also produced a largely classless perspective on Canada. They have tended to accept Lord Durham's dictum on the Canadian struggle: "a struggle between two nations warring in the bosom of a single state . . . a struggle, not of principles, but of races."[4] Thus, the English Canadian may hear much of the injustices of British rule over French Canada, but the inequities are seen as temporary injustices, consequences perhaps of racial bigotry, and not as the events of a class struggle. Similarly, the building of the railroads is depicted as a courageous conquest of a rugged terrain, the fur trade is remembered as a series of rather romantic adventures, and the pioneers are described as stout-hearted individualists. Whether or not these descriptions have truth, they do not provide an interpretation of Canadian history that would induce the reader to consider the nature of industrial classes or the relationships between classes which might cause conflict.[5]

The ideology allows us to expect differences between individuals, since achievements lead to differences in wealth, power, and access to goods and services, but it does not allow for an expectation of consistent and persistent differences between identifiable groups whose common characteristic is socially, not individually, defined. If we find, in fact, that high income and power are highly concentrated within a small sector of the population, and that access to education, or the congruence between rewards and educational achievement differ systematically by ethnic group, sex, place of birth or family of origin, then to that extent we are faced with evidence that cannot be explained through the prevailing ideology. Also to that extent, the ideology obstructs our vision, explains superficially and inadequately facts which derive from circumstances not recognized within that ideological framework.

3

Contrary to the general belief that Canadians form one vast "middle class," there are considerable and measurable differences between sectors of the Canadian population. We will first consider differences in wealth.

At the top of the income distribution, an elite consisting of about 2% of the population holds nearly one-third of the total wealth, as well as the majority of significant decision-making positions in the economic institutions. John Porter in the 1960s, and Wallace Clement in the 1970s, provided evidence of strong homogeneity within this class.[6] The members tend to be related through marriage, and families tend to inherit both wealth and position. By descent, they are almost exclusively British. By occupation, they are mainly in financial, professional, and managerial positions, and their income is not derived mainly from salaries or wages as it is for other groups in the population: it is derived from inheritance and investment profits.

In 1983, there were 9 363 individuals with reported taxable incomes over $250 000. A total of 55 147 individuals with incomes above $100 000 comprise 0.5% of Canadian taxpayers (a total of 15 302 940). About 4.4% pay taxes on incomes of $50 000 or more.[7]

There is a considerable gap between this class of wealthy taxpayers and the rest of the population. Nearly half (48.5%) of all taxpayers received less than $13 000; and 70.6% received less than $22 000. Over time since 1977 (as reported in the second edition of this text), the proportion with incomes over $250 000 has increased, but of course, inflation has also increased so that $250 000 in 1981 is substantially less real income than in 1977. Over the same period, the proportion with less than $13 000 has also increased, though the extent of this is not clear because Revenue Canada shifted from calculations based on all returns instead of only taxable returns after 1979. This would alter the lower-income figures more than the upper-income, since more lower-income individuals would pay no taxes. The 1984 data show an increase from a third to nearly a half of the population in this low-income category since 1977, but this shift makes comparisons problematic.

With reference now to family incomes, the trend during the years 1977–1984 is toward a decline in shares of total national income received by the lower groups and an increase in the share received by the top group. Figure 2 shows the 1984 figures, with the 1977 figures in brackets, for shares of total income going to the population of families. These figures represent only reported taxable income. As the discussion further on in this chapter indicates, the taxable income of the wealthy is less representative of their true incomes than is that of the poor.

Taxable incomes are reported for individuals. Since many adults share family incomes, the distribution of income for family units

FIGURE 2

Family income quintiles, 1984 (1977 in brackets)

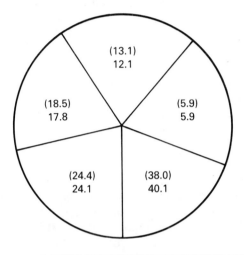

Family population divided into equal fifths; percentage of total income to each fifth.
Source: National Council of Welfare, *Poverty Profile 1985*, p. 65.

may better indicate the distribution of wealth and poverty in Canada. In 1984, the top fifth, or 20% of families, earned just over two-fifths, or 40%, of the total national income. This share was not very different from that of 1951. From this top fifth, there is a sudden drop in share of the total wealth. The distribution is shown in Table 1, and a pictorial description is shown in Figure 2. As can be seen, the bottom fifth of the population (including as many families as the top fifth) earned under 6% of the income.

In 1969, the Senate established a poverty committee whose task it was to determine how many Canadian families had incomes that did not permit them to live at a "reasonable" standard, and what were their characteristics. The method of determining a reasonable level was to estimate what it costs to feed, house, and clothe a family of a certain size in Canada for any given year, and still have any discretionary income for education, medicine, recreation, and such other items as allow people to participate in the industrial society. Then the number of families who were unable to meet the requirements for food, housing, and clothing were computed. The committee estimated that one-quarter of the Canadian population lived below the poverty line. The poverty rate for single persons living alone was 38.7%; for families, it ranged between 15.6% for four-person units to 28.5% for larger units.[8] The Economic Council of Canada estimated that 29% were in this position in the same year, and some estimates exceeded this.[9]

Since these studies were published, there has been a much greater concern about poverty in the midst of affluence, and further studies have continued to describe its existence. Among the more thorough of these have been a series of publications by the National Council of Welfare.[10]

This series includes a detailed examination of "the working poor," that is, families in which one or more income earners regularly bring home wages insufficient to raise a family outside of poverty. The Council estimates that 60% of Canada's poor derive the greatest part of their income from work. Of all families with children, 8% are among the working poor.

The National Council of Welfare estimated that in 1984 there were over 1.2 million children under the age of 16—one in five—in low-income families. This was an increase of 35% since 1980.[12] Poverty, clearly, has not been eradicated in Canada, and its incidence appears to be increasing throughout the 1980s.

Where, then, is the middle class? Porter suggested a cut-off point of $8000 annual family income as the bottom of the middle class for 1961. He defined the middle class as one with a fairly affluent life-style, including the ownership of a house, a car, and possibly a boat or a summer cottage, with the chance of occasional holidays abroad or the capacity to maintain a university student. This is the image of the middle class portrayed on American television. Yet less than 20% of the population of 1961 had an annual income of $8000 or more. The mean income was $5317. In the mid-1980s, the dollar figure would be much higher but the proportion able to afford such a life-style would be, if anything, smaller than in 1961.

Another definition of middle class is: all families and individuals whose major source of income consists of wages and salaries or self-employment income, and whose welfare and investment incomes are both less than 10%. In other words, the working class. This definition would include all but the top 2% and a bottom 10% who must live on welfare. By this definition, classes are not defined by wealth—though there is a great difference in their income positions—but by their relationship to the productive mechanisms of the society. The top class owns those mechanisms; the plants, the mills, the resources, the commercial enterprises; in short, industry. The working class is employed at wages to operate the mechanisms. The bottom class is marginal to the industrial mechanisms, un-employed and *therefore* unable to maintain itself. Within the working class as a whole, an important development has been taking

TABLE 1

Share of total family income received by each quintile of the total population of families. Selected years, 1951–84. *

Year	Lowest fifth %	Second fifth %	Middle fifth %	Fourth fifth %	Highest fifth %	Total
1951	6.1	12.9	17.4	22.4	41.1	100.0
1954	6.5	13.5	18.1	24.4	37.5	100.0
1957	6.3	13.1	18.1	23.4	39.1	100.0
1959	6.8	13.4	17.8	23.0	39.0	100.0
1961	6.6	13.5	18.3	23.4	38.4	100.0
1965	6.6	13.3	18.0	23.5	38.6	100.0
1967	6.8	13.3	17.9	23.5	38.5	100.0
1969	6.9	13.0	18.0	23.4	38.7	100.0
1971	5.6	12.6	18.0	23.7	40.0	100.0
1974	6.3	13.1	18.2	23.6	38.8	100.0
1977	5.9	13.1	18.5	24.4	38.0	100.0
1979	6.1	13.0	18.4	24.3	38.3	100.0
1981	6.4	12.9	18.3	24.1	38.4	100.0
1984	6.1	12.3	18.0	24.1	39.5	100.0

	Upper limits 1980s					Average $
1981	15 126	23 767	31 783	42 514	N/A	30 440
1984	16 473	27 084	37 140	50 228	N/A	35 583

* For years 1951–61, these refer to non-farm families and total non-farm income. For subsequent years, all families are included. A family is an economic unit of related individuals sharing a common dwelling-unit.
Sources: Staff study, D.B.S., *Incomes of Non-Farm Families and Individuals in Canada, Selected Years 1951–65* (Cat. No. 13-529), Tables 4 and 12; Statistics Canada, *Income Distributions by Size in Canada, 1977* (Cat. No. 12-207), Table 72 and 1984, Table 74. Average Family Income from National Council of Welfare, Poverty Profile 1985. Reproduced by permission of the Minister of Supply and Services Canada.

place. The number of wage-earners per family has increased, although the total distribution of incomes has not appreciably changed since 1951. To earn the same relative income, families require more wage-earners today than they did in 1951. According to the National Council of Welfare, there would be an increase of 51% in the number of poor families in Canada if families now existing on two incomes were obliged to live on one.[14] In other words, for many families it is absolutely essential that two adults earn wages if they are to maintain a standard of living above the poverty line. In 1984, 43.6% of the families with incomes of $60 000 or more had two or more income-earners. Of families earning under $12 000, 2% had two or more income-earners. Clearly, one income for a family is insufficient; a $12 000 income in 1984 was about a third of the average income for all families and was inadequate to meet the reasonable standards established by the various councils on poverty. At the average income level, 12.5% of families had two or more income-earners.[15]

A definition so comprehensive masks the considerable differences in wealth between the individual who earns $100 000 as an employee, and the individual who earns $5000 and keeps a family only by pooling earned income with another member of a working unit. Both may be working class or, by this definition, middle class, but clearly their experiences of Canadian life will be very dissimilar. As well, there are differences in status and authority, as between the manager and the production worker or service worker, which are too important to ignore in describing the nature of a class. A modified description of the middle class by life-style definition, together with that by relationship to the productive mechanisms of the society, would provide a middle class consisting of most of the population earning over the mean income level; that is, about 40% of Canadian families.[16] The ideology which suggests one homogeneous middle class has no way of explaining the circumstances for the remainder of the population.

The question is, though, do these differences persist over generations? Are the children of the rich born to be financiers and managers in their turn, and are the children of the poor doomed to inherit poverty? The ideology argues that all have equal opportunity and that the opportunity is experienced within the educational system.

4

When we examine the university population, we discover that it is not evenly distributed over the total population of families. Students tend to belong to families whose heads have high incomes and high status occupations as well as high educational levels. A detailed study of the 1961 census data revealed that children of professionals and managers made up half or more of all students in the professional schools, although their fathers comprised about one-sixth of the labour force. At the other end of the scale, the children of labourers were scarcely represented, although their fathers comprised one-tenth of the labour force. Students in law and medicine were disproportionately the children of professional fathers. The largest proportion of children from homes where the fathers were farmers and

TABLE 2

Highest Education Attained by Education of Respondents' Fathers, Canadians Aged 17–64, 1984.

| | Education of Respondents' Father | | | | | |
Highest Education Attained by Respondent	Elementary only	Some Secondary	Completed Secondary	Some Post-secondary	College Completed	University Completed
No College or University Education	77.1	63.2	51.8	46.5	40.9	28.5
College and University	22.9	36.8	48.2	53.5	59.1	71.5
College including some Postsecondary	16.9	26.4	30.9	34.1	40.0	37.0
University	6.0	10.3	17.3	19.5	19.1	34.5

Source: Statistics Canada. Unpublished data from the *Adult Education Survey*, Labour Force Supplement, 1984.
Note: Totals may not add up to 100% due to rounding.

labourers were enrolled in education faculties, general arts and science programs, and engineering. Thus, even among those who reached university there was some stratification by parents' occupation.[17]

Between 1961 and the mid-1980s, the general level of education has greatly increased. University education has been heavily subsidized during that period; loans and other financial aids have been increased, and community colleges have been expanded. Yet university students are still far more likely to be the children of university-educated parents than the children of parents with less education. A 1984 study of the distribution of education of fathers compared to the education of respondents shows a very high relationship: of fathers with elementary education, 77% of children did not obtain college or university educations; of fathers with university educations, 71.5% of children had university/college educations (Table 2). An earlier study in the mid-1970s indicated that the proportion of university students whose fathers had university degrees had increased over the previous five-year period.[18]

If no children from the homes of labourers and low-income families ever entered university, a class system would be easily recognized. Some children from these backgrounds do enter university, and some from more privileged backgrounds do not. However, the process of inter-generational mobility via the educational channels is less effective for the lower income groups than for the middle-income groups. Where fathers are clerical workers and in skilled trades, there is a much better chance of their children attending university than if the fathers are in primary industrial sectors or agriculture and are employed in labouring jobs. The congruence between a father's occupation, and attendance at university leads to questions about the social, rather than the individual and private, reasons. Such reasons may include the costs of university attendance, regional disparities in educational facilities, cultural influences of homes, and conditions in the school programs and surroundings that lead to disadvantages for children not in the "middle" class. Whatever the explanation, an assumption of equal opportunity is not valid.

It is of some interest that these same relationships were examined by a pioneer in sociology in Canada, Leonard Marsh, in 1940. Marsh noted then that the relationship between school attendance past the age of 14 and the class of parents was marked. For example, 50% of the children from the managerial class in a 1930 survey were in school after that age; only 20% of the children from the unskilled, manual class continued their education beyond 14 (class here being defined as parents' occupation).[19] What has occurred in the meantime is that the average educational levels have increased and the majority of young people remains in school until near or full completion of their secondary education. But with the rising average, the proportional representations by parental class have not significantly changed at either end of the scale.

Education is a major component in the success story, as the ideology suggests. The economic elite studied by Porter and Clement consists of very well educated men (not women). They are engineers, scientists, lawyers, chartered accountants, and financial experts, or people who have already achieved successful careers in political, military, and other professional areas. The political elite—those who have occupied cabinet positions over the 1940–70 period of these studies—are also highly educated. Porter found that 86% had university educations, and 64% of these were lawyers. Of those whom he identified as having the top positions in the federal civil service, 87.5% had university degrees, and in the intermediate positions in the federal service, professionals in law, science, engineering, and the social sciences were the usual incumbents.[20]

The disparity between the ideology and the reality does not come with its linking-up of education with success, but in its assumption that all have equal chances of gaining an education, of entering university, and of reaching the most powerful positions even with university educations. These positions—the corporate directorships and the heads of dominant companies—are overwhelmingly reserved for the children of those who already occupy top positions. The disparities between groups in access to education and in access to directing heights in the economy are not all attributable to the same cause. There are disparities by sex which cannot be attributed to class. There are disparities by ethnic origin which may be partially but not wholly connected to class. And there are disparities which, when all of these other factors are equal, can only be attributed to class. That is, they can be best explained in terms of where, in the spectrum of wealth and power, an individual is located at birth or in childhood. Let us look at the disparities by sex and ethnicity.

5

Regardless of the jobs they fill, and regardless of their educational attainments, women earn considerably less than men. So much less, indeed, that the differences between the sexes are greater at each level than those between men at different levels of education and occupational standing. Table 3 shows comparisons between the sexes' incomes by occupation and education for high-income recipients; Table 4, for low-income recipients. More detailed breakdowns by specific jobs show that income inequalities attributable only to sex can run as high as 120%. That is, men earn two and one-fifth more than women in the same jobs.[21] The differences are particularly marked in industries for which high education is not required, and where employees have very low bargaining power, as in low value-producing manufacturing industries (e.g., leather products, furniture and fixtures products).

In addition to these differences in income, there are differences between the sexes in access to many jobs. According to the 1981 census, women comprised 40.9% of the labour force, but of all managerial workers, they comprised 27.3%.[22] This is a rise since 1971, but equality remains a long way off. Women are employed in clerical, service, and low-paying professional jobs, especially teaching and nursing. These are not only low-income jobs; they are not on the hierarchical ladder that leads to high positions.

Women are disproportionately represented amongst the poor and the working poor. The National Council of Welfare has published data showing that four out of ten families headed by women are

TABLE 3

Representation of men and women at income levels of $30 000 or more within selected occupations and educational levels, 1984.

	Men % Earning $30 000 or more	Women % Earning $30 000 or more
Occupation Group		
Managerial	55.9	17.9
Professional	50.1	20.6
Clerical	21.9	3.8
Sales	26.3	5.4
Service	17.1	1.6
Farming	13.1	4.9
Processing and Machining	30.7	1.7
Product Fabricating	25.6	2.2
Transport	26.0	2.7
Construction	26.6	(insufficient number)
Educational Level		
University degree	59.2	26.1
Post secondary diploma	33.6	7.8
Some post secondary school	23.7	5.2
Some secondary school	20.9	2.8
0-8 years	12.9	1.2

Source: Calculations based on *Income Distribution by Size in Canada, 1984*, Table 60 & 61, Cat. No. 13-207 (Ottawa: Information Canada).

poor, compared to one in ten headed by men. The poverty rate in 1984 for families headed by women was 42.9% compared to 11.3% for those headed by men. Unattached women have a greater chance of being poor than unattached men, their poverty rate being 43.3% compared to 32.4% for men. Women comprise 57.2% of the elderly in Canada, but 70.7% of the elderly poor.[23]

It is apparent from these figures that many women are unable to earn sufficient incomes to keep either themselves or their families. If they are not married to an income-earning man, their chances of living in poverty are extremely high.

Men also live in poverty; many also earn incomes too low to keep their families. But the greater proportion of women in this category indicates the greater proportion of jobs performed by women which are low-paying, and the lesser access to jobs or other means of subsistence in our society.

TABLE 4

Representation of men and women at income levels of under $9000 within selected occupations and educational levels, 1984.

	Men % Earning under $9000	Women % Earning under $9000
Occupation Group		
Managerial	4.7	13.4
Professional	11.5	19.8
Clerical	17.4	29.0
Sales	23.9	52.9
Service	34.9	60.1
Farming	36.3	58.1
Processing and Machining	12.4	40.6
Product Fabricating	14.6	31.4
Transport	19.2	40.9
Construction	19.5	(insufficient number)
Educational Level		
University degree	9.9	23.9
Post secondary diploma	17.2	35.2
Some post secondary school	33.7	49.9
Some secondary school	28.0	52.9
0-8 years	33.1	70.9

Source: Calculations based on *Income Distribution by Size in Canada, 1984,* Table 59, (Ottawa: Information Canada).

6

There are considerable differences in educational attainment for various ethnic groups in Canada. The majority of native Indian and Inuit people of working age have no, or minimal, elementary education. Asiatic, Jewish, and British people have relatively high proportions whose educational attainment includes university. The Italian, Ukrainian, and French people have relatively high proportions whose educational attainments are less than secondary school level.[24]

Differences in educational attainments carry through to occupational and to income differences. The British, Asiatic, and Jewish groups have greater representation at the high levels and lower representation at the lower levels of the occupational ranking scale than the other ethnic groups. The total population of Jews and Asians is small, and in fact the majority of high-ranking positions are held by British descendants. At the bottom of the occupational and income scale are the native populations, the vast majority of whom are engaged (if they are in the labour force at all) in primary industry (fishing, trapping, logging, mining), or as labourers and service personnel.

These results may be explained in a number of ways (differences in cultural background, differences in motivation to obtain high educational standings, differences in access to educational institutions by region, language differences, and religious influences), but they cannot be explained in terms of individual characteristics.

The income distribution presents more puzzles when ethnic groups are compared. At the end of the 1960s a startling difference still existed between French-speaking and English-speaking peoples. Using the index of mother tongue, the differences in income in 1969 greatly favoured the Anglophones—which was not surprising considering the occupational structure. What was more surprising was that those whose mother tongue was French, and those who were bilingual and of French origin, earned less than those who were unilingually English. The Royal Commission on Bilingualism and Biculturalism studied this evidence and concluded that it could not be explained in terms of differences in education. Regardless of education, Francophones were likely to earn less than their Anglophone counterparts.[25]

According to Porter and Clement for the period up to the mid-1970s, people holding the major economic positions were still predominantly English and Protestant, and this was so even though that group represented a lower proportion of the population with each decade after 1950. Less than 7% of the economic elite were French Canadian in the 1950s, though French Canadians comprised a third of the total population.

There have, however, been some changes since the 1950s. Through the 1960s and 1970s, the major changes were in Quebec, where a steadily increasing proportion of French Canadians either owned substantial businesses or controlled public investments and public enterprises through the Quebec government and its crown corporations, and a "new middle class" was beginning to emerge.[26] As the 1970s drew to a close, French Canadian investors were increasing their presence in the larger Canadian and North American markets.[27]

The greatest differences by ethnicity in the 1980s existed between the European immigrant population and the native peoples. While the Europeans were still stratified with the British descendants at the top and central and southern European descendants at the bottom, the various populations were much more mixed than in previous decades. In the middle ranks especially, all ethnic groups had representation in sufficient numbers to suggest that within the European immigrant population and its descendants, ethnicity had ceased to be an important criterion of success. However, outside this population, native Indians remained and remain now as a separate population.

Native people, unlike immigrants, were never incorporated into industrial society. As European society encroached on their tribal territories, they were pushed further and further north, and contained on reserves. The hunting and fishing economic bases for their cultures were eroded. They have existed in great poverty throughout northern and western Canada, and until the late 1960s, they were a silent minority. After that time, and aided by transportation and communication links, various groups began to organize resistance movements. Where there were no treaties, they made the claim that their aboriginal rights had never been extinguished and that they held property rights to territories now being exploited by non-Indians. In the early 1970s, the James Bay Cree Indians took the Quebec government to court in connection with the proposed development of their region. In the mid-1970s, Justice Thomas Berger's Royal Commission on the Mackenzie Valley Pipeline proposal brought the dilemmas of the northern Dene and Inuit to the attention of many Canadians. These and other land claim cases and public inquiries have not resulted in great improvements in the situations of natives, but they have informed a much larger public that native peoples have legitimate complaints and unattended needs.

In the 1980s, the ethnic origins of the Canadian population are changing rapidly. European immigration has declined, while immigrants continue to arrive from all other areas of the globe. (See Table 5.) A global shift in trade and investment patterns has some impact on Canada's demography. Atlantic trade has diminished, and trans-Pacific trade has dramatically increased in the past decade. More and more immigrants to Canada are from Asian countries. Canadians have a sad history of discrimination against people of Asian origins, with "anti-oriental" legislation throughout the early 20th century, exclusion of many groups from trade unions and jobs, and the expulsion of the Japanese people from the West Coast during the Second World War. With the influx now of immigrants from Asian countries, other Canadians are facing new tests of their capacity to deal with ethnic differences.

For our inquiry at this stage, the question is, how do we explain differences in income and occupational distributions for different ethnic groups? As long as we see distinctly different distributions, we know that the patterns cannot be explained simply in terms of

TABLE 5

Source of Immigrants 1980–81 to 1984–85.

Region	Fiscal Year				
	1980–81	1981–82	1982–83	1983–84	1984–85
Europe	41 555	48 006	41 646	22 124	20 709
Africa	4 093	5 112	4 336	3 567	3 638
Asia	63 317	48 655	39 298	37 791	41 260
Australasia	1 491	1 248	817	482	545
North & Central America	11 195	11 609	11 290	10 728	10 846
Carribbean	7 304	9 604	8 261	6 480	5 638
South America	5 720	6 288	6 561	4 363	4 033
Oceania	947	1 002	1 146	668	615
Not stated	0	12	113	0	29
Total	135 622	131 536	113 468	86 203	87 313

Source: Canada. Employment and Immigration Commission, *Annual Report 1984–85*, Cat. No. MP1-1985 (Ottawa: Ministry of Supply and Services, 1985), Table 15, p. 64.

individual differences. An explanation in terms of "discrimination" is not really an explanation at all, it is a description of the process. Discrimination has to be explained. Such explanations reach beyond simple ideologies.

7

There is another dimension of inequality attached to birth and childhood but neither a "natural" condition such as sex nor one attached entirely to an individual's position within the industrial production system. It is region. Within Canada, the differences in income, employment rates, and types of employment are much too large to attribute to individual causes. The probabilities of being unemployed, of working in primary or service industries, or of earning a low income differ systematically by region.

Prior to the "oil era" in Alberta and Saskatchewan, these two provinces were among the poorest regions of Canada. Between the 1950s and the late 1970s, Alberta became a relatively wealthy region because of its oil royalties. However, it still lacked secondary industry and thus remained dependent on the export of a non-renewable resource. When the oil boom suddenly ended in the early 1980s,

Albertans experienced a rapid decline in living standards. British Columbia has had a similar experience, its boom period being dependent on the export of forest products. Like the Prairie Provinces, it lacks secondary industry, and is dependent on markets outside its borders. As the forest industry went into decline after 1980, British Columbians, like Albertans, have experienced a rapid decline in their living standards. The Atlantic Provinces have suffered the greatest poverty of all regions, and this has persisted throughout the 20th century. Rural Quebec has also known great poverty. The southern urban areas of Quebec and Ontario have been the industrial heartland of Canada throughout Canada's lifetime. It is only in these regions that manufacturing industries in large numbers are located—about two-thirds of all manufacturing industries are situated there.

These differing economies provide different opportunities to the resident populations. Wealth allows a population to establish and maintain high quality educational and other cultural institutions. It allows young people to stay in school for longer periods of their lives. Manufacturing industries provide a wider range of jobs for well-educated or highly skilled workers, and in general (though not always) provide more stable employment than do resource industries. Thus, people raised in a wealthy region have better opportunities to obtain education and high-paying jobs than those raised in poorer regions. Table 6 shows the distribution of wealth by region in 1984.

8

These data suggest that there are dimensions of inequality that are not well explained in terms of individual motivation and achievement. The explanations that are offered for those which do not contradict the more general ideological premises are of two kinds: one, cultural and historical conditions of a "happenstance" nature; and two, conditions of nature and geography. These explanations do not challenge the liberal theory; they supplement and modify it.

With respect to the ethnic differences between European descendants, for example, an historical explanation of inequality may be provided. One can point to the conquest of 1760, the dominance of the Catholic Church and the seigneurial system of tenure in Quebec throughout the 19th century, the *quasi*-feudal nature of Quebec right into the 20th century, the classical colleges in that province which could not compete with the business schools elsewhere on the continent, and the wages of English-speaking, and particularly, of American, immigrants to the commercial cities during the critical years

TABLE 6

Distribution of family income by province, 1984.

	% Total	Atlantic				Centre			Prairies		Coast
		% Nfld.	% P.E.I.	% N.S.	% N.B.	% Que.	% Ont.	% Man.	% Sask.	% Alta.	% B.C.
Under $12 000	10.4	15.2	10.7	13.8	15.2	11.9	8.1	10.0	12.2	10.0	10.7
$12 000–24 999	25.1	36.5	35.6	31.0	30.0	26.5	22.4	27.9	29.6	22.7	24.9
$25 000–34 999	20.2	19.5	23.1	21.6	21.3	21.1	20.4	20.4	19.0	19.2	18.7
$35 000–59 999	32.9	23.0	25.7	26.6	27.4	30.3	36.0	32.4	29.0	33.7	34.2
$60 000+	11.5	5.6	5.1	7.1	6.0	10.3	13.2	9.4	10.2	14.5	11.6
Total	100.0	100.0	100.0	100.0	100.0	100.0	100.0	100.0	100.0	100.0	100.0
Average Income	35 767	28 003	29 183	30 820	30 191	33 911	38 464	33 783	33 090	37 670	35 944
Median Income	32 167	24 255	26 400	27 332	27 032	30 567	34 571	30 800	29 216	34 145	32 696

Source: Adapted from Statistics Canada, *Income Distributions by Size in Canada, 1984* Cat. No. 13-207 (April, 1986), Table 2, pages 48, 49. Reproduced with permission of the Minister of Supply and Services Canada.

of the British colony. These historical events may be used as explanations for the present inequalities between the English and French charter groups. Other ethnic groups entered Canada at different periods, and according to their settlement patterns, the skills they brought with them, their original wealth, and their ability to fit into the dominant Anglo-Saxon and English-speaking world, they obtained their respective ranks. Of recent date, the great population and technological sophistication of the Americans have made them a dominant power, and their large degree of control of the economy of Canada may be explained in these terms.

Supplementing the historical explanation are cultural explanations of stratification by non-utilitarian measures (ethnicity and sex). Various groups perceive the world and themselves through particular cultural interpretations which disadvantage them in competing with other groups. Languages, religions, and world-views differ in their emphasis on material goods and public power, on the place of the individual and the rights of the collectivity. They also provide different evaluations and even measurements of time, space, and humankind as a part of nature.

Industrial man is distinguished from pre-industrial man in his view of the individual as a distinct entity with personal prerogatives over which the community has no rights, in his pursuit of personal wealth and power, in his division of time into minute portions to be parcelled out with utmost care, and in his systematic exploitation of nature. Industrial society has divided the world of experience into work and non-work, into the economy and the social sectors. A male member of this society gains his status from his work role, and obtains his material wealth from that role. Other roles tend to be subordinated to that one, and it is seen as somehow distinct from his other roles as father, husband, friend, neighbour, and member of non-economic institutions such as churches and social clubs.

Industrial woman is distinguished from pre-industrial woman in her lack of a clearly defined position in an income-oriented society. Buffeted by cartoons depicting a little girl attending to the demands of a little boy which are labelled "Love is . . . ," and pressed simultaneously by the increasing need for a second income in a family and by the pervasiveness of the tie between personal status and paid work, she is fully rewarded neither for fulfilling the roles of lover and mother, nor for competing with men for economic status.

This is an arrangement alien to pre-industrial societies, where work and communal activity were consonant, and where economic activity was simultaneously religious, political, and family activity. It is not "natural" to seek private possessions at all costs, to have no strong links with a community, to live life at the pace of the white rabbit in *Alice in Wonderland* or to separate work from other aspects of life. These are part of a learned ethos and one, as far as we can understand of history, that arose painfully during the Industrial Revolution. It was not the ethos of the North American Indian societies, nor of many of those from which Europeans migrated to Canada. These people, then, were at a disadvantage in competing with those European immigrants who came from industrialized areas, people who already shared such an ethos.[28]

Conspicuous among the latter were British Protestants who inhabited the New England States and who, after the American War of Independence, came to Canada as the Empire Loyalists. These people were already urban dwellers, used to a money economy, and imbued with what has since come to be known as "the Protestant Ethic."[29] Whether the religious ethic promoted the spirit of capitalism, as Max Weber argued, or simply grew out of it and supported capitalism, remains a central debate of Western thought. Weber contended that Protestantism, by emphasizing individual responsibility for sin and redemption, and by insisting—in its Calvinist form—that each man must prove his eligibility for heaven, gave rise to the characteristics that underlie an industrialized and capitalistic economy. Catholicism, on the other hand, by concentrating on the rewards of the afterlife and the essential equality of all sinners in this life, maintained the characteristics necessary for the feudal, community-oriented economy.

The differing concepts of life and the individual, combined with historical circumstances, may be thought to have given rise to the present inequalities of positions in the Canadian society. Protestants and Jews (who share the present- and individualistic-oriented ethic) have reached the top positions because they first and most consistently held the beliefs and sentiments suitable for an industrial society. Catholics of French, Ukrainian, Italian, and Irish descent have lower positions because they clung to future-oriented and community ethics. Native Indians were left far behind because they shared none of the sentiments that paved the way for industrialism.

A similar argument may be made with respect to differences between the sexes. Socialization of boys and girls takes different forms, so that while boys are taught to want certain social goals that lead to wealth and power, girls are taught to want other goals such as love, children, and homes dominated by men. These are cultural differences, even though the same culture distributes the two versions of appropriate goals and values.

Cultural differences could also be cited with respect to the disadvantages of children from low-income families. Low-income occupation and low education are frequently associated with particular ethnic and religious group members. The children in families characterized by these memberships may not attend universities because their general cultural orientation puts them at a disadvantage with respect to individualistic and commercial pursuits. But beyond this, for low-income families of all ethnic groups, the general cultural awareness within the family may fail to motivate children to seek a higher level of living than their parents.

With respect to regional inequalities, the conventional explanation is that various regions are differentially endowed by nature with resources. Richly endowed regions are better able to develop industry and thus to feed and maintain their populations. Supplementing this explanation, one may point to the historical development of Canada from the centre toward the West, a development that made the West, until it reached maturity with the oil economy, necessarily dependent on initiatives taken in the central regions.

These explanations allow for a modification of the bargaining or functionalist model without challenging its major definitions of the social structure. Reformers who work within these explanations may debate the specific rankings of different jobs, or may point to the obstacles encountered by underprivileged groups which are contrary to the belief in equality of opportunity. They may attempt to change people's beliefs about the needs for certain jobs, or about the respective merits of the sexes or of the ethnic groups. They may also attempt to change the self-images and goals held by the different sexes and ethnic groups. Action toward reform may be directed toward removal of barriers to education for certain groups, or toward the raising of incomes of certain occupational groups. Or it may be directed toward a redistribution of the benefits of industrial development, through various welfare schemes.

9

With respect to these reforms, the liberal society has instituted what is often referred to as a "progressive income tax," and, for purposes of reducing regional disparities, an "equalization" system. In addition, since the 1930s, Canada has provided a number of income supplements for those living below the poverty line, and since 1940, has maintained an unemployment insurance system to aid those without wages.

As the income data presented earlier suggest, these many attempts at redressing the income inequalities have not succeeded. Since 1951, the distribution of income has not altered the relative shares of income for the rich and poor. In a detailed study of the taxation system the National Council of Welfare argues that it is in fact a "regressive tax" system, and that, contrary to beliefs, the larger part of welfare payments actually go to those with wealth.[30]

This may seem a most unacceptable argument to those who assume that the tax system taxes the wealthy at a higher rate than it taxes the poor, and that "transfer payments," or "welfare," are exclusively given to poor people. The argument rests on two facts. One is that while the rate of taxation does increase with income, so do the allowable deductions. Only the wealthy can afford to deduct capital expenditures, work-related expenses, retirement savings plans and investments of various kinds, credits against tax, and deferrals of tax. Tax subsidies in the form of, for example, exemptions on portions of investment income, are available only to those who can afford to invest income. Thus the poor do not receive these subsidies.

The Council estimated in 1974 that 17 of the 60-odd of these subsidies were distributed so that the income group earning over $50 000 was able to deduct nearly $4000 per tax filer; those earning under $5000 deducted about $250. In percentage terms, 70% of tax filers, all earning below $10 000 in 1974, received 40% of benefits from these subsidies; the top 11% of tax filers, earning in excess of $15 000, received 33%. This accounts for only 17 of the estimated 60 tax subsidies because the Council could not obtain information from the taxation authorities regarding the distribution of other subsidies.[31]

These figures ignore some of the extreme examples of legal tax evasion. In 1974, approximately 250 individuals earning incomes over $50 000 paid no income tax at all. In 1983, 8102 individuals with incomes over $50 000 paid no taxes.[32] Among the explanations for this are numerous tax shelters built into the income tax provisions which can be utilized only by those with wealth.

The second fact cited by the Council is the condition of taxation laws that cause both the poor and the wealthy to deduct the same amount for necessary costs such as child care, or to obtain tax credits differentially according to income. As well, there are the equal welfare payments such as family allowance and pensions which are given to poor and rich alike. These do not reduce the inequalities between the two extremes; they maintain it.

As a consequence of these various aspects of the direct taxation system, the shares of income *after* taxes are almost identical to those *before* taxes. If one adds to this the indirect taxation systems, such as sales tax, the remaining disposable income begins to diminish much more rapidly for the poor, since they pay exactly the same amount as do the wealthy. The same is the case for consequences of provincial health insurance premiums, contributions to the Canada/Quebec Pension Plan, and the Unemployment Insurance premiums. The Unemployment Insurance program is perhaps the least equitable of these schemes, in that the low-income workers pay the highest rate for the lowest coverage.[33]

The persistence of inequalities by ethnicity, sex, region, and income position of parents in spite of the growth of a welfare system and equalization schemes may still be explained by the liberal as defects in the system rather than endemic conditions of the system. There are, none the less, several structural conditions of the system that are unexamined in that explanation. Two of these factors are ownership rights and group bargaining powers, both of which are hard, objective economic conditions and not ones attributable to "cultural" or ideological causes. Those who accept the conventional perspective on the basic organization of the society, but recognize the inequalities, may identify these factors as irrational or accidental forces which distort the overall structure, but they are less easily explained away than ethnic and sex differences.

Different incomes, for example, are held to motivate competent people to take on the most important tasks in society. Yet the total wealth of individuals is not the same as earned income. Two additional sources are inherited wealth and investment profits. While high income may act as an initial motivator to potential recruits for functionally important jobs, high income over time generates new income from investment sources and confers on the wealthy a range of ownership rights. Ownership rights include the purchase of labour and the profiting from the products of others' labour. Those who become most wealthy need not be those who could best perform important tasks, and indeed the tasks for which they gain an income may become less important to them as a source of wealth than their investments. Wealth, in addition, can be transmitted to another generation. Wealthy young people are not receiving high rewards for their functional position in society, but for their inheritance rights.

In addition to these differences in access to wealth, the liberal theory tends to ignore differences in bargaining power held by groups in the society. Conventional wisdom treats groups as aggregations of individuals who share common histories and cultures. But industrial society is not made up only of individuals all seeking, within their varying conceptions and possibilities, their share of the available goods and services. It also consists of organized groups which act as single units vis-à-vis the rest of society. These groups include corporations which have virtual monopolies over certain sectors of the economy, government corporations, organized professional associations, employers' associations, and labour unions.

Within the liberal framework, we are led to a view of society which has many of the attributes of a free market. Each individual or each group sells a commodity at the best price and buys at the best price. As the more talented manage their market affairs more efficiently, they push out the less capable and these must accept lower rewards for lesser talents. In a sense, the entire process is a bargaining system. However, these organized interest groups cannot be treated as free and open to all comers where these organized interest groups exist.

Whatever the importance of their task to the industrial society, any group which possesses the collective right to strike or to set prices has greater bargaining strength than any individual. Dentists, for example, have remarkably high incomes, second only to doctors and judges on the occupational ranking scale. It seems odd that they should have higher incomes than professors and kindergarten teachers, if in fact the educational mobility channels are so important to the maintenance of society. Although much discomfort can be occasioned by a toothache, few careers are lost for the sake of a tooth. The difference between dentists and teachers is organization. The dental associations in Canada have a monopoly on the teething of the nation. Teachers, until very recently, tended to form very loose associations with no bargaining power and no binding agreements between employers and the individuals represented by the associations.

The same inequality of bargaining power is evident between clerical workers (mostly female) and truck drivers, construction workers, and longshoremen. Although as a group, labourers have a low average income, these particular groups within that occupational category have relatively high incomes. Clerical workers, on the other hand, are not organized in any large numbers, and this is particularly true for workers in offices which contain mainly female employees.[34]

Similar organization affects the incomes and power of any group of employers who act collectively vis-à-vis the workers in any industry. If only one firm provides employment for a certain class of worker, or for all the workers in a given region, that firm is in a position to establish wages which may be higher or lower than those offered elsewhere, and which are not necessarily in line with the overall distribution of incomes by occupation and education. In addition, those who have a monopoly of capital may, given sufficient technological expertise, establish industries that are capital-intensive, that is, which require very little human labour for their operation. Where this is possible, labourers have no service to sell and no bargaining power.

These organized interest groups cut across the institutional sectors, and while they provide for a hierarchy of incomes that is roughly congruent with education and occupation (modified by sex, ethnicity, and age), it is doubtful that they provide for a hierarchy of power that fits the functional model. Power becomes the property of organized groups, and these are not evenly distributed nor do they balance one another within the various institutional sectors.

The ideology places the blame for failure on individuals. Yet the data we have surveyed suggest that many of the inequalities are structural, that is, embedded in the very nature of the economy itself. There are fewer jobs available than there are workers to fill them, and thus even if every single available job were filled there would be unemployment. The unemployment would be particularly severe in regions where there are few industries or mainly seasonal employment. Further, many jobs provide incomes below the poverty line; thus, though one or two workers in a family provide their labour, their families live in poverty. These low-income jobs are held especially, though not exclusively, by women; thus many women live in poverty and raise their children in poverty even though they work for income. The puzzle in this is that in spite of an ideology of equality, and the promise of material recognition for industry and participation, employers remain both willing and able to pay low wages for work done. That cannot be attributed to culture, socialization, or lack of ambition on the part of the wage-earners.

The ideology suggests the openness of the system to reform in its assumption that this society is not yet perfect but is capable of perfection. Yet the major reform measures have failed. Regional inequalities persist in spite of equalization payments; poverty persists in spite of a welfare system; the taxation system is finally unable to redress the considerable imbalances between the rich and the poor. These are puzzles that the liberal ideology, with its emphasis on individual achievement, equality of opportunity, a marketplace for competing talents, and an openness to reform, cannot explain.

Further, it cannot adequately explain regional inequalities since, in fact, Ontario and Quebec are not better endowed with resources than the Western or Atlantic Provinces, and historically, the Atlantic region was more industrialized prior to Confederation than Central Canada. The explanation for the movement of industrial capital to Ontario, first from the Atlantic region, then from the West, and more recently from Quebec, is not a simple function of geographical location. In order to explain this, one has to move outside the liberal paradigm.

Finally, what is unobserved by a focus on individuals is the remarkable lack of secondary industry in Canada. Outside of Ontario, scarcely any manufacturing industry exists. After over a century of political independence, Canada's economy remains dependent mainly on resource extraction and export of raw materials. Given the natural wealth of the country and a well-educated, industrially skilled population, one is obliged to ask why.

3 FREE ENTERPRISE IN (RELATIVELY MORAL) NATION STATES

The liberal theory of economic development for a new country such as Canada in the 19th century postulates an incremental growth process whereby a nation first exploits its raw materials for an export market, and obtains sufficient capital from these transactions to invest in the construction of infrastructure (roads, canals, railways, and public institutions such as schools). On the basis of this construction, it can extract more resources and accumulate greater wealth, at each juncture investing further in the basic conditions for the development of industry. Finally, the country will have a fully developed infrastructure and will be able to invest in both the industries which manufacture the means of production (e.g., agricultural machinery for a wheat economy, or logging machinery for a timber trade), and industries which produce new products from raw materials (e.g., flour and baked goods from wheat; furniture and paper from timber). As these industries develop, the population grows and demands more consumer goods, thus providing the basis for a diversification of industry. As new industries "spin off" from the original base, the country becomes fully industrialized. This theory has been advanced by numerous neo-classical economists and historians, by governments, and by *quasi*-governmental institutions such as the Economic Council of Canada.[1]

A number of assumptions are built into this theory. The most essential is that the society acts as a cohesive unit. Investment is determined by "the people" acting in the interests of the total national unit, and acting rationally with reference to the ultimate industrial growth for the total society. There are no classes and no class interests involved in the process. The second is that investments are always ploughed back into the same society, which would follow only if the first assumption were true. The third is that there are no external pressures or other inducements to invest capital obtained through the extraction of resources in one country into the manufacturing industries of another country. This implies that each nation acts out its own linear development pattern entirely independently of the others. This in turn implies that there are no great imbalances between the products of one nation and those of another.

53

If Canada exports timber, then it imports manufactured products but the costs and prices of these exchanges should be roughly equal.

Canada did not, in fact, develop in this fashion. The surplus from the fur trade was, indeed, invested in infrastructural development such as canals and railways, and the new resource trade in wheat was opened up in the 20th century, but after that the postulated growth of secondary industries failed to materialize. Manufacturing industries were established primarily in Ontario, but by 1920 a very high proportion of these were owned by American companies and were subsidiaries of American parent firms. The rest of the country continued to extract resources for export markets, and continues to be dependent on these export trades to the present time. A large part of the surplus obtained from the resource extraction industries was invested outside Canada in the growing manufacturing industries of the United States.

If one is going to explain the actual history of Canadian industrial development, the liberal theory of incremental growth patterns is patently inadequate though it continues to be accepted and promulgated by most public agencies. In order to both explain the actual history and explain why the theory continues to be believed, it is useful to consider the nature of a liberal democracy and the population's more general beliefs about the role of government and private capital.

1

The liberal ideology rests on three distinctive organizational features of the societies in which it is held. The first is that these societies support one or another form of representative government within the framework of the nation state. This support involves periodic elections of members of a government by the population inhabiting a given territory. The second is that their economies are not directed exclusively or even mainly by the governments, and profits from economic transactions may be legally retained—subject only to tax-ation laws—by private citizens or privately owned corporations. The third is that judicial courts evaluate the merits of individual, corporate, and government actions with reference to legislation provided by governments, when any two individuals or other entities disagree on the nature of their prerogatives.

The first of these conditions underlies a range of beliefs and values widely held. One of these is that majority rule is achieved when governments are elected through majority votes of the people, and that rule by majority vote is both democratic and just. In part this belief in justice reflects the further belief, discussed in the second chapter, that there is general equality of condition among the people, so that a government's decisions will equally affect all members. The majority and the minority are assumed to belong to the same, homogeneous population. Also involved is the belief that, since all people have the same single vote, a government does not represent the interests of any one sector of the population, including the wealthy sector. Since there are no classes, parties cannot be class organizations nor governments the means of promoting class interests.

There is a certain contradiction at the core of the liberal view of government. On the one hand, governments are the managers of the system, subject to the wishes of the majority and acting in their interests. On the other, the economy is not directed or managed by governments. Governments, to be sure, are able to enact various kinds of legislation that affect the economy, but such legislation is expected to be regulative and to restrict in no fashion the rights and privileges of the owners and directors of the major economic institutions. Free enterprise means, essentially, private business or business not directed by governments. It is assumed, and often argued, that where a large number of people pursue private profits through individual initiative, the net result is a prosperous and free society. The corollary of this belief is that those societies in which governments own or control large segments of the economy are neither prosperous nor free.

The contradiction is not resolved by the functional model of society postulated within the liberal ideology: a model of independent but interacting institutions, each balancing the others and responding to actions taken in the other sectors. The difficulty lies in the fact that only one of these institutions is subject to electoral vote, and the institutions of the economy are neither required nor expected to subject themselves to majority control. The managers of the system, then, must respond to the directors of the economy and must account for their responses to the citizens; the directors may or may not respond to the managers and are not accountable to the citizens. To the extent that economic institutions influence the daily lives of citizens independent of government management, governments do not govern. Their independent actions are restricted to other spheres, or to responses rather than initiatives in the economic sphere. Majority government, then, does not mean—as it is assumed to mean—direction and control of the society by representatives of the majority.

The precise role of governments is not altogether clear, but the general direction of their actions is, according to the ideology of the liberal state, to provide the framework of legislation by which individuals may pursue their private objectives successfully. As stated by a former Prime Minister of Canada:

[The problem] is posed in the necessity of preserving the independence and self-reliance of the individual, driving home the realization that he stands above the state, which is the essence of liberalism, with the obligation, in the complicated organization of society which we have today of the state to protect the individual when protection is required.[2]

The beliefs in the rights of the individual and the supremacy of the individual over the society are intimately linked to the restriction on government action in the economic sphere. The assumption, then, is that government control of the economy would restrict private freedom, independence, and individual self-reliance. The assumption lies behind the words of John Stuart Mill in 1849:

There is a limit to the legitimate interference of collective opinion with independence. . . .

The sole end for which mankind are warranted, individually or collectively, in interfering with the liberty of action of any of their number, is self-protection.[3]

It was more explicitly stated by Lester Pearson in 1958: "No intervention of the State in the affairs of the individual is justified if it doesn't liberate and release the forces of the individual so he will be better able to look after himself."[4]

Mill talked to recent converts and lingering skeptics in an England torn between the remnants of a land-based class system and the needs of an industrial and urban society. Sentimental attachments to the feudal aristocracy remained. Ideologies do not die easily, and Edmund Burke's eloquent defence of the past written half a century earlier bespoke a passionate attachment to stability, order, and community still felt by many English working men as well as by Lords.[5] Yet the conditions had irrevocably changed, and the change predated Burke's appeal. Burke might rail at the pettiness of the commercial entrepreneurs, at the tragedy of Marie Antoinette's pretty head, at the loss of religion and sense of propriety signalled in the French Revolution. But it was Mill who caught the flavour of the new industrial state. It was a flavour of motion rather than stability, freedom rather than control, personal salvation rather than the collective good. Let a man choose his way of life, he preached, and the collective good will result; let a man act as he pleases, and it will please him to serve his community; let a man serve himself and all men will be well served. Enlightened self-interest—a catch-phrase for the *laissez-faire* economic doctrine of the 18th-century philosopher Adam Smith—became an exciting new venture as Bentham, Mill, and others of the school called "the Utilitarians" preached the new ideology of individualism and efficiency.

The liberal state of the 1970s and 1980s expresses little admiration for the feudal aristocracy. It has labelled "good" those events of history that brought it to an end: the Industrial Revolution in Britain, the French Revolution, and the American War of Independence, the development of colonies, the extension of the franchise, the creation of a landless and mobile labour force, and the establishment of public schools. Individualism is so well entrenched, indeed, that those who called themselves revolutionaries in the 1960s were able to do little more than proclaim the virtues of this creed. To do one's own thing was thought of as remarkably novel, though it was precisely what the leaders of the liberal revolution were doing two centuries earlier.

The threat to individual freedom in this long-developed creed is from governments; governments, therefore, must be restricted. If governments are restricted, then it cannot be assumed that governments, acting supposedly in the interests of the majority, will have the power to direct surplus capital gained in each development stage toward a planned and rational industrial economy. That task is left up to those who control the capital. Since there is no conception in this theory of a class, and capitalism is ordered by discrete individuals each acting in their own interests, one must assume that these interests lie with the growth of an independent nation state.

2

In defining Canada as a nation state, it is assumed that the government of the territory may take independent action even if it cannot control the economy, that the economy is under the control of the citizens of the territory, and that the citizens are sovereign in every other respect. These assumptions were modified in the post-war world by a general recognition that nation states are interdependent through trade and cultural ties, and that peace and international law require the co-operation, and sometimes the waiving of sovereignty, of all nations. These modifications give rise to a high value being placed on internationalism, by which people appear to mean openness or tolerance of other nations and other ways of organizing society. Internationalism, however, depends on the existence of independent nations, and nationalism is its prior condition.

Independent nation states engage in trade: the importing and exporting of goods. Canada's most important export market is the

United States. While a nation state is dependent on its export trade with other countries, and while its dependence is more delicate when its trade ties are predominantly with one other country, this kind of dependence is not, in itself, a threat to national sovereignty. Neither is investment in a nation's industrial assets by non-nationals when the investment takes the form of loans. Canada borrowed money from British investors throughout the late 19th century: this led to foreign indebtedness and high interest rates on the loans, but it did not preclude Canadian ownership of the industries so financed. The outright purchase of Canadian industries through what is known as direct investment is a different process, and unlike trade or portfolio investments (loans), it does pose serious questions about Canadian sovereignty. Throughout the 20th century, the dominant form of investment in Canada has been direct investment, and the investors have been mainly, though not exclusively, American nationals.

The development of an economy in which foreign-owned subsidiaries form an ever larger share of the total assets began shortly after the turn of the century. Reverses in Britain and the remarkable growth of the United States economy pulled Canada into the American orbit. In 1904, tariffs were erected by Canada on certain manufactured goods precisely for the purpose of inducing American firms to set up Canadian subsidiaries. Of this tariff, the finance minister of the Laurier government asserted:

We have some evidence of a gratifying character that the tariff, without being excessive, is high enough to bring some American industries across the line, and a tariff which is able to bring these industries into Canada looks very much like a tariff which affords adequate protection.[6]

By 1945, about 40% of all foreign long-term investment in Canada took the form of direct investment. The process accelerated during the 1950s, and by 1967 this had increased to 60% of which 85% was American and 10% British.[7] (Including all forms of foreign investment in 1967, 81% came from American sources.) This direct investment by the late 1960s created an economy in which at least two-fifths of all non-financial assets (industrial assets outside the sector of financial institutions) were owned, and a somewhat larger proportion were controlled by non-Canadians.[8] The intention of the Laurier government in the early part of the century was to create employment by inducing the firms to establish in Canada. By the second half of the century, these firms owned a significant share of the Canadian economy.

The pace of take-overs of Canadian firms and overall increases in foreign control reached a peak in the early 1970s. Since then, the proportion of foreign ownership in Canadian industry has decreased, and we will discuss the reasons for this trend in Chapter 9. Even with the drop in foreign ownership, non-Canadian firms still held about a quarter of all assets in non-financial industries in 1983, down from 30% in 1977, and they obtained about 44% of all profits in 1983 (Figures 3 and 4).

Measuring the overall totals actually tells us less than measurements for the leading enterprises, because foreign ownership rises sharply with the size of firms, and is greatest in the high-value industrial sectors. Of the leading 500 enterprises in Canada in 1983 (an enterprise consisting of all corporations under the same parent firms), 240 were foreign-owned, and these accounted for 24.3% of all sales for all firms in Canada. They held 18.9% of total assets and generated 37.4% of total profits. The 246 Canadian privately controlled enterprises among the top 500 accounted for 23.7% of all sales, 30.1% of all assets, and 21.9% of all profits.[9] (See Table 7.)

American ownership continues to be dominant, accounting in 1983 for 71.5% of the assets, 76.6% of the equity, 76.2% of the sales, 88.2% of the profits, and 87.5% of the taxable income for all foreign-controlled non-financial corporations.[10]

Foreign ownership and control are especially dominant in the resource industries and manufacturing. Petroleum and natural gas, mining and smelting, chemicals, rubber products, transport equipment, and tobacco products are owned and controlled mainly by non-residents. Other industries with high degrees of control include electrical products and machinery. Canadian ownership tends to be in the less strategic and technologically less advanced industries such as leather products, wood, textiles, and food and beverages.

Once an industry has passed through its initial establishment phase, the need for additional capital investment is greatly decreased. The industry generates profits and these profits are reinvested in improved and enlarged facilities, research and development, and the creation of supplementary industries. Thus, when foreign companies expand or take over existing firms through their subsidiaries in Canada, they need not generate any large amount of new money from their home base. Of the total financing to foreign firms in Canada over the period 1960 to 1967, only 19% was obtained abroad. The remainder came from retained earnings, that is, profits which have not been distributed to shareholders, from capital consumption allowances and depletion allowances in Canada, and from Canadian investors through Canadian financial institutions.[11] In the same period, referring only to expansion funds, 38% came from retained earnings and 21% from Canadian investors. Thirty-three

FIGURE 3

Distribution of Assets of Leading Enterprises, by Control, 1983

LEADING 25 ENTERPRISES

LEADING 100 ENTERPRISES

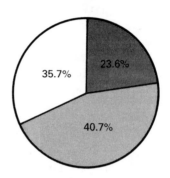

LEADING 500 ENTERPRISES

ALL ENTERPRISES

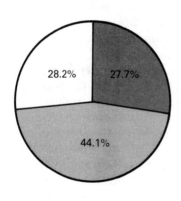
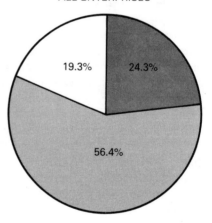

LEGEND

FOREIGN   CANADIAN–   CANADIAN–
                 PRIVATE   GOVERNMENT
                 SECTOR   SECTOR

Source: Corporations and Labour Unions Returns Act, *1983 Report*, (Ottawa: Statistics Canada, 1986) Part I, p. 46: Figure vii.

FIGURE 4

Distribution of Profits of Leading Enterprises, by Control, 1983

LEADING 25 ENTERPRISES

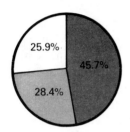

25.9%

45.7%

28.4%

LEADING 100 ENTERPRISES

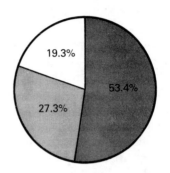

19.3%

53.4%

27.3%

LEADING 500 ENTERPRISES

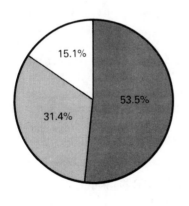

15.1%

53.5%

31.4%

ALL ENTERPRISES

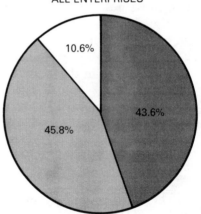

10.6%

43.6%

45.8%

LEGEND

FOREIGN   CANADIAN– PRIVATE SECTOR   CANADIAN– GOVERNMENT SECTOR

Source: Corporations and Labour Unions Returns Act, *1983 Report*, (Ottawa: Statistics Canada, 1986) Part I, p. 47: Figure viii.

per cent of the expansion funds came from the owning countries as new capital investment.[12] In dollar terms, this amount was less than the outflow of capital from these companies to shareholders and in management fees and interest rates. In other words, a foreign company once established in Canada can expand and take over other firms without bringing into Canada any substantial amount of capital. At the same time, it uses the Canadian capital which might otherwise be provided to new and competing firms owned by Canadians. Kari Levitt, in an early study of foreign ownership, gave evidence that in the critical area of mining and petroleum, where American investment increased steadily, only 15% of the new funds for expansion between 1957 and 1964 came from United States' sources. Seventy-three per cent came from retained earnings and depreciation reserves, and 12% was provided by Canadian banks and other financial institutions in Canada.[13]

With this reinvestment potential, the same corporations which owned major resource extraction industries (e.g., mining rights) could establish processing firms either in the dependent nation or in the mother country, and could buy into the transportation, communications, research, distribution, and sales firms which were all connected with the processing of the original resource to its final form as a product for consumption. It is this process of expansion from an original base in Canada which underlies the fact that Canada has a higher degree of foreign control than any other industrial nation. As pointed out in the Gray Report on *Foreign Direct Investment*:

If the government should wish to deal with the rate of growth in foreign control completely, it would not be sufficient to look exclusively at new direct investment. It would also be obliged to take account of the finances obtained from Canadian capital markets and the application by the individual firms of the internal cash-flow.[14]

The organization within which much of the foreign ownership and control is located is the multinational or transnational enterprise. This is an enormous corporation which straddles several different countries and whose major form of control is direct investment. This investment is intended to bring raw materials needed by a parent company from another country, or to extend a manufacturing empire from a home base to outlying areas. The majority of the transnational corporations are still based in the United States, but over the past decade the number of Japanese and European firms successfully competing with American firms has steadily increased. The top 200 corporations account for about 80% of all American foreign direct investment, about 30% of which is in Canada.[15] We will discuss this competition further in Chapter 8.

A giant corporation extending over several countries may form a partial or a complete industrial process. Often operating under a variety of names, and listed as separate firms, the total process may include everything within a single industry from the extraction of the raw material, primary processing, shipping, manufacturing, to sales. Subsidiaries buy from the parent firm or sell to it, so that even where the subsidiary appears to lose money in any one year, it may be a profitable link in the chain for the parent company. The parent company, moreover, can afford to lose money on a subsidiary for a period of time if the loss eventually results in the deterioration of competing firms which cannot likewise afford losses. Subsidiaries do not require research and development facilities or expenditures: they become arms of a parent which maintains the research facilities on the home base. Thus, to the extent that an economy is dominated by subsidiaries, it is not generating competition or new technologies: it is imitative and supportive of the parent firm.

The transnational enterprise is not, in fact, multi-national in any respect other than that it produces materials through subsidiaries in territories other than its home country. Subsidiaries are located, funded, moved, used, and directed according to the needs of the parent firm and its major market, not according to the needs of the dependent countries.

There are several reasons for Canadian concern over the degree of foreign control of their economy, but one of the critical concerns is the loss of the decision-making power that this implies. Those who control the industries also have the right to make major decisions about their location, their employment practices, the kinds of skills to be used in the subsidiary as contrasted with those needed in the parent firms, the amount of technological research to be done, the wages and prices to be paid or received, and the conditions for continued operation. To the extent that Canadian industry is dominated by non-Canadians, these decisions are not within domestic control. This raises a serious question about the sovereignty of Canada. Political sovereignty which does not include the right to make major decisions affecting workers, investment, or location of industries is not a very strong form of sovereignty.

Canadian sovereignty has another dimension which is also affected by her economic situation and by the role played in that situation by American transnational corporations. This is Canada's international role as an independent nation state. Since the Second World War, Canada's military forces have been largely integrated with those of the United States, and her manufacturing enterprises in the arms and strategic industries have come under American ownership and control.

The production of arms and military equipment in Canada is tied in with the *Defence Production Sharing Agreements*, formally signed in 1959. The stated objective of these agreements is:

> ... to increase the participation of Canadian industry in the production and support of North American defence weapons and equipment. The continuing long-term objective is to coordinate the defence requirements, development, production and procurement of the two countries in order to achieve the best use of their respective production resources for their common defence in line with the concept of interdependence and the integration of military arrangements.[16]

The military arrangements were aimed at preventing Soviet attacks on the United States. Canadian government spokespersons of the 1950s asserted that the defence of the United States was congruent with Canadian defence.[17] They did not, therefore, consider a policy of neutrality during the "cold war," nor did they perceive the power distribution of the post-war period in terms other than those stated by American leaders.

The armaments, aircraft, and electronics industries, together with those industries which provide essential minerals for armament production are dominated by American subsidiaries operating in Canada. In some of these industries, aircraft particularly, Canadian firms strove to compete with American firms for defence contracts in the early 1960s. Although the Canadian government financed much of their research, provided capital grants, and purchased war materials, the major purchaser was the United States Defence Department. However, Canadian-owned manufacturing firms competed on unfavourable terms with American firms for American contracts. They tended to either shift over to production of component parts, thus becoming segments of an American industry, or to sell out to American corporations already dominant in the field. By 1963, nearly 80% of the aircraft industry was foreign controlled, and similar proportions of other industries connected with defence production were under foreign—mainly American—control. With respect to the aircraft industry this meant, for example, that American corporations built aircraft in Canadian subsidiaries for sale to the American Defence Department. Furthermore, they were supported financially by the Canadian government, through that government's purchases toward continental defence, and through grants for research and development which totalled nearly 50% of all financing of the industry.[18]

In 1975, the federal government announced its purchase of de Havilland Aircraft of Canada from the Hawker-Siddeley Group of London, England, and its intention to purchase Canadair from General Dynamics of St. Louis, Missouri. The overall objective was the "restructuring [of] Canada's aerospace industry." The announcement stated that the government would subsequently turn these companies over to "responsible Canadian interests," that is, private Canadian corporations.[19] In 1979, a new Conservative government announced its intention to "privatize" these same industries, but an election forestalled any such action. In 1986, another Conservative government sold Canadair to Bombardier of Quebec and de Havilland to Boeing of Seattle, U.S.A. Both firms continue to depend on American defence contracts. This history of purchases and sales raises serious questions about the role of government and the use of public funds.

Coincident with the integration of defence production industries, Canada has joined alliances and undertaken contracts which provide for an effective integration of her military forces with those of the United States. Under the NORAD agreements of 1957, Canadian military forces came under the command of an international body headquartered in Colorado Springs. One test of national sovereignty under such agreements occurred during the Cuban missile crisis in 1962. Although the agreements specify that Canada should be consulted in advance of important NORAD actions, there is considerable evidence that Canada was not consulted in advance of American action, and that when Canada's Prime Minister refrained from giving the orders to the Canadian military forces to go on alert, the military went on alert anyway, under orders from Colorado Springs.[20]

Foreign ownership and integration into the overall military policies of the United States undermine the economic and political sovereignty of Canada. To begin with, the subsidiaries of American firms are subject to American laws, specifically with respect to export contracts. Under the American *Trading with the Enemy Act*, subsidiaries of American firms must obtain their government's approval for export sales, and may not sell any goods to countries defined by the United States as enemies. A great many items produced in Canada are either produced by American subsidiaries or are dependent in various ways on United States supply routes. Thus, to the extent that Canadian industry in general, and the arms industry in particular are owned by American corporations, Canada may not export goods outside the sphere of the United States, and enemies of the United States are by definition enemies of Canada.

Secondly, Canada cannot maintain neutrality in American wars. Although maintaining an official neutrality in Vietnam, the Canadian government subsidized, the Canadian workers produced, and the Canadian people accepted the production of war materials for Vietnam in American subsidiary operations in Canada. Throughout the war, the United States purchased millions of dollars worth of arms from Canada.[21] Many of the Canadian materials were parts, small arms, bombs, and chemicals. But the more strategic materials were minerals essential to the continuation of the war and to the military stockpiling in the United States. Canada has no control over the uses of these materials once they have left her territory.

3

We have concentrated on those aspects of the economy which affect the nation state, because the assumption that Canada is an independent nation state is fundamental to the notion that the Canadian government governs, and governs subject to the wishes of Canadians. The erosion of the nation state, however, is more in the nature of a result than a cause. To understand why it should have occurred, we must return to the second condition of liberal democracies: the system of private enterprise.

Private enterprise means private ownership of economic resources, the means of production, and property, and the right to profit from such ownership. Those who invest money in enterprises are the owners. Those who work in enterprises are not the owners. In a system of totally private enterprise, governments own no shares in industry. Most liberal democracies support some forms of government ownership, however, usually in the non-profit spheres, such as postal services. Where this occurs, the economy is mixed: private and public. Canada, in part because of the sparseness of population and the vastness of territory, in part because of the slow development of capitalism and a capitalistic labour market,[22] and in part because of the rejection of the American model by the Empire Loyalists and the Family Compact, has developed a liberal democracy in which government initiatives in the economy have been more readily accepted than they have been in the United States.[23] Private enterprise has been supported by public enterprise, and in some vital areas—utilities, transportation, communications—governments have held control of significant parts of the industry. Free enterprise in Canada, therefore, means private enterprise in the profit-making sector; public enterprise in the non-profit sector; and public support for private profit-making ventures: a mixed economy, with emphasis on the private sector.

Free enterprise and private enterprise are often used interchangeably, by way of indicating the absence of government intervention or ownership. Free enterprise also means, however, an economic market system in which all comers compete equally for the attention of consumers, and the consumer, through a free choice of products, is sovereign. Within such a system, it is believed that laws of supply and demand will operate: when the supply exceeds the demand, some firms producing the item will fold, leaving the field to the most efficient producers. Likewise, when the demand exceeds the supply, there will be room for new firms to enter the field. The profit margin is determined by consumer sales. The market, in theory, is self-adjusting and the price of goods represents their relative value to consumers. Those who invest their labour in firms receive an income, the income level to be determined by the value of particular skills to the owner. This, in turn, is determined by the value of the product and the profit margin: what it is worth to the owner, given what price he receives for the product. Ultimately, then, wages and prices are determined by consumers in a free and competitive market.

The assumption that such a free and competitive market is alive and well in Canada is illustrated in the comments of a former cabinet minister in Liberal governments:

Liberalism seeks the welfare of all Canadians. In economic affairs, it values the efficiency that springs from free initiative, and from the prevention of monopolistic power. . . . Liberalism opposes the concentration of economic power in a few hands. It rejects all measures that profit special interests by sheltering them from competition; it rejects politics that help business corporations or other organizations to become unnecessarily big and powerful.[24]

It is not important that the speaker is a politician for a particular party, and the word "liberalism" as a political party label may be ignored: if the speaker referred to the Conservative Party, the underlying assumptions would be the same. They are that free initiative operates in the market-place, that concentration of power is not good, and that government is not a coalition for the benefit of special interest groups.

The theory of competition and free enterprise rests on the belief that there are a great many separate businesses competing for the consumer's attention. Competition rests on an equality of condition: that is, equals may compete equally. When, however, there are a few enormous corporations sharing among them a very large proportion of the total market, together with a large number of very small businesses sharing the remainder, it is no longer accurate to talk of a single competitive market. Such is the case in Canada.

The top 25 enterprises (parent firms together with all subsidiaries) accounted for nearly a quarter of all sales and a third of all assets, equity, and profits in Canada in 1983. The top 100 enterprises accounted for nearly two-thirds of all sales and over half of all assets, equity, and profits. Of all separate corporations reporting to Statistics Canada in 1983 (397 965), the top 100 enterprises owned 1398 or 0.003% (Table 7). These data are consistent with trends documented by Statistics Canada throughout the past two decades and with studies going back to the 1940s.

The levels of concentration differ by industry. Four enterprises account for 93.5% of all sales in tobacco products, 91.9% of all storage industry sales, nearly 70% of sales in communications and transport equipment, and between 50 and 65% of all sales in petroleum and coal products, primary metals, rubber products, and public utilities. The industries which are not controlled by a very small group of enterprises are retail and wholesale trade, furniture industries, services, clothing industries, agriculture, and construction.[25]

An enterprise may include corporations in entirely different sectors of industry. Brascan, for example, was once primarily engaged in transportation and communications industries outside Canada, and breweries in Canada. It has since expanded into the resource sectors, and is the major owner of Noranda (which owns mining and forestry companies) and other companies. Olympia and York, owned by the Reichmann family, was primarily engaged in real estate but has more recently moved into resource sectors and the financial sector. Such enterprises may also be known as "conglomerates," firms owning subsidiaries in a range of unrelated industries.

Where a few corporations—transnationals and the banking institutions of Canada—control the majority of industrial enterprises in the country, one must have serious reservations about an ideology promoting the belief that there is free enterprise and competitive capitalism. There are, in fact, two distinct economies: the centre, which controls most of the wealth, and the periphery, which competes for the remainder. The degree of competition at the centre is open to debate. In some areas, the number of independent corporations is so small, or the degree of concentration is so great, that a virtual monopoly exists. In others, the situation is better described as oligopolistic: a number of extraordinarily large firms sharing most of the market between them. There may be competition within an oligopolistic market, but there are also very effective means by which the large companies can reduce their competitive risks. Among these are vertical integration, that is, the buying-out of companies which

TABLE 7

Leading enterprises in terms of sales of non-financial corporations, by control, 1983.

		25 Leading Enterprises			100 Leading Enterprises			500 Leading Enterprises			All Non-Financial Enterprises		
		Foreign	Canadian	Total	Foreign	Canadian	Total	Foreign	Canadian	Total	Foreign	Canadian	Total
Enterprises	No.	9	16	25	44	56	100	240	260	500	3399	387 813	391 212
Corporations	No.	133	452	585	480	918	1398	1241	1929	3170	5239	392 726	397 965
Sales	%	9.5	14.0	23.5	16.3	22.9	39.2	24.3	30.5	54.8	29.6	70.04	100.00
Assets	%	5.7	28.3	34.0	12.3	39.9	52.2	18.9	49.3	68.2	24.3	75.7	100.00
Equity	%	8.1	25.0	33.1	17.3	37.0	54.3	26.4	45.8	72.2	32.9	67.1	100.00
Profits	%	14.9	17.7	32.6	28.0	24.4	52.4	37.4	32.4	69.8	43.6	56.4	100.00

Source: Corporations and Labour Unions Returns Act, *Report for 1983*, Part I—Corporations, Cat. No. 61-210, Statistics Canada, 1986. Text Table viii, p. 43. Reproduced with permission of the Minister of Supply and Services Canada.

provide the raw materials or service the production company, or provide parts, or undertake the sales of the main company. A vertically integrated corporation reduces its risks by setting its own prices in the supply areas and determining its own costs from the extraction of the material right through to the sale of products. Another method is to create the needs and demands of the market: thus the disproportionate amount of corporate funds given over to advertising. Corporations do not simply wait for consumer demand: they introduce new products and advertise these for purposes of creating new demands.

When one attempts to determine who actually owns the largest corporations, an incredibly intricate pattern emerges. A parent company is owned by one or more finance companies which may or may not all be in the same country, though one of these will have the controlling interest. This parent company in turn may wholly own some 20 companies which in turn wholly or partially own another 20 or more companies, which yet again themselves partially own yet further companies. Some of the finance companies are themselves owned by other finance companies.

Decision making has several levels in this complex structure. While decisions about the production within a subsidiary firm may take place within its own board of directors, those directors in turn are appointed by the corporations which own the subsidiary. Their decisions will reflect their own corporate policy and ultimately the interests of the investors in the parent corporation: increasingly, this parent is a financial corporation, not a production corporation at all. It is often thought that these shareholders are numerous and representative of the total population. Nothing could be farther from the truth, especially in Canada. The investment class is small, and the elite within it which holds controlling shares in the major industries is extremely small. The representatives of that investment class may be found on the boards of directors of the major financial institutions. According to John Porter, for the period 1948 to 1950, some 907 individuals shared among them 81% of the directorships in the nine chartered banks, and 58% of those in the life insurance companies.[26] According to C.A. Ashley in a 1955 study, 97 individuals who were directors of Canadian banks held 930 directorships in other corporations in every sector of the economy.[27] Wallace Clement identified the 231 Canadian residents with bank directorships in 1972, who between them held 306 directorships in other dominant corporations, accounting for 25% of all such positions held by Canadian residents. The 145 directors of the 11 most powerful insurance companies also held 220 directorships in other dominant corporations. Bank and insurance company directorships were interlocking for a high proportion of these persons.[28]

Have ownership patterns changed since these studies were conducted? Apparently not. The *Globe and Mail* reported in 1985 that one family (the Bronfmans) directly and indirectly controlled almost one in ten of the publicly traded companies in the Toronto Stock Exchange composite index, including (through Edper Corporation), Brascan, Tizec, Labatt, and Noranda (which in turn owns Macmillan Bloedel and many other corporations); and, through another branch (Cemp), Seagram and Cadillac Fairview. The other major families in Canadian business, and their major corporate holdings, are: Ken Thomson (International Thomson, Thomson Newspapers, and Hudson's Bay); Paul Desmarais (Power Corporation, Canadian Pacific, CP Enterprises); the Reichmann brothers (Olympia and York, Abitibi, Hiram Walker); Galen Weston (George Weston, Loblaws); Conrad Black (Argus, Dominion Stores, Norcen); Southern (Atco, Canadian utilities); and Seaman (Bow Valley).[29]

These families represent the Canadian investment class, and by every measure they wield enormous economic power in Canada. Said the *Globe and Mail* in one report: "Some sectors are concentrated in so few hands that all the controlling shareholders would not make a noticeable difference to the lineup in a bank on a typical Friday afternoon."[30] These same individuals or their representatives are directors of the five largest chartered banks (with about 90% of the assets of the chartered banking industry), life insurance firms (five hold about three-fifths of assets in that industry)[31], and other financial institutions which have provided much of the financing for foreign-owned firms in Canada. Their own corporations are frequently engaged in co-ownership arrangements with foreign firms of subsidiaries in Canada or elsewhere. Thus, we cannot separate the phenomenon of foreign ownership from that of high concentration of ownership, nor neatly separate foreign from domestic corporate holdings.

Whether decision making is done by Canadians or foreigners, there is one important difference between the decisions made by corporate owners and those made by governments: corporations are not accountable to an electorate in any way. They may or may not make decisions that benefit the general public, but they are not required to demonstrate, defend, or even publicly announce those decisions to a Canadian (or other) population. Indeed, in Canada, they are not even required to report fully their financial standing. They make decisions that affect not only their shareholders (whose controlling shares are typically owned by very few individuals or organizations), and not only their employees (whose numbers may be very considerable), but the entire population, and the economic environment and political possibilities of the entire nation (indeed, of many nations). Yet they make those public decisions in private and with reference to private goals and private profit. The ideology of private enterprise is invoked at precisely this point, even though the private enterprise may be financed by government institutions and may be well past the point of competitive enterprise and consumer control.

4

As the data and history discussed in the previous sections indicate, an incremental theory of development is an inadequate explanation for Canadian growth patterns. As with the theory of the classless society, those who hold this view of development processes provide additional and supplementary explanations for the misfit between theory and fact.

The most widely held belief is that growth is ultimately dependent on the natural resources available in a region. It is assumed, therefore, that the regions of Canada which have failed to establish industrial conditions are deficient in this respect. Lawrence Copithorne has demonstrated that contrary to this belief, natural resource endowment is not a major cause of regional disparities in incomes and unemployment in Canada, and is not the cause of differential industrial development. Newfoundland, long the poorest region of the country, is not a resource-poor province with its hydro-electricity, and the largest provincial output of iron ore, and fish. Copithorne argues that in terms of the value of primary production per employed worker, the four poorest provinces (the Atlantic region) and the four western provinces are blessed with greater natural resource endowments per capita than either Quebec or Ontario. He concludes that it is productivity in the non-primary trade-goods industry sector that most critically affects the wage levels in a province.[32]

Productivity in the manufacturing industries would depend on, first of all, the establishment of such industries. Given their establishment, the means of selling the goods would be required, and transportation which is not of such great cost that it makes the goods non-competitive on the world market. Thus, the problems of entry into world markets which are already dominated by multinational corporations, and the costs of transportation from such areas as the Atlantic region to dense population areas such as Ontario and Quebec, or the United States, would be major factors in explaining regional disparities.

In explaining why some regions have failed to establish manufacturing industries, some of the factors advanced are disincentives to investment such as unappealing tax laws; an untrained labour force, or a labour force with inappropriate skills; population densities which are either too small for the growth of local markets and labour pools, or too large to simultaneously meet their welfare requirements and create investment surplus for further development; wage demands that outstrip productivity; and cultural attitudes that are not conducive to technological development and growth.

These explanations rest on the assumption that private interests have the right to choose where surplus will be invested and that the task of government is to create "the conducive atmosphere" for investment in local industry. Thus, the proposed solution to such problems includes improving the tax laws, creating incentives, and inviting foreign industries to establish subsidiary plants in underdeveloped regions. As well, there is encouragement to improve the marketability of resources through government aids to industry for technological development. Other reforms would involve improvement in public services, upgrading the educational standards, wage controls, and the encouragement of emigration if none of these reforms results in an increase in employment. All of these measures, together with extensive propaganda, have been tried by various provincial governments in Canada. Newfoundland, with all its rich resources, has undertaken extensive development of the regional infrastructure and upgrading of the educational system; retraining of the labour force for industrial work; relocation of outport fishing populations to urban centres in order to create both a labour pool and a domestic market; and the provision of numerous and costly incentives for industry. The net result before the discovery of oil off-shore from the island was increasing unemployment and an even greater gulf between its people's standard of living and that on the mainland.[33]

The Newfoundland experiments indicate the problem of attempting to develop an economy in a vacuum, that is, working on the assumption that an economy can be developed entirely from within. This would require that its investors return their surplus to the local economy rather than put their capital into more lucrative ventures already established outside, and that outside investors, the multinational corporations, take as their primary responsibility the employment of the local population and full development of the local industry. If one does not assume that these investors and corporations will act in this way, then one asks rather different questions and arrives at rather different notions of what would constitute reform for this provincial economy. For example, it is of some interest that there was a flourishing fish industry in Newfoundland in the 19th century, and that it did provide subsistence for the population. It was only as very large fishing boats were introduced, and large, corporate fish-packing companies became dominant in the industry, that the stocks became depleted and the industry fell into decline. It is also of interest that there were two pulp mills in Newfoundland, both with 99-year agreements signed in 1902 and 1923, which leased 60% of all forest lands in the province, and there were several large mining companies. If these companies had been reinvesting their surplus from these resource industries into manufacturing in the province, then it should not have been necessary for the government to offer large tax and other incentives to foreign companies to establish there.

Newfoundland represents a miniature case-study of a more general problem that affects the whole of Canada. Alone, it cannot create an industrial economy in an economic environment dominated by large corporations and controlled in such large measure by an investment class which has the right to invest according to its own interests. In terms of an ideology, given all of the assumptions of liberalism which we've discussed, it is understandable that its failure to develop should finally be blamed on unskilled workers, cultural backwardness, and government policies, but it is precisely because the beliefs that give rise to these perceptions of the problem are so widely held and accepted by governments that the problems themselves remain unsolved. Ideology, then, becomes one of the contributing factors in the maintenance of an underdeveloped economy.

5

Finally, we can return to the proposition that governments are representative of the majority of the population within the territory of the nation state. Granted their limited powers in the economic sphere, it remains within their prerogative to enact legislation. It was, for example, a government which entered the *Defence Production Sharing Agreements*. It was a government which created the *Combines Investigation Act*. It was a government which gave life to the Canadian Broadcasting Corporation, the National Film Board, and the many regulatory and cultural bodies which do affect the lives of the electorate. Can we at least agree with the prevailing ideology that the government is an independent institution representing everyone equally, and not the interests of one sector over others?

There are three impediments to this belief. One is that political parties are financed by particular interest groups. The Liberal and Conservative parties receive most of their funds from corporations and individual businesspeople. The New Democratic Party receives between a third and a half of its income from trade union sources.[34] While such funds are not overt acts of bribery, they obviously imply an expectation that the party, should it gain power, would act in the interests of the funding organizations. A party which acted otherwise, or a party which those with wealth expects to act otherwise, would not be funded. Only well-funded parties can survive in democratic electoral systems, so that many interests are never represented in political parties. They cannot present their platforms to an electorate or wage a campaign. Election campaigns may, as a result, have different parties, all of them representing the same interests and backed by the same funding organizations; this effectively removes political alternatives prior to the election.

The second problem is that recruitment to political office is not evenly distributed throughout the population. No matter whom politicians purport to represent, they are inclined to diagnose problems and make choices through the perspectives of their own positions in society. Where all are representative of the same positions in society, some perspectives are never taken. If, moreover, their positions are all, or mainly, in an elite sector of society, they cannot, willing though they may be, represent the total population.

John Porter's study of elites indicated that those who enjoy political careers, especially those who occupy cabinet positions in the federal government, are not representative of the population at large in terms of educational level, occupation, or income. Of those persons in the political sphere who had occupied cabinet positions during the 1940–60 period, 86% had university educations, and 64% of these were lawyers.[35] These persons are of both "upper class" and "middle class" origins as defined by family wealth and parental occupations. Dennis Olsen has examined the origins of this elite in a more recent study, where he found that, in 1973, approximately 22% of the politicians and judicial elites came from the upper class; 69% from the middle class, and 9% from below the middle class. He defined middle class as persons who attended private schools, persons whose fathers held substantial professional or managerial positions, and persons with university degrees. In terms of current class positions rather than social class origins, Olsen found that 83% of federal cabinet ministers were lawyers, businessmen, farmowners, physicians, or other independent professionals. The remaining 17% were salaried professionals before becoming politicians.[36]

A number of the cabinet leaders have, on retiring from politics or losing an election, moved into top corporate positions and directorships, a further indication that there are many affinities between the political and corporate elite. The candidates for office are chosen by political parties, not by the population at large, and this again reduces the chances for the average citizen to exercise political power or to choose representatives who can articulate his or her needs, his or her perspectives.

The third problem is actually the most serious. It is that even if political parties were not financed by particular interest groups, and even if the majority of political offices were not held by upper middle and upper class representatives, Canadian governments have always acted with reference to the interests of the investment class and the large corporations which control the economy. It is at least arguable that in Canada, where governments have had a more active role in the economy through public corporations, and where the population is more accepting of that active role than are the populations of many other liberal democracies,[37] both the federal and provincial governments might have taken a more entrepreneurial role in developing the economy. At the present time, the governments of Saskatchewan and Alberta, through different crown agencies and in spite of two very different ideological perspectives, are both attempting to become more active managers of provincial economies; whether they succeed, and what success would mean for our understanding of government's role, is yet to be seen.[38] But, for the past, what is clear is that governments have accepted the constraints imposed by the ideological premises of capitalism: that it is not they, but private investors, who have the right to make decisions that affect the employment conditions of the society. As long as that assumption is made, governments must continue to act in the interests of the most powerful economic actors, even while advancing the theory that they are governing in the interests of the majority. We will return to this problem and further explanations of it in subsequent chapters.

6

The strength of the liberal ideology lies in its apparent accommodation of diversity. All people are equal, all choices are legitimate, all alternatives are worthy. Good and evil are relative terms, and the latitude for personal action is wide. Life is a market-place of competing claims for the attention of consumers. Having no apparent philosophical commitment to a hierarchy of values, the liberal must pose all problems as questions of strategy. Such questions are solved by the application of scientific research and the probing of the general will. For this reason, liberalism never appears to its adherents as an ideology. Marxism, communism, conservatism—but not liberalism. Liberalism appears to them as simply a common-sense approach to life. After all, it is their common sense. The "end of ideology," heralded by the American writer, Daniel Bell, in a book by that title, seems an appropriate title for the liberal age—to the liberal.[39]

Yet, when each man can choose his own moral obligations, there are no guarantees that a variety of social demands will be met. No lord is responsible for the poor, no employers for the unemployed, no upper class for the lower class. The young are not obliged to care for the old, the healthy for the sick, the educated for the ignorant. The moral obligations of manufacturers to consumers, corporations to employees, universities to the public, the mass media to viewers and readers, and governments to voters are all extremely vague.

To answer that the solutions are matters of strategy is to assume that without moral obligation, and in spite of the ideology of achievement, individualism, material profit, and personal success, people and institutions will somehow ignore their private interests and act on behalf of the society as a whole whenever the two pose different requirements. Strategies are worked out after values and goals are chosen; they are means to desired ends. Desires are translated into action to the extent that people are able to make this translation. In a society where wealth is of utmost importance, those with wealth can translate more desires into actions than those without wealth. There is no reason to expect them to put the desires of others above their own, and it is not surprising if they assume that their own desires are congruent with the social good.

The thesis of moral relativity provides a view of society as a collection of individuals whose interaction requires a co-ordinating body to ensure fair play. The question for the liberals is: when is intervention justified? When is protection required? Mill was famous for his defence of the principle that another man's liberty stopped short of this one's nose, but the room for abuse is far in excess of physical force. Is one's liberty impaired by polluted water, by political parties financed through organized corporations and international unions, by noise, by expropriation rights of governments acting in defence of other property interests, by tax spending on military defence, by control of industries by non-nationals, by the concentration of wealth and power? Whose liberty is impaired when corporate directors make decisions in the interests of the corporation which are not in the interests of their workers or the communities in which they operate? The liberal can have no philosophical answer to such questions, since liberty itself is defined in relative terms. Social good becomes whatever the will of the majority defines it to be, should the majority find a way of entering its competing claims, and subject to the decisions already made within the economic sphere not by the governments at all but by non-elected directors whose liberty is unimpaired by democratic procedures.

4 THE PREROGATIVES OF A RULING CLASS

The liberal ideology, by its assumption that governments are merely representatives of the people and that governments actually regulate the economy, inhibits the examination of economic power. If there is no ruling class, there is no need to consider its prerogatives or responsibilities.

By contrast, a conservative ideology assumes the existence of a ruling class, and by implication, of at least one other class. The definition of the ruling class may change, as from landowners and merchants in the 19th century to corporate industrialists and financiers in the 20th century. Whatever its specific composition, the claim to power is control of the economic resources of the society.

A ruling class, unlike a democratically elected government, is expected to serve the interests of those who control the economy. But it is also expected to look after the population, to ensure that its workers are housed and fed, and to ensure that foreigners do not reap the benefits of the paternalistic society. There is an assumption embedded in conservatism that the people are not able to make decisions on their own behalf, that they are not endowed by nature with that capacity, and that it would be unnatural and against the laws of the universe for common folk to have a say in the decisions that affect them. But there is also the assumption that because of this, the natural rulers have obligations to shepherd their flock.

The essence of this perspective is contained in comments by Sir Francis Bond Head, Lieutenant-Governor of Upper Canada in the 1830s. In response to the eruption of an unsuccessful liberal rebellion, he wrote these words to the Colonial Office:

The dispute on this continent is not, as it is in England, which of two parties shall attain the honour of conducting the government of their Sovereign; but here the great mass of society is striving to secure to their children the blessings of the British constitution, which a small party, from self-interested motives, is endeavouring to pull down . . . in the United States the will of the public has become stronger than the power of the law. Public credit, life, and property hang therefore upon the conduct of a dense mass of men, in no one of whose hands can it be wise that such vast interests should be committed.[1]

In defence of the "family compact" Sir Bond Head had this to say:

The "family compact" of Upper Canada is composed of those members of its society who, either by their abilities and character have been honoured by the confidence of the executive government, or who, by their industry and intelligence, have amassed wealth. The party, I own, is comparatively a small one; but to put the multitude at the top and the few at the bottom is a radical reversion of the pyramid of society which every reflecting man must foresee . . . can end only by its downfall.[2]

There was no single occasion in Canadian history when the liberal ideology symbolically made its maiden speech. The debates on Confederation are a mixture of conservative beliefs in the natural rights of hierarchy, and the emerging liberal beliefs in *laissez-faire* economic policies and the freedom of merchants to amass wealth. There was no Declaration of Independence, largely because the creation of Canada was a function of Britain's desire to dismiss her responsibilities to a colony which, in mid-19th century, had become more of a burden than a benefit. There were no stirring sermons on the rights of individuals, the virtues of freedom, or the great benefits of parliamentary democracy. The moulders of the new Dominion were not particularly literate men; their objective was to make money out of the expansion of territorial control to the West, and their liberalism was marked by its opportunism much more than by philosophic depth.

Along with industrialization and the influx of large American manufacturing companies in the early 20th century, liberal ideas were spreading amongst the urban population. These ideas included the notion that workers had a right to organize and to bargain collectively, that there should be free and competitive enterprise, and that religion had no place in the economic life of the people. In Quebec, these ideas met with the opposition of a strong Catholic Church.

1

The conventional history of Quebec assumes that the Catholic Church was always the dominant power. More recent histories question this view, and some historians date the emergence of the Church as the most powerful institution in the life of the Francophone population to about the turn of the 20th century.[3] In any event, during its reign, it was the mediating agency between the Anglophone merchants, who controlled the economy, and the largely rural population. It interpreted the former to the latter but as well shielded and protected the French farming population from the materialistic values and individualistic way of life which the Anglophone conquerors maintained. The Church controlled the educational system, through which it taught such Christian values as the subordination of humans to God, the superiority of the collectivity over the individual, and the importance of the family unit, the parish, and the school itself, as institutions with legitimate authority over individuals. Spiritual growth was portrayed as a more humane and proper goal than material welfare. The Church, in fact, took on many of the welfare functions that elsewhere were the tasks of governments. This provision of basic survival materials was an act of charity by the leaders for their flock. It was improper for the people to demand more, since their reward for obedience, faith, and living by Christian values would come in another world. This conservative, and in many respects feudal, ideology remained dominant in Quebec as long as the population remained largely rural.

It was the ideology of pre-revolutionary France, as described by a participant and leading writer in 1908: "At the present time there are two Frances, the radical France and the conservative France, the France of unbelievers and Catholic France, the France that blasphemes and the France that prays. The second France is our France."[4]

Industrialization penetrated Quebec as well as the rest of Canada in the early 20th century. A continuing stream of rural workers arrived in the cities. These French workers obtained service and labouring jobs which provided them with regular wages, but at the same time deprived them of many of the paternalistic and mutually protective ties of the rural society. In the cities they competed with other French Canadians for jobs, and as well with immigrants from other countries. None of these workers had much in the way of job security, they had no organizations to bargain for higher wages, and they were extremely vulnerable to unemployment when market swings caused employers to reduce staff. In the rural society these fluctuations were less severe because much of the farming was subsistence, that is, it was designed for self-maintenance of a family rather than for a market. Yet even there, as the industrial world penetrated ever more into Quebec as elsewhere, an increasing proportion of farms were being transformed into grain and other crops dependent on export markets for their viability. Thus the French-Canadian farmer, like the worker, was experiencing increasing insecurity at the same time as real wages and profits increased. The rural way of life was slowly undermined by these developments.

The Church responded to these changes by repeatedly urging the farmers to stay with their subsistence farms, and the workers to return to a rural way of life.[5] It defined competitive enterprise as evil, thus removing the French workers from the temptation to become more integral parts of the industrial world. At the same time, it defined the authority structure as God-determined, thereby establishing the right of materialistic Anglo-Canadians to maintain their empire. In return for a careful policy of non-interference from the authorities, the Church ensured that its members in the industrial labour force would be passive. The workers had the right to demand a decent salary to feed a large family, but no more than this:

. . . the fundamental rights of workers include the right of freedom of conscience with respect to life, to moral surroundings, to the rest prescribed by God, to a salary adequate for a family as well as the right to organize into an association.[6]

The association in question was the Confederation des Travailleurs Catholiques du Canada (CTCC), organized by the Church.

If the message needed clarification during the unemployment of the 1930s, special directives were sent out warning that the CCF was communist-inspired, and that non-Catholic unions were materialistic. The message of the Catholic Nationalist union was that:

. . . a Catholic cannot allow neutral unions because the latter consider all the problems of work as economic so that moral considerations do not enter into the solutions to these problems. They are guided only by self-interest which does not always coincide with justice.[7]

The Church spoke out against business as well as international unions, and on much the same grounds:

The archbishop of Quebec deplored the system in which a worker was viewed as a production machine, devoid of human dignity, or a soul, and where the company owners ignored the workers' responsibilities to God and to his family.[8]

As these quotations suggest, the Catholic Church in the early 20th century was attempting to infuse the new urban society of its parishioners with the same spiritual values as had permeated the rural society. The process was frustrated by the harsh conditions of life in cities. Large kinship groups and large families could not be supported by urban workers. Relationships between bosses and workers were entirely contractual. French workers were surrounded by events that could not be interpreted in terms of the Christian values they had learned, and for which appropriate responses could only come from a different set of assumptions. In spite of these frustrations, the Church remained a dominant institution in the life of French workers and was, through to at least the end of the 1930s, largely successful in its ideological persuasion. How was it possible to maintain a conservative enclave within a liberal stronghold, even while the capitalist society was in daily contact with the French workers?

According to some commentators, the Church, as a property owner and major shareholder among the corporate elite, was spreading the ideology of the ruling class through active suppression of all alternatives and a monopoly on the socialization institutions. According to others, the French workers simply lacked the skills to enter the industrial labour force and so succumbed to Church control. Both views can be accommodated with a third: the religious version explained the conditions of life to a colonial people as liberalism did not.

To begin with, it explained why there were two separate hierarchies in Quebec: that for the English-speaking, and that for the French. The explanation was a conquest. The Conquest of 1760 has earned a reputation in Canada that it scarcely deserves. The difference in population between the settlers of the New England states and those of New France, together with the vast differences in economic circumstances between the two groups, made the outcome of the war superfluous at any level other than symbolism. At that level, however, it was an important event. It clearly identified the enemy, and in ideology it accorded him the rights of the victor. His ideology was inappropriate precisely because it was his: it belonged to the Anglophones. This is expressed by two scholars in an interpretation of French-Canadian society:

What is crucial is Quebec's being a colony, not in the political-geographical sense of the term, but in the human, social and economic senses. It is an entity controlled from outside, a society which can act and decide only within limits circumscribed by the colonizer.[9]

With no power, no mobility, no individual hopes for change, shared servitude, the religion of the collectivity made more sense of life than the religion of free enterprise. The Church was the instrument not only of the elite for keeping the colonials in hand, but also of the colonials themselves for maintaining their explanation of what they experienced.

The role of the provincial government in Quebec is more ambiguous than that of the Church during the early 20th century. The political machinery was, as in other provinces, that of a liberal democracy. Members of the legislative assembly were Francophone. However, unlike the Church, the governments perceived their function to be the facilitation of industrialization. Also unlike the Church, the institution of government did not command the allegiance of the people. It was an alien institution.

A Liberal government in Quebec from 1921 to 1935 promoted industrialization, and acted on the tenets of liberal ideology with respect, at least, to the "neutral" role of government. These policies increased the pace of industrialization and as well the growth of foreign capital in the province. It hesitated to introduce social welfare legislation and only under pressure, and then with weak legislation, introduced minimal collective bargaining rights. The influx of French workers from rural Quebec was used by foreign business in service and labouring capacities still; management positions were held by imported workers or Anglophone residents. Thus the dominant Church continued to be the protector of the workers well into the 1930s.

In response to these policies, the Church became increasingly concerned about foreign ownership, and the threats to national sovereignty, as well as the conscience of the workers, that these foreign industrial corporations imposed. As well, the Church became concerned, as the depression of the 1930s advanced, with the growth of socialist organization elsewhere in Canada. The Church pressed for reforms, and published a list of these including government credit aids to farmers and French-Canadian small businessmen, incentives for urban workers to return to the land; minimum wage laws, a revision of the *Workmens' Compensation Act*, health insurance, old age pensions, and other social reforms for urban workers; the destruction of monopoly industrial trusts and other, especially foreign, large business interests; and various electoral reforms. Where this list of reforms differed from the Co-operative Commonwealth Federation platform was in its general assumption that while foreign ownership and massive industrialization were "bad," capitalism, or private ownership at least, was still acceptable. These, then, were reforms to the system rather than a new system which the Church advocated.[10]

This set of demands was adopted by a dissident group from the Liberal Party, consisting in large part of intellectuals. The Conservative Party, under Maurice Duplessis, struck a coalition with the splinter group, agreed to adopt the Church reform measures, and thus obtained the unofficial blessing of the Catholic clergy. With that came the support of various nationalistic organizations, the farmers' organizations, co-operatives and credit unions, youth organizations, the Catholic trade unions, and numerous cultural groups. Renamed the Union Nationale, this conservative party nearly won its first electoral campaign in 1935, and did win an election in 1936.

Over the next three years, it ousted the splinter group of Liberals, and while it enacted some minimal social welfare legislation in accordance with the agreement it had made, it did not proceed to enact legislation contrary to the interests of foreign industrialists. It regained power in 1944 and remained in power until 1960.[11]

The Union Nationale Party is of interest to us because it represented a peculiar mixture of conservative and liberal ideological justifications for government action. After ousting the splinter Liberals who had provided him with the necessary coalition, Premier Maurice Duplessis sponsored conventional fiscal policies, co-operated entirely with foreign business, and spoke with conviction about the virtues of private enterprise, the free market, and individual achievement. Its labour legislation was repressive, including one Act providing for the government's right to abrogate collective labour agreements without the consent of both parties, and a minimum wage law which allowed wages to be set below the level achievable through collective bargaining. These actions have been labelled "economic conservatism" by most writers on the subject, and the labelling is accurate enough, but they were not performed with conservative ideological justifications. Quite the contrary: the rhetoric was liberal in tone and content. It was not because of God's will that Duplessis helped the industrialists in Quebec during the 1930s; it was because it was good business.

During the Depression, before Duplessis came to power and before the nature of his administration could be ascertained, another and much more conservative movement gained prominence. This was the fascist movement under Adrien Arcand. It may be of some passing interest that one must name Arcand, Aberhart, and Duplessis because they led movements which were to a considerable extent their personal creations; one can talk about the Communist Party of Canada without a discussion of Tim Buck, and the CCF without a discussion of J.S. Woodsworth although both were very important to their respective parties. In the latter two cases, policies were perceived by their followers to be of greater moment than personalities. Perhaps this is part of the explanation for the persistence of antagonism toward these left-wing parties by established parties, in contrast to their remarkable tolerance for extreme right-wing movements such as the fascist movements in the 1930s.

2

The fascist movement was characterized not only by an authoritarian and charismatic leadership, but also by its attacks on supposed enemies of Christianity, including particularly Jews and socialists, and by contempt for parliamentary democracy. Where Aberhart in Alberta attempted to style government as a selection pool for technical experts, these movements talked of the corporate state. In this state, government consists of selected representatives of industry, technicians, and possibly unions to act as advisors to the supreme leaders. There is a descending hierarchy of councils, each one chosen by the group above. The objective of this arrangement is to avoid the uninformed choices of an electorate and pressures from below on the superior judgement of knowledgeable leaders, and to give the leaders a free hand in establishing and maintaining a healthy and efficient economy. This remains a private enterprise economy. The role of government is not to own industry but to ensure that it runs effectively. The sentiments that back up this corporate state are patriotism, the Christian faith, order and efficiency, the sanctity of the family, and belief in free enterprise.

Arcand was, from the outset, stridently anti-Semitic.[12] His campaign against Jews was so successful that in 1932 two Jewish MLAs in the Quebec legislature introduced a group libel bill. In terms of the history of civil liberties in Canada this was an important occasion. Civil liberties then as now were defined largely in terms of individual rights rather than group rights. It remains a contentious issue. To draw a modern parallel: for the Francophones today, a collective right claimed under the language legislation is the civil right to conduct all affairs in French. The opposition to this is framed in terms of individual rights, i.e., the individual right of parents to choice of language of instruction for their children. If individual rights are given predominance, then the collective right to conduct affairs in French is undermined. A similar case can be made about such matters as the employment of minority groups. If employers have quotas on the proportion of women they are to employ in order to create an equivalence for women and men, then men's individual rights to employment and non-discrimination are violated. Thus any legislation concerning group rights becomes contentious.

In this case, as in many others, the group right of the Jews to collective protection against hate campaigns ran contrary to the civil right to individuals to publish their beliefs. Libel laws are problematic in these cases; they reflect the liberal bias in favour of individual liberties. If an individual is libelled he or she has a much better chance in the court system of arguing his or her case, than if a group is libelled. The bill was greeted with hostility in the Quebec press. The press claimed it was an attack on their freedom. For example, *Le Devoir* ridiculed it in these words:

Some people lack all sense of measure, like the sponsors of the bill on outrageous subject-matter. Does John Bull get upset when he reads in a Quebec paper that Napoleon called England a nation of shopkeepers? Or Jacques Bonhomme when he reads in a Montreal daily that the French are a race of frog-eaters? Or does Sandy become angry at the Scotch jokes in the Gazette, *or Pat when he reads a story about Irish drinking habits in the* Star? *But is Isaac angry when* La Patrie *writes that the Jews have been and continue to be bankers exacting higher interest from everyone and that they have a penchant for usury. Quick, to the nearest lawyer. There the vexed man will demand an injunction against the paper and he will get it.*[13]

As one might sense from this, the reaction included a strong undercurrent of anti-Semitism. In fact, the proposed bill brought forth considerable support for the Arcand movement that had not previously been apparent. A bitter debate took place in the Legislative Assembly, concluded when the Liberal government killed the bill with the statement that "public opinion is not ready to accept such a radical measure."[14] This dismissal of the problem was similar to the reaction in Ontario in 1937 when a group libel bill was put forward, also to protect the Jewish population from group slander. There *The Globe and Mail* called the bill, "not the British way."[15]

The Arcand movement became publicly affiliated with Hitler by 1932. Arcand wrote that Hitler was the "champion of Christianity." He became active in distributing copies of the "Protocols of the Elders of Zion." This document vilifies the Jews by purporting to be a Jewish plan for the take-over of the world. It was, in fact, a document written by the Tsarist police to be distributed to the underground revolutionary groups in an attempt to cause them to splinter through their distrust of their own Jewish members. After the 1917 revolution, some emigré Russians brought out copies to the West and used them as anti-Bolshevist propaganda, arguing that the revolution was a plot by the Jews. They were exposed many times as a forgery but Arcand in the 1930s and numerous others right through the 1950s continued to point to them as proof that the Jews were intent on destroying Christianity.

Swastika clubs and bands of shirt-wearers became evident in Ontario and Manitoba after Hitler's rise to power in the spring of 1933. A Master's thesis in 1933 on attitudes toward Jews in Toronto provided survey-type data to the effect that businessmen and self-employed professionals were the most prejudiced against Jews. There were supporters of Fascism in all classes of society, amongst the working class and independent professionals, amongst students, and amongst ex-military personnel. Many middle class workers were willing to sacrifice constitutional liberties and to condone Hitler in order to do away with what was called "the Jewish problem".[16]

In Canada's West the anti-Semitism could be equally virulent, but support for the Fascist movements was less great than in Ontario and Quebec. This may have been due to the greater mixture of ethnic groups in the West. Jews were better represented amongst professionals in Winnipeg than in Toronto or Montreal. Organized labour very early opposed fascism in Winnipeg, and pushed the National Congress to maintain opposition to it. However, it was in Winnipeg that the branch of Fascism imported from Britain and known as the "Black Shirts," or "the Mosleyites" after its British leader Sir Oswald Mosley, had its greatest appeal. Here the racist undertones were less pronounced, and the emphasis was on efficient, businesslike government.

Corporatism in this form was very appealing to the business sector. It promised to eliminate strikes, class divisions, and inefficient democracy. The model was provided by Mussolini in Italy. In 1934, *Fortune* magazine devoted an issue to a favourable analysis of the corporate state in Italy. Some prominent Canadians spoke well of that style of government. Democracy appeared to be inefficient at generating economic security and prosperity, and government by technicians and industrialists appeared as a solution.

The fascist movement grew steadily in Quebec and Ontario throughout the 1930s, though the approval for Mussolini dissipated with Italy's invasion of Ethiopia in 1936. In Quebec it was aided by the strong denunciations of communism by the Church: fascism looked respectable because it, too, condemned communism. In 1937, the new Duplessis government introduced the *Padlock Act* against dissemination of communist literature. The communist paper, *La Clarte*, was closed and the editor's house padlocked, together with its printing company and leftist bookstores. Private libraries were also ransacked. No action, meanwhile, was taken against the Fascist party, though its affiliation with Hitler was becoming more suspect as war with Germany became more likely. In 1937, *The Globe and Mail* was still calling Arcand "the brilliant young French-Canadian,"[17] and the number of followers in Quebec was still increasing.

After war was declared in 1939, and after Britain had imprisoned Sir Oswald Mosley, the RCMP raided the offices of Arcand's newspaper. Arcand was finally imprisoned as an enemy agent, and both the fascist and communist movements were declared illegal. Following the war, Arcand worked as an editor for Maurice Duplessis.

By way of explaining the sudden rise of the fascist ideology in Quebec, sociologist E.C. Hughes wrote:

Observation throughout the period leads me to conclude that the symbolic Jew receives the more bitter of the attacks which the French-Canadians would like to make upon the English or perhaps even upon some of their own leaders and institutions. . . . Many of the accusations made against the Jew in Quebec—with the obvious exception of Communist leanings—would be justified if made against the English. The department stores, chain stores, banks, and large industrial and utility corporations have been introduced and are controlled by Anglo-Saxons. The Jew in Quebec is the physically present small competitor rather than the hidden wirepuller of high finance and big business. The Jew operates and competes upon the French-Canadian businessman's own level; it is the English who have introduced the new forms of economic enterprise which threaten the French-Canadian way of living and working.[18]

While this explanation is helpful in explaining the small businessman's support for anti-Semitism, it is inadequate for explaining the more extensive willingness to destroy the liberal democratic machinery. This occurred not only in Quebec, where the machinery was imposed by colonizers, but as well in Ontario where it had long had the support of the majority of the population. To reach beyond this explanation, one is obliged to consider the possibility that liberal democracy, or more specifically, the liberal sentiments on which it is based, is supportable only as long as it actually appears to produce upward mobility for the middle class, increasing prosperity, and economic growth. Unfortunately, we do not have a detailed study of the membership of the Fascist party and its unregistered followers, so that we do not know for sure which segments of the population were most willing to abandon liberal premises during a depression. In her path-breaking study of the movement, Lita-Rose Betcherman notes that small businessmen were indeed amongst the early followers, that nationalistic students joined in as the depression prolonged their anxiety about the future, and that a large proportion of the Italian community supported the movement mainly because of the high respect held for Mussolini before 1936.[19] As a minority group in Quebec, and one which also competed with the French Canadians for urban jobs, this group may have had some motivation to pin-point an enemy in yet a third competing labour pool; thus its support for an anti-Semitic program.

The opposition to group rights legislation highlights one of the contradictions of capitalism. On the one hand, it is purported that the liberal machinery allows for the protection of minorities. It is supposed to do this through tolerance for minority viewpoints. Tolerance for minority viewpoints, however, permits both majorities and minorities to discriminate against other minorities and in the name of freedom to be protected by the state while doing so. This is a contradiction at the level of ideology; it is less one at the level of real action. In fact, action against groups which have the potentiality for seriously challenging the state and the status quo has frequently been taken by governments. The Padlock Laws are an example. The imposition of the *War Measures Act* on other occasions provides other examples. There is a practical limit to tolerance for diversity, but in practice that limit does not appear to be determined by moral and intellectual concerns for minority rights; it is determined, rather, by the interests of those who control the economy.

Both the penetrating conservatism of the Catholic Church and the more populist right-wing movements during the 1930s occurred against an economic background that included a very high degree of ownership and market concentration in major industrial sectors. A scholarly study by L.G. Reynolds in the mid-1930s summarized the concentration.[20] This indicated that in the automobile industry three firms controlled 89% of all output; in agricultural implements, four firms controlled 75%. One cement firm controlled 90% of the output, two canning firms controlled 83% and three fertilizer firms controlled 70%. Three electrical equipment firms controlled 100% of that industrial sector, and similar degrees of concentration were found for most of the mineral industries, meat packing, milling, and several consumer products such as silks, sugar, and tobacco. Many of the dominant firms were, by that decade, American companies.

These companies were establishing the prices and had a monopoly of the sales to the 300 000 independent farmers on the prairies. There was no converse monopoly for the farmers, who necessarily competed with one another in the sale of their produce.[21]

This "real" situation may have appeared more tolerable to small commodity producers and other small businessmen, to farmers and to wage-workers when for them, at least, there was some opportunity to move up the economic scale within an expanding economy. With blocked mobility, they became concerned with such realities. Their expressions of concern were not necessarily embodiments of realistic solutions—to blame the Jews for the situation was manifestly unfair, in a social situation where one would be hard put to find a single Jewish industrialist or financier—but they were protests against monopoly insofar as its dimensions were known to them.

3

In Alberta, as in Quebec, the Depression created a painfully insecure population. Dependent on exports of wheat, the farmers of the prairies were impoverished with declining grain prices. The onset of a drought increased their misery. Their costs for manufactured products from central Canada remained high, since the manufacturers weathered the depression by cutting production rates rather than decreasing prices.

By the 1920s, farmers had organized themselves into political protest groups whose hostility to the manufacturers, bankers, and railroad owners of central Canada was their cohesive ideology. A United Farmers' Party had been elected in Alberta in 1921, and was still in power there at the height of the Depression. However, this government, like others the world over, was unable to cure poverty, drought, unemployment, and falling wheat prices.

An evangelist, William Aberhart, captured the voters' imagination with his interpretation of the monetary reform theories of a British mechanical engineer, Major C.H. Douglas. His new party, the Social Credit, was elected in 1935, and remained in power well past his death until 1971.

What is important about the movement is not the monetary theories. These were never actually brought to life, partly because Aberhart rejected them and partly because those that were attempted were judged to be *ultra vires* by the Supreme Court (outside the jurisdiction of a provincial government in accordance with the *British North America Act, 1867*, and constitutional precedents). The importance of the movement was that its values and methods were entirely out of tune with liberalism and the theory of liberal democracy. Early in his initial campaign, Aberhart declared:

A democracy can suggest but it has not the power to execute, and that is what anybody would be doing when you start to decide what your government should and should not do when it is elected. Don't try to tell your government everything they should do. The minute you start to talk about the policing of the country you are out of order. The one great thing you have to do is keep together.[22]

The role of the citizen, in Aberhart's view, was to vote for results. He asked them to think about what they wanted, such as the end of poverty, the onset of prosperity, freedom, and happiness, and to inform their legislators of these wants. They should not bother themselves with the details on how such ends were to be obtained.

Then always vote for the RESULTS you want. For if you vote for any theme whatsoever you will merely be passing your opinion on it. And you may be sure that there will always be others voting for some OTHER plan and so nothing vital will be done. But add your WILL to that of other Alberta voters, and together we shall gain power that will move mountains—that

most assuredly will abolish poverty—easily—for it is just a bad dream.
Facts, the REAL things, have only to be straightened up a little, rearranged,
and poverty will cease to exist.[23]

Once a government was in power, Aberhart's plan was that it
should employ technical experts to advise on how ends could be
achieved. The job of the politicians, then, was simply to facilitate
technical expertise.

Combined with this program was a promise that all electors would
receive a monthly dividend of $25 once Social Credit theories had
been put into practice. In the midst of the Depression, this promise
was alluring. It was not clear whether everyone would receive the
credit, however. There was a strong undercurrent of thought to the
effect that it would go only to those who believed in and voted for
the party, and those who worked hard. Aberhart warned that a State
Credit House Inspector would be employed to ensure that recipients
worked. Any citizens who "squandered their dividends and were
hungry or improperly clothed" would be warned that they were
"abusing their rights and privileges" and the dividend would be
stopped. As well, a person who "did not wish to join with the Social
Credit idea . . . would not receive any monthly dividends."[24]

Another departure from liberal parliamentary practice was the
demand by Aberhart that candidates for the party be chosen by
himself and an advisory committee. Thus, Aberhart ensured that
his potential colleagues in parliament would be persons selected for
their willingness to accept his leadership and platforms. This arrangement was accepted by the movement, as evidenced in this
resolution of the Southern Alberta Social Credit Convention in 1935:

Whereas we must always maintain the fundamental principles of true
democracy; and
Whereas there is a tempting opportunity afforded under the old political
lines for candidates to use wire-pulling tactics; and
Whereas we believe that it is fundamental under true democracy that the
people directly, or indirectly through representation, are qualified to in-
dicate the general course of their desires, but that execution of them must
be left to experts,
Be it therefore resolved that in the nomination of candidates in each con-
stituency we agree to nominate three or four—and that our leader together
with his advisory committee be empowered to decide the candidate from
those nominated by the constituency convention.[25]

In summary, this movement promoted as its values, the supreme
authority of a charismatic leader, the obedience and faith of followers, and acceptance of expertise outside parliament for choice of

means to obtain agreed-upon ends. These values were reinforced through a continuing evangelical crusade, in which Aberhart assured the people that Social Credit and Christianity were the same thing. Christianity, being an ideology much diluted over time, provided a complementary set of values: humility of the mass of people before the authority of God and his chosen representatives; the protestant work ethic; the necessity for faith. These values still underlaid the movement a few years later, when members of the party became possessed of the belief that Jews and socialists, together with (or possibly embodied in the same persons) atheists and fascists, were engaged in a world plot to destroy Christian democracies. Major Douglas ended his life propagating these beliefs.

C.B. Macpherson, in his classic study of the Social Credit movement in Alberta, argued that the success of this party and ideology was due to the "one class" composition of the population.[26] The one class consisted of independent prairie farm producers who were insecure, had long-standing grievances against the established powers in central Canada, and equally long-standing immersion in fundamentalist Protestant sects or an essentially authoritarian Catholicism. The combination of their grievances, religion, and socio-economic condition predisposed them to support a movement specifically addressed to their situation. The theory proposed by Aberhart amounted to a belief in modern technology to solve the problems these independent commodity producers experienced, without fundamentally altering the structure of private enterprise. The Alberta population at that time was predominantly rural: about 48% of the people were engaged in farming or ranching. Urban centres were small, and much of their business was dependent on farm produce and imports of manufactured items from central Canada.

By the end of the war, with the post-war boom and the discovery of large oil deposits at Leduc, the Social Credit Movement lost much of its momentum. The party became a conventional political party within a somewhat "right-wing" tradition of liberalism, and as such continued in office with conventional fiscal policies.

These manifestations of insecurity during the Depression represented the frustrations of small businessmen, independent farmers, an impoverished working class: the victims of the cyclical downturn in capitalism. Their protest movements were not pegged to carefully considered, examined philosophical beliefs as was the case, for example, of the Catholic Church in Quebec. They were "right-wing" movements in the sense that they espoused values contrary to the dominant themes of liberalism, and sought solutions outside the framework of liberal democracy in the direction of authoritarian rule by a charismatic leader and an absence of democratic checks on that rule. But even at their most strident moments, they espoused such values as individualism (if only for an elite) rather than collective welfare. While they offered panaceas contingent on this or that change in the monetary system and parliamentary machinery, they did not provide a systematic critique of capitalism, nor a comprehensive vision of a genuinely different society.

4

By contrast, the Catholic Church in Quebec did provide such a vision and such a critique, even when it was willing to accept cohabitation on earth with an anti-Semitic Fascist movement. The Church continued through the Depression to argue that authority flows from God, and that there is thus an eternal legitimacy to the hierarchical class society. Well into the post-war period of prosperity, the Church remained genuinely conservative in its vision:

> *Sovereign authority, by whatever government it is exercised, is derived solely from God . . . It is therefore an absolute error to believe that authority comes from the multitudes, from the masses, from the people, to pretend that authority does not properly belong to those who exercise it, but that they have only a simple mandate revocable at any time by the people. This error, which dates from the Reformation rests on the false principle that man has no other master than his own reason.*[27]

Yet the Church could not stem a transformation of society. Quebec, by the end of the war, was not a rural, agricultural society any more. Thousands had left the farms for manual work in the cities. It is estimated that the rise in the number of manual workers in the 1940s was greater than the increase over the entire previous century. Industrialization proceeded at a rate greater than that of Canada as a whole.[28] As the impact of changed realities began to challenge the official interpretation, there emerged a restlessness with conventional wisdom. The Church stood for a world that could no longer be seen to be believed.

Within the period of roughly 1945 to 1960, Quebec went through the process that the rest of Canada experienced between about 1830 and 1920. But with one difference: its economy was already dominated by an external elite, and its most obvious and evident opposition came not from that source but from the remaining supporters of the old regime. The search for new rules began, therefore, with condemnations, litanies of grievances, and strikes that failed to bring forth any strong class ideology because the industrial conflict was confused by the intermediary presence of the remaining church, the remaining authority in the form of the Union Nationale, and the remaining faith. The 1949 Asbestos Strike seems to have been the breaking point.

This strike against the Johns Manville Company in the little town of Asbestos was a violent one and had the pattern of other strikes at earlier periods in both Quebec and other parts of Canada at those times and places where union development had been impeded. Police intervened on behalf of employers, strike-breakers were brought in, strikers were arrested and beaten even in their own homes. The *Riot Act* was read and strike leaders were arrested on conspiracy charges. Five months after it began, the strikers returned to work with a wage increase and the recognition of their union (the Catholic Confederation).

Apart from its violence and the massive use of force by police, the remarkable feature was the sources of outside support received by the strikers. The most significant source was the clergy.

Archbishop Charbonneau of Montreal used strong words in a sermon at Notre-Dame-de-Montreal to express his support:

The working class is the victim of a conspiracy which wishes to crush it, and when there is a conspiracy to crush the working class, it is the duty of the Church to intervene.

We wish social peace, but we do not wish the crushing of the working class. We are more attached to man than to capital. This is why the clergy has decided to intervene. It wishes that justice and charity be respected, and it desires that more attention cease to be paid to financial interests than to the human factor.[29]

Students, journalists, and other workers supported the strikers, and support from both Catholic and international trade unions provided the strikers with living funds over the long period. One year after this strike, the bishops of Quebec issued new directives on the relations between employers and employees. "This document was a landmark in the development of social thought in Quebec" was the judgement of historian Mason Wade.[30] The document recognized, as no earlier Act had done, that Quebec had become, and would remain, an industrial society.

Le Devoir, La Presse, and *Le Standard* had openly published accounts of the Asbestos strike in 1949, which allowed a reading public to know of the workers' situation. During the 1950s, these established papers continued to exercise a previously unknown degree of press freedom. Radio, television, and a National Broadcasting System under federal control completed the overthrow of monopoly control on the thoughts of the nation. Universities became places of political debate, and *Cité Libre* was established. A group of intellectuals, journalists, and trade unionists of liberal and socialist persuasions gathered together to devise a strategy to oust the Duplessis government. All of this activity held a theme of liberalism: free speech, freedom to organize, the legitimacy of private pursuits, freedom of religion, and freedom to engage in trade were the components of the revolutionary ideology. While the main thrust of the movement was an attack on the traditional ideology of the church, the elite, and the corrupt politicians, the models for reform appeared as Ottawa and the United States.

Repression did not abruptly end any more than it had in 1837. Sir Francis Bond Head had his parallels in 1957, and they were more openly ruthless in opposing reform. But in the long run, the gulf between reality and ideology could be bridged only by an ideology that made sense of changed circumstances. In 1960, the Liberal government was elected. The educational system was overhauled, a middle-class bureaucracy was developed, and the state actively intervened in the economy with the nationalization of electric power.

It should be understood that we are not here arguing that the liberal ideology did in fact take into account all of the "realities" of the Quebec situation, any more than it did or does now of the economic realities elsewhere in Canada. What it did, rather, was explain those realities that people could see, feel, experience: it established goals that were obtainable, addressed itself to problems people lived with, redefined the world in a way that seemed indeed to coincide with the world of daily activity. It was an ideology for urban workers on the way up, an ideology for those who were receiving salaries and buying houses and supporting students, an ideology for industrialized people who were no longer so sure where the classes began and where they ended.

Liberalism is a useful ideology for a large middle class, for urban workers, white-collar workers, skilled craftsmen, technicians, professionals. But to maintain its dominance, it must provide either the reality or a very successful illusion of unlimited mobility. Elsewhere in Canada, partly because the United States could always absorb the talented with no place to go in Canada, the illusion and to some extent the reality have been maintained. It is only since the publication of Walter Gordon's book, *A Choice for Canada*, and the Task Force Reports on concentration of control and foreign domination, that knowledge of the extent of foreign control has become public property. It is still only the property—the mental experience—of a minority in the English-speaking population.

In Quebec, the barriers to the top were always apparent. Under

the corporate theology, the barriers were explained: they were established by the collective enemy. Under the liberal ideology, their
continued existence begs further justification. Liberalism came under attack almost before it became established in Quebec, and sooner
than in English-speaking Canada. By 1970, the attacks in the various
forms of separatist, nationalist, socialist, and Creditiste ideologies
were creating a lively and sometimes vicious debate.

5

The perceptive French-Canadian sociologist, Hubert Guindon, argued in 1964 that the liberal regime was giving rise to a bureaucratic
class employed largely within the public sector. The political power
of this class and its upward mobility did not match its growing
economic wealth and expectations. Control rested with the same
old elites, and the Anglo-Canadian directors and managers were all
too apparent as they blocked the way to this growing class of professionals and bureaucrats. It was this class, in Guindon's opinion, that
sponsored separatism:

*Separatist leaders as well as their rank and file are to be found among the
better-educated, younger, professional and semi-professional, salaried, white
collar ranks. This class constitutes the core of its support. The nature of
separatist grievances also underlines its class bias. Separatist discontent,
in the final analysis, boils down to protest against real or imagined restricted occupational mobility. The objects of separatist indictment are
the promotion practices of the federally operated bureaucracies, of Crown
and private corporations. This class bias is also the reason why the separatist appeal has gone by largely unheeded by the rural classes and the
lower social strata of the cities.*[31]

A year later, the same theme was developed by Charles Taylor:

*I have maintained that the new nationalism . . . is mainly a middle-class
phenomenon, largely the creation of what I have called the intelligentsia,
that its roots are to be found partly in the situation of this class, competing
for promotion and careers in a modern economy which is in origin and
stamp largely Anglo-Saxon . . . Nationalism has little intrinsic appeal to
classes lower in the social order, worker or peasants; it appeals only when
it is linked with the solution of deeply felt economic ills.*[32]

It was the Creditiste Party that appealed to the rural population,
and especially to the rural working class. In an extensive study of
the Creditiste movement, Maurice Pinard has shown that this was

a protest of those who were excluded from the new regime, against the liberals, the middle classes, the elites, but not specifically against the foreign elites and not a movement that could be mobilized by the middle classes in that direction. Nor was this an ideological rejection of liberalism as a philosophy. Pinard argues that it was a pragmatic protest against the new establishment by those who were dispossessed.[33]

There was another event in progress at this time which did not become apparent until much later, though its effects were already being experienced in the 1960s. This was the movement of capital from Montreal to Toronto. It was not for ethnic and language reasons that this movement occurred; it was simply that Montreal had ceased by the 1940s to be at the Canadian core of the financial and industrial world. Industry was located in Ontario, the banks had followed industry, and cumulatively, other industries which had originally located in Montreal, followed the same route.

Jane Jacobs, in a probing three-part series of articles on Quebec separatism, has documented this movement.[34] She points out that the City of Montreal more than doubled its population between 1941 and 1971. The influx of population included immigrants, but the major influx was from rural and small-town Quebec. This had several important effects on the city. It became transformed into a French-Canadian city, where it had previously been an English city with French-speaking workers. An indigenous French culture developed which blossomed in the 1960s. Meanwhile, rural Quebec, though losing thousands of people and especially the young to Montreal, became the food producer for a much larger urban population. Agriculture in Quebec became mechanized.

Meanwhile, Toronto was also growing. Beginning as the smaller city, it expanded as American industry penetrated Ontario. Its financiers took on the financing of new mining ventures and the support of American manufacturing. By the 1940s, the volume of stocks traded in Toronto exceeded the volume in Montreal. Rapid as the growth of Montreal was during the post-war period, that of Toronto and its industrial suburbs was even greater. Its immigrants included many people from other parts of Canada, and its suburban "satellite" towns became, themselves, major urban centres. Montreal, by comparison, did not create major satellite towns because its industry was not growing to the same extent. In Jacobs' view: "Montreal, in spite of its growth, was losing its character as the economic centre of an English-speaking Canada and was simultaneously taking on its character as a regional, French-speaking metropolis."[35]

Jacobs argues that Montreal as a regional Canadian city would not have a promising economic future. Capital would not be invested in the development of many manufacturing industries. If Montreal stagnates economically, her culture will also subside. Given her now well-educated, industrially skilled urban population, her future would be more dynamic as the centre of a French-Canadian nation than as a secondary city within the financial and commercial economy of English Canada. Thus in her view, the separatist movement cannot be explained simply with reference to the growth of a technocratic class. Its economic base lies in a more dramatic change than the internal class structure of Quebec. We will return to this issue in Chapter 7.

5 THE EXPOSURE OF A RULING CLASS

The dominant ideology, which we have called liberalism because that is the name given it by its leading philosophers and political exponents, is the ideology of a capitalist society. It represents that society as one in which equality is both valued and experienced, individualism is an absolute good and individual freedoms are a general property; there is no ruling class, the rule of law and of parliament co-ordinates the total activity of the society, and the political life is ultimately subject to the will of the majority of the population. As we have seen, these representations of the society are not accurate as descriptions of reality.

Skeptics may observe this inconsistency between ideology and fact. Some skeptics become scholars, documenting the nature of the "real" society, attempting to match that against the ideology in order to arrive at something they might be able to call "truth." Their production may take the form of "theory," that is, an internally logical statement of the relationships between the elements and institutions of a society which is subject to comparison against factual evidence.

They may choose to abandon the scholarly activity, which by its nature is somewhat frustrating because truth is elusive, facts contestable, and certainty unattainable. They may, experiencing disillusionment with the fantasies of the dominant ideology, project beyond contemporary society to a Utopian society in which the values they hold are actually realized. Their version of what kind of society would be perfect is always in part a reflection of their understanding of the contemporary society and its historical development.

The combination of critique of contemporary society, projection of Utopian values to a new society, and interpretation of the transition from the first to the second comprise the elements of a counter-ideology.

In Canada and elsewhere in capitalist economies the major counter-ideology has been socialism. The chief (not the first) theorist within the socialist tradition was Karl Marx. His theories, and his interpretation of the next stage of social growth, have provided the basis for both intellectual theories about contemporary society and popular ideologies.

It is sometimes difficult to separate the theories—which are by definition internally logical propositions about the nature of the system or the process of history—and the ideological perspectives, which are expressions of belief, statements of what are taken to be self-evident truths, and prophecies about the future. It is particularly difficult because the popular versions of Marx's theories are intertwined with ideological statements. Before examining the history of socialism and socialist thought in Canada, it may be helpful to consider some of the basic arguments proposed by Marx in the 19th century and some neo-Marxist arguments published in our own time.

1

In Marx's view, man is distinguished from other animals by the fact that he must produce his own means of subsistence. (It should be noted that Marx uses the terms "man" and "men" rather than a generic term for both sexes.) Men collectively produce subsistence in different ways over historical time. The various ways, that is, the organization of people and techniques, are called the modes of production. The techniques, including whatever is used for energy and all machinery or other capital goods, are called the means of production.

The history of man is the history of the successive epochs which are each characterized by a distinctive mode of production (though other, earlier, modes may be simultaneously present in any given society). Modes change over time because the means of production and the relationships between people to which each mode gives rise create contradictions. The contradictions cause social pressures to change conditions, and the resolution to the contradictions of any particular mode is the successive mode.

The motive force of social change—the essence of the social pressures—is class struggle. A class structure is the total organization of the society around the means of production such that some members control the labour power of others. In Marx's view, all historical societies have been characterized by classes and their essential conflict:

The history of all hitherto existing society is the history of class struggles. Freeman and slave, patrician and plebeian, lord and serf, guildmaster and journeyman, in a word, oppressor and oppressed, stood in constant opposition to one another, carried on an uninterrupted, now hidden, now open fight.[1]

Capitalism is a mode of production within which one class—the bourgeoisie—owns the means of production and employs labour on a wage; the second class—the proletariat—has no ownership of productive mechanisms and thus must sell its labour-power in order to survive. In its early phases, the two classes are buffetted, and the class struggle obscured, by the existence of middle or transition groups, and groups which exist beyond the realm of the industrial sector, remnants of the feudal stage. The middle groups include, for example, small business owners and merchants whose capital is insufficient for long-term investment and who will, in due course, be bought out by larger capitalists and become, in their turn, wage labourers; professionals who earn high incomes but are not in positions to reinvest or gain control of the economy; intellectuals and civil servants who, in blindly serving the interests of the status quo, are unable to realize that they are akin to wage labourers; artisans and white-collar workers in the private sector who likewise identify with bourgeois capitalists. Outside the sphere of industrial society, there is a peasantry: the rural agricultural workers and farmers, who will inevitably be lured to cities and become the proletariat (wage workers). Within the industrial society but not included as wage workers are the unemployed. They form a critical group in the maintenance of the class structure, since their existence provides a labour pool from which capitalist employers can withdraw the numbers required and so keep down the wages of employed workers.

The production relations between classes are translated into distribution relations as well as political relations. It is for this reason that many other theorists attribute to income or other rewards the distinguishing features of class. Marx emphasized ownership of productive mechanisms as the distinguishing feature of the classes and objected to the less strict uses of the term:

The vulgar mind commutes class differences into "differences in the size of purses," and class conflict into "trade disputes." The size of the purse is a purely quantitative difference, by virtue of which two individuals of the same class can be opposed quite arbitrarily. It is well known that medieval guilds quarreled with each other "according to trade." But it is equally well known that modern class differences are by no means based on "trade." Rather, the division of labour has created very different types of work within the same class.[2]

Marx argues that those who control production will also control distribution, such that they will not determine how much of what is to be produced, but how much of what they will receive, and how much the workers will receive. Income, forms of property other than the means of production, prestige, honours, and non-economic positions are all within the control of the bourgeois owners.

Capitalism emerged from feudalism, and from the class struggles of that epoch. As the feudal nexus between lords and serfs dissipated with the emergence of the bourgeoisie, the beginnings of capitalism developed. This ultimately led to conflict between bourgeoisie and nobility, culminating in the bourgeois revolutions in America and France. The bourgeoisie continued to grow, developed new means of production, and caused the development of a large class of wage labourers.

Capitalism in its early forms was a system by which individual entrepreneurs sought to enlarge their private fortunes through increasing their share of the market. They did this by producing better products than their competitors, by mass-producing cheaper products, by paying low wages to workers, by introducing new products, and by creating a demand for their products. But as the development of a fully commercial market economy occurred, some capitalists gained sufficient wealth to buy or push the smaller capitalists out of the market.

This process was enhanced by a feature of capitalism that is unique to such a system: periodic depressions. The business cycle of booms and busts occurs because the unregulated conduct of business gives rise to overproduction. Markets are glutted, capitalists lay off workers, workers cannot consume products, some businesses go bankrupt. These cycles are coincident with an ever-increasing use of technology to change the nature of production. "The bourgeoisie cannot exist without constantly revolutionizing the instruments of production, and thereby the relations of production, and with them the whole relations of society."[3]

At each juncture in this process of manipulated social change, the smaller enterprises disappear, and the greater enterprises appropriate large areas of the total production chain. Their capacity to capitalize technology gives them a continuing edge over smaller competitors. Competitive capitalism then gives way to monopoly capitalism, dominated by that segment of the bourgeoisie which controls industrial capital on a very large world scale. "The need of a constantly expanding market for its products chases the bourgeoisie over the whole surface of the globe. It must nestle everywhere, settle everywhere, establish connexions everywhere."[4] As it grew, it inevitably centralized the population, the means of production, and property; ever fewer owners control ever-increasing territories and industrial capacity.

The necessary consequence of this was political centralisation. Independent, or but loosely connected provinces, with separate interests, laws, governments and system of taxation, became lumped together into one nation, with one government, one code of laws, one national class-interest, one frontier and one customs-tariff.[5]

Thus competitive capitalism within nation states has given rise to monopoly capitalism within an imperialistic framework; diverse and scattered populations each having their markets have come under the control of centralized corporations and a controlled market; cultural diversity has given way to cultural uniformity, with the world, rather than the community or the nation, purchasing the same products from the same producers and working in the same relationships to the owners of the means of production. Monopoly capitalism is the contradiction of early competitive capitalism, and has destroyed its original mode of production. Under monopoly capitalism, the two classes emerge in stark contrast, all other classes having been demolished. This polarized structure would, in Marx's view, provide the situation within which the proletariat could perceive its situation and actively struggle to change it. From monopoly capitalism, then, would arise the communist mode of production.

___

2

This quotation is attributed to Cecil Rhodes of Boer War fame by Lenin:

I was in the East End of London yesterday and attended a meeting of the unemployed. I listened to the wild speeches, which were just a cry for "bread," "bread" and on my way home I pondered over the scene and I became more than ever convinced of the importance of imperialism . . . My cherished idea is a solution for the social problem, i.e., in order to save the 40 000 000 inhabitants of the United Kingdom from a bloody civil war, we colonial statemen must acquire new lands to settle the surplus population, to provide new markets for the goods produced in the factories and mines. The Empire, as I have always said, is a bread and butter question. If you want to avoid civil war, you must become imperialists.[6]

Perhaps these words catch, as clearly as the sophisticated analysis of Lenin, the meaning of imperialism. Imperialism, like capitalism, has stages. One stage is the export of surplus populations, usually supported by the military presence of the imperialist nation. A second stage, and it is this to which Lenin addresses himself, is the export of capital for purposes of exploiting natural resources, labour, and commodity markets in other countries. With this form of economic imperialism, Lenin argues that the world becomes divided among the biggest capitalist powers through monopolies in various industrial sectors. Those who own and control the monopolies are the financiers, whose base of operations consists of finance and holding companies, banks, insurance corporations and similar enterprises.[7]

The few imperialist powers identified by Lenin in 1915 were Britain, United States, and Japan. These countries, he argued, carved up the world into their colonial territories, from which they extracted raw materials for their manufacturing industries and through which they provided wage employment for the people in their nations at the expense of the colonial peoples. Thus the world became one divided between the haves and the have-nots, the rich nations and the poor nations. The First World War was, in Lenin's view, a struggle between the capitalists of these nations for the division of territories and spoils, brought on by the growing strength of Germany. Lenin expected that the growth of monopolies following that war would enslave nations until the workers of all countries united in rebellion against their imperialist masters. The contradictions within monopoly capitalism—such as the enormous surpluses created by the poor nations—would eventually give rise not only to revolution but to decay from within the system. "Monopoly . . . inevitably engenders a tendency to stagnation and decay."[8]

These early theories of imperialism have modern extensions. With reference to the global activities of the modern corporation and its expansion into the underdeveloped world, both neo-Marxist and other social scientists identify an unequal relationship between the metropolitan core nations (e.g., the United States) and the peripheral nations (e.g., Latin American countries).

Branch-plant economies are dependent economies. Their control, ownership, direction, research, expansion, markets, and manpower allocations are determined elsewhere. Foreign companies obtain access to natural resources, and through reserving the rights to process these into manufactured products, increase their profits very rapidly without encouraging the development of competing national industries. Though such firms must repay the loans, or interest on the loans floated for purposes of the initial purchase, and must as well pay taxes and wages for local workers, they can in very short order so increase their profits that they no longer require additional investment funds in order to continue expanding. Their expansion tends to provide for vertical integration of their industry: that is, they move into supporting industrial areas such as construction, transportation, manufacturing of tools and machinery, research and retail sales, and so gain a large degree of control over the total industry. This inhibits growth of potential competition, it inhibits local investment in local firms, and creates a spiralling dependence of the local labour force on the foreign industry. This process is frequently referred to as modern economic imperialism. It involves very little outright force, depends instead on the co-operation and aid of a small elite within the dependent country, and does not require the export of its own nationals in any large numbers or as settlers.

Following the lead of André Gunder Frank, some writers refer to this form of imperialism as "the development of underdevelopment" because where it is successful, it necessarily underdevelops or hinders the development of an independent economy in the host country while fully developing the central or imperialist economy.[9] The host country, or the branch-plant economy, is referred to as the periphery, the satellite, or the hinterland, because its economic development is geared to the policies and practices of another country. The other country is referred to as the metropolis, the centre in which the major economic decisions are made and to which the lion's share of the profits is delivered.

This process is replicated at the local level within a country. The metropolis at any level is simultaneously the hinterland at another level. Thus Canada as a whole is regarded as a hinterland to the United States, but within each of these countries, the large metropolitan areas use the resources of their respective hinterlands. In Canada's case, the hinterland to the Toronto—Montreal axis includes the Canadian Prairies and the East Coast; the hinterland to Calgary and Edmonton in Alberta (themselves hinterlands to the United States and Ontario) include Northern Alberta and, increasingly, parts of the Northwest Territories and British Columbia.

As any centre grows, it attracts the most capable people from surrounding territories. The city attracts workers from rural areas; the large metropolitan areas attract, as well, the most talented intellectuals, artists, writers, technicians, researchers, and administrators. In return, the metropolis feeds the hinterland its own surplus products, including people who cannot find jobs in their homeland. These people take over the subsidiary plants and staff the other institutional sectors of the hinterland economy; the media, the universities, the schools, and the theatres. This asymmetrical flow of excellence toward the metropolis[10] was essential to the development and maintenance of the Roman empire, the Austro-Hungarian empire, and the British empire, and it is argued within this theoretical framework that it is still an important factor in the present imperialist empires. The consequence for the hinterland areas is that their potential leaders are drained off, and they are, instead, led by people whose allegiance is to the metropolis, not to the hinterland and their decisions and influence create a replica of the metropolis, rather than an independent or culturally different society.[11]

This theory, in addition, attributes a share of unemployment in the hinterland areas to the exploitative nature of economic imperialism. Large corporations, in order to continue developing their products and creating ever more products and markets, engage in various kinds of research and development. This is the area in which skilled technicians and scientists are employed. The unique contribution of American capitalism has been its capacity to create markets where none existed, to create demands for new products, to constantly refine and alter the nature of existing technology so that new products are always required to meet new conditions. The capacity of innovation depends on the maintenance of considerable investment in research and development and on the monopoly of these processes so that the parent firms are always one step ahead of potential competitors in other nations. This can be done by maintaining all important research and development processes within the parent company and on home territory.[12] Subsidiary firms are not generally engaged in any basic research, and their promising technicians are provided with better paying positions within the parent company. Unskilled workers and skilled workers, on the other hand, are dependent on the continued interest of the parent firm in the subsidiary. If market conditions tighten up, employment is more likely to be curtailed in the colony than in the metropolis. Thus both the technicians and the labourers experience insecurity in their employment conditions within a branch-plant economy.

The dominant ideology of underdevelopment (a theoretical interest that has largely emerged since the Second World War) involves the premise that countries are in varying stages of the same industrializing process. This theory, articulated particularly by W.W. Rostow, and discussed in Chapter 3,[13] has it that there are stages of industrial growth. At some particular point, the turn of the century for Canada, technology, population, and means of transportation coalesce in some fashion to abruptly alter the concatenation of productive forces in the society. It "takes off" into the industrial cycle and leaves its agricultural underdeveloped base behind. This theory is the natural extension of the liberal framework discussed in earlier chapters. But it is also implicit in the major writings of Marx. He said in the preface to *Capital*: "The country that is most developed industrially only shows to the less developed the image of its own future."[14] Although he identified the contradictions that moved society from the competitive to the monopolistic and imperialistic stage of capitalism he did not consistently recognize the qualitatively different positions of imperialist and colonial territories.

The general theory of imperialism as advanced by Lenin, and that presently is being forwarded by others, suggests quite a contrary process. As one country enters an intense phase of industrialization, those countries which provide it with raw materials and manpower lose their relative strength. They are depleted in their productive capacity and of necessity become exporters of raw materials and fuel, importers of consumer products and surplus goods. Their economies are truncated, their talent drained off, and their political independence eroded. They are not on the road to industrialization, and they are not merely underdeveloped versions of industrial societies.

3

Labour in a bourgeois society is alienated. The term alienation means "sold" or "removed from the control of the owner," and is used by Marx to refer to the incapacity of labour to identify itself historically and socially because the institutions of the society and the dominant ideology deprive workers of self-understanding. This is an objective condition rather than a subjective feeling. In Marx's view, when the production of subsistence in a society is carried on by workers who sell their labour, as in a capitalist system, then the worker becomes a commodity, a thing rather than a fully social being. His worth is determined by a competitive labour market. He is obliged to do one task in a labour process that allots separate phases of a total production system to individual workers, and in producing his small task repetitively he loses a sense of himself as a whole being and of his social relationship to other workers. He is, in Marx's words, "a most miserable commodity."

The worker becomes poorer the more wealth he produces, the more his production increases in power and extent. The worker becomes a cheaper commodity the more commodities he produces. The increase in value of the world of things is directly proportional to the decrease in value of the human world. Labor not only produces commodities. It also produces itself and the worker as a commodity, and indeed in the same proportion as it produces commodities in general.[15]

In contrast to this alienated condition, Marx envisions a communist society in which all people would be equal producers and owners of the means of production, the division of labour would be overcome, and workers would no longer be alienated from their own work and the communal interest. He describes this society:

In communist society . . . where nobody has an exclusive area of activity and each can train himself in any branch he wishes, society regulates the general production, making it possible for me to do one thing today and another tomorrow, to hunt in the morning, fish in the afternoon, breed cattle in the evening, criticize after dinner, just as I like, without ever becoming a hunter, a fisherman, a herdsman, or a critic.[16]

This does not mean that no one has duties or obligations, and that one can simply work or not work as he chooses. It means, rather, that the necessary work of society, that is, the carrying out of productive tasks so that subsistence is provided for all, becomes the work of all equally. No one person can unilaterally determine the division of labour, no class owns the work of others, and the division is not constant. Thus an intellectual would also be, at some times or seasons, an agricultural worker; the management of factories becomes the social responsibility of the community, and so forth. Those who are provided with specialized training would be engaged in providing the fruits of the training to the community, as agents of the community rather than as private practitioners: thus, for example, a doctor, trained at the expense of the society, would then be engaged in the practice of medicine for the society rather than for his own material enrichment. The essence of this communist society would be that the objective is the social well-being of the total community, not the material well-being of a privileged few.

How precisely this transition is to take place is not clear. Marx argues that the empirical forms the transition would take cannot be predicted in advance; what he is attempting to do, rather, is argue, on the basis of a theory of history and on the assumption that history is a progression of resolutions of the internal contradictions of each previous stage, that the stage following full monopoly capitalism would be communism. The chief mechanism for the struggle of the workers against capitalism would be the very centralized labour pools created by capital, and the extreme and stark divisions between the two polarized classes. This would be the condition which would demonstrate to the workers their own alienation.

4

The production relations between classes determine the way in which people interpret their social world, that is, their ideological perspective. The mode of production by which subsistence is created differs from one epoch to another, and it is the specific mode at any time which determines the organization of the society and moulds the perception of life itself.

The production of ideas, of conceptions, of consciousness is directly inter-woven with the material activity and the material relationships of men; it is the language of actual life. Conceiving, thinking, and the intellectual relationships of men appear here as the direct result of their material behavior.[17]

Thus, "consciousness does not determine life, but life determines consciousness."[18] This argument has been frequently misinterpreted to mean that individual consciousness is determined by one's position in the economic system. Marx, however, is not arguing such a deterministic case. He is arguing, rather, that the overall social view, the pervasive ideology of a society, is generated from the real and material conditions by which subsistence is produced; individuals are enveloped in this pervasive ideology and interpret their own positions relative to it. This is also true of intellectuals, of whom Marx claims that in each historical epoch they have shared in and advanced the dominating illusion of the period.[19]

While ideological perspectives grow out of the material conditions of any mode of production and the relationships of producers to one another, at the same time,

In every epoch the ideas of the ruling class are the ruling ideas, that is, the class that is the ruling material power of society is at the same time its ruling intellectual power. The class having the means of material produc-tion has also control over the means of intellectual production, so that it also controls, generally speaking, the ideas of those who lack the means of intellectual production. The ruling ideas are nothing more than the ideal expression of the dominant material relationships grasped as ideas, hence of the relationships which make the one class the ruling one and therefore the ideas of its domination.[20]

This has also sometimes been misinterpreted to mean that the ruling class consciously and deliberately manufactures lies which will pre-serve the status quo. This does not appear to be Marx's argument. It is, rather, that the ruling class interprets its reality, its ruling position, in an idealized way, and through appropriate symbolism and language, passes this on through the ideological channels which it controls. This class, like the class or classes it rules, perceives its own situation through the material relations and modes of produc-tion. Marx offers by way of example a situation in which royalty, an aristocracy, and a bourgeoisie are contending for domination, and in which the ideological expression of this is a doctrine of the sep-aration of powers believed to be by these groups, as well as by those whom they dominate, an "eternal law." A similar idea has been explored by non-Marxist writers since this was written, one of the hypotheses being that monotheism as religion is most likely to characterize a highly centralized political state; polytheism, a decentralized or more tribal organization.[21]

The fact that the ruling ideas are idealized versions of the ruling class and its relationship to the modes of production is one generally not understood. In considering the history of ideas, intellectuals (themselves being normally allied with, if not actually part of, the ruling class) turn the idealized version of reality into complete abstractions with a life of their own. There is then a tendency to suppose that ideas have an entirely independent capacity to cause action, that people are actually working out their ideas rather than the reverse.

If, in considering the course of history, we detach the ideas of the ruling class from the ruling class itself and attribute to them an independent existence . . . we can say, for example, that during the time when aristocracy was dominant the concepts of honor, loyalty, etc., prevailed, during the dominion of the bourgeoisie, the concepts of freedom, equality, etc. The ruling class itself generally imagines this to be the case.[22]

With any upheaval in the society, a new class emerges. This new class has to discard the prevailing ideology of its predecessors in the course of overthrowing the material conditions of the previous epoch. To do this, it must express its interests as the interests of the total society, and it will do so in an idealized form just as the preceding dominant class did.

The ruling class may or may not be conscious of its domination and of its class membership; this would depend on how it actually rules and whether that mode of ruling gives rise to an idealized version of social organization which includes the existence of classes. An aristocratic society, for example, by which individual lords directly and legitimately rule over serfs or peasants and in which the class of lords has stated prerogatives, would be expected to create a version of society in which there are natural rules and a class structure, possibly supervised by an omnipresent god. A bourgeois society, however, in which economic power is institutionally divorced from political power and where ruling is a less obvious condition would be less likely to idealize bourgeois rule in class terms; thus the bourgeoisie might deny even to itself that it is a class.

The working class in a bourgeois society is unlikely to view itself as a class since its material conditions stratify its members, provide some with authority and wealth, others with entirely subordinate roles and poverty; and since it exists within an ideological framework of classlessness. This is the essence of its alienation: that it lives with a false class consciousness, and that its material conditions, its relationships to the means of production, prevent it from recognizing its social condition. None the less, in Marx's view, this class will eventually recognize its class situation. Its members, increasingly impoverished, will become more aware of their common plight and organize around mutual material interests, first in trade union associations and then in political organizations. As workers in different trades and with different statuses recognize their common bondage to ever fewer capitalists, the grip of the bourgeois ideology will weaken and the class struggle will become an open conflict.[23]

5

Capitalism and its extension, imperialism, require for their smooth operation the existence of a state. A state is not the same as a society; it is a particular institution which has a monopoly of force within a given territory. With the emergence of capitalism there also emerged nation states, and because of the competitive nature of early capitalism, the institution of the nation state took the form of a parliament to which members were elected, first by the aristocracy and bourgeoisie, then by the total population. Marx characterized the executives of this state as "but a committee for managing the common affairs of the whole bourgeoisie,"[24] a phrase that has frequently been interpreted to mean that the state automatically acts in the interests of the capitalist class. Since Marx did sometimes suggest that this was how he viewed the state in a bourgeois society, the interpretation may be correct. However, the modifier "whole" also suggests another interpretation, consistent with other aspects of the total theoretical framework. In describing the bourgeoisie, Marx pointed out that at any one time it was not necessarily cohesive. Some of its members would be concerned with the development of industry, with ownership and management of the productive mechanisms, and with the accumulation of industrial capital; other members would be concerned with the creation of profit from the circulation of capital, i.e., with banking and finance; yet others with the buying and selling of industrial and other commodities. Furthermore, the total world class would be divided in function and power according to their regional positions within the imperialistic system. These various fragments of the bourgeoisie do not necessarily have identical short-term interests. Legislation beneficial to the banker might be highly detrimental to the industrialist, and so forth.

The state, if it were acting in the common interests of the whole bourgeoisie, would have to co-ordinate these various interests, to determine which of them or what other considerations might lead to the enhancement of the long-term interests of the entire class. Thus a state, acting in the interests of the bourgeoisie, might enact legislation protecting the right of workers to a minimum wage. This might reduce the short-term profits of employers, but in the long run might reduce the likelihood of a proletarian revolution or the loss through emigration and early death of too large a portion of the working class. The "common affairs of the whole bourgeoisie" means the long-term interests of the total class. One of the central questions of contemporary Marxist studies is, what is the nature of the state in a society dominated by corporations and structured by fragmented ruling and working classes?

Many Canadian Marxists argue that there are three primary functions of the state. These are: (1) *the accumulation function*, that is, the provision of conditions that will permit private capital to continue with its extraction of surplus value; (2) *the legitimation function*, that is, the maintenance of a climate of social acceptance for the private accumulation of capital, and of social stability so that it can occur without interruption; and (3) *the coercion function*, that is, the monopoly of legitimate force.[25] The accumulation function may be performed through taxation legislation, grants to corporations for expansion, research, and development, the building of infrastructure, regular banking laws, trade laws and practices, and laws and regulations, governing the labour force. The legitimation function may be performed through effective socialization agencies which turn out a trained and disciplined labour force, welfare practices that reduce the extremes of poverty, and successful propaganda. The coercion functions are performed when the legitimation functions fail to achieve success, as when there are disruptive strikes or when there is illegal trading on the stock market.

These functions are not necessarily congruent. It can happen that a government is faced with a fiscal crisis, as American James O'Connor argues is true of governments in capitalist economies today,[26] and that they cannot simultaneously provide the conditions for increasing the rates of profit and conditions of labour stability. In such a case they may be obliged to resort to force in order to shore up the economy, thus giving rise to a "crisis of legitimation," that is, a situation in which a significant proportion of the population loses its faith in the system.

The way in which a government will deal with such contradictory pressures will depend upon both the external context within which it operates, and the internal balance of powers between the various fractions of the ruling class. In a seminal group of essays on the

Canadian state, Leo Panitch has stressed that the state is not merely, and perhaps not importantly, the government:

The point here is that the extent to which a government effectively controls the power of the state, indeed even the extent to which it can speak authoritatively in the name of the state, will depend on the balance of forces within the various institutions of the state, such as the bureaucracy, the judiciary, and the military, in terms of the classes they represent and the values they hold. This will determine how far governmental power is circumscribed by state power.[27]

This argument follows on a study of the capitalist state by Ralph Miliband, in which it is argued that the state consists of the civil service, public corporations, central banks, regulatory commissions, the judiciary, and many other institutions.[28] As Panitch points out, in Canada these institutions are particularly extensive because provincial governments are large and significant governing institutions, with all of the state sector replicated in each province. The peculiar circumstance in Canada is that, by virtue of remaining so long a British colony and because of its early control by a financial elite and that group's control of the regional development, the central state and the provincial states are frequently in conflict, as noted in the previous section. Thus the central state in Canada reaps the effects of its early subordination to American industrial capital by a weakened capacity to control internal forces and a balkanized country with a fragmented capitalist class.

While the central state is weak and the capitalist class fragmented along regional lines, there is, none the less, uniformity of objectives within that class in the sense that all are clearly within the ideological framework of capitalism. The role of the state vis-à-vis these fractions is the same for the Parti Quebecois and occasional provincial NDP governments whose planning includes a more overt state participation in the economy, as for the federal and Alberta or other provincial governments which use the state as the entrepreneurial agent to facilitate entirely private accumulation. The internal rivalries represent the aspirations of the remaining petit bourgeoisie and the rising managerial class of the corporations and state bureaucracies, but they do not lead in the 1980s, any more than in Alberta of the 1930s, to control by these groups. As Alberta bargains for higher oil prices against Ontario's claims on lower energy costs for its manufacturing plants, both ultimately represent monopoly capital with a foreign home base.

As an integral part of this state-business relationship, the federal state is called upon to aid large companies when falling rates of profit diminish their strength. Thus Ford obtained funds for its plants in Canada, though it provided no guarantee of the jobs for Canadians in the negotiations and subsequently reduced employment at its Canadian plants.[29] The federal government is caught in a classic dilemma of capitalism; if it fails to bail out the companies, the unemployment rate and community instability may well create a legitimation crisis—a situation in which the workers rebel. If it does support the companies, even if this were accompanied by a guarantee on existing jobs, it would sustain the high level of foreign control over Canadian industry and the high level of concentration in the economy as well as making it apparent to the general public that it is the underwriter for private corporate profit.

If the North American economy entered a major depression, many companies would either go bankrupt or reduce their investments. The major victims would be small companies, the service sector for the large companies. But as well, some large companies, such as Chrysler, could not continue to operate in an economy where they are technologically outclassed. After a period of severe unemployment, falling prices and falling profits, fewer very large corporate structures would remain, each with a much larger share of the total market. But these large structures would require extensive state support, and in order to re-establish themselves they would need to increase their technological investment around changing energy sources. In that event, the role of the state could change—from that of support system to that of major actor. State capitalism differs from private capitalism in that the state is openly allied with business and plans the economy together with business. Where that situation occurs, as it did in Italy, Spain, Portugal, and Germany during the 1930s and early 1940s, there arises a serious gap between the ideology of democracy, in which the state ostensibly acts in the interests of all the people and via majority votes for a government, and the reality. During the 1930s, when this occurred in Europe and when businessmen in Canada experienced the effects of the Depression, the proposed solution was the corporate state.

The corporate state, as a political form, has been defined by Panitch as:

... a political structure within advanced capitalism which integrates organized socioeconomic producer groups through a system of representation and cooperative mutual interaction at the leadership level and mobilization and social control at the mass level.[30]

This political form would normally involve various planning organs which are not elected but which are paramount in the management of the economy. These would include organized labour and other business interest groups. The planning would have as one of its objectives, full employment; the return for employment would be wage controls, and no-strike labour contracts. The objective of this form would be to reduce class conflict while retaining the prerogatives of private property.

Several Canadian writers have argued that the state in Canada has always played a major role in the economy, and that it has been a much more overt and active participant than the state sectors in most other liberal democracies. Reg Whitaker has termed this history, "private ownership at public expense."[31] Herschel Hardin has argued that Canada has always had a uniquely entrepreneurial central state in which crown corporations have been the major state actors.[32] The explanation for this has been the structural weakness of the Canadian bourgeoisie in both the British and American imperial empires. However, these writers are not arguing that this large state role has constituted state control or even state management of the economy. The state provided extraordinary largesse to the Canadian Pacific syndicate in the 1880s but did not become a controlling director of the railway or the businesses generated from that gift; similarly, the state provided a substantial share of the financing for the Syncrude project in Alberta in the 1970s, but has only minority voting power as a shareholder.[33]

A corporate state, then, does not apply to Canada throughout this history, despite the role of the state in the economy. It is a more specific political form, and would involve a change in the organization of government, the nature of a liberal democracy, and the explicit relations between business, labour, and government. This was the proposal advanced by the Union Nationale and the fascist parties in Canada during the 1930s.[34] These groups did not actually implement their proposals in the 1930s, and Canada was closer to the corporate state during the war under the Liberal administration with its powers to co-opt (or be co-opted by) business leaders for wartime purposes. The 1930s and 1940s, however, were unlike the 1970s and 1980s in that the corporate empires were considerably less extensive and continental policies had not yet included the entire military establishment.

Marxists argue that the present stage of capitalism constitutes an "advanced monopoly"—advanced in the sense of extreme rather than progressive—and that in this stage the contradictions of liberal capitalism exceed the capacities of the democratic state to manage the affairs of what are no longer national economies. If that is the case, then one of the possible outcomes is a corporate state more divorced from national electorates than the present democracies.

6

Marx assumed that history is cumulative, not unlike the assumption of the liberal society, but complicated by internal contradictions in its development. He differed in his view of the stages of that history and in the mechanism that causes social change. He also assumed the virtue and basic compatibility of two major liberal values: equality and individualism. His demand for equality, of course, exceeded that of the liberal society, but his view of individual rights was remarkably similar to the idealized view of the individual within liberalism. Where he most fundamentally differed from the liberal view was in his insistence that there is a ruling class, that it maintains its rule not by force of intellect or hard work but by exploitation of the surplus created from other people's labour, and that the ruling class in capitalism consists of the bourgeoisie. This, together with a version of the future that would discard the privileges of that class and make all industrial property social rather than private, is what makes Marx's ideas and the socialist ideologies that follow it appear threatening to those members of the capitalist society who believe themselves to be beneficiaries of private ownership, and appear accurate to those who believe themselves—or whose conscience causes them to believe others—to be victims of the system.

The core of Marxist theory is the labour theory of value, patterned after theories already advanced in what has since become known as classical economics. This has been subjected to continued debate since Marx published. The objections to it are many, including the discounting of entrepreneurship and managerial skill, the failure to appreciate market operations in the evaluation of goods and the creation of profits, and the specific mathematical formulation provided by Marx for working out the rate of exploitation (the rate at which surplus value is extracted from labour). At one level there is some agreement: labour must produce value over and above the amount required to maintain and reproduce itself, since otherwise there would be no accumulation of profit. That surplus is not controlled by the wage labourer; it is controlled by the owner of the means of production who employs the labourer. But at another level there is a problem: the market price of goods is not simply determined by the amount of labour time embedded in its production. Numerous other conditions affect prices, and goods may sell at well above the costs of production or may not sell at all even though much labour time is embedded in them. A theory of prices and profits, therefore, cannot be deduced from a labour theory of value.

Using the first level of insights, we can arrive at an understanding of the basic division between an owning and a wage-labouring class. Marx's arguments on the social relations of this class system remain today powerful analytical tools for an understanding of capitalism. However, we have to go beyond Marx to understand the relationships between groups within these classes, groups not adequately defined in either of these classes, and groups not defined by class at all.

The first of these include, for example, managers who earn wages, and public-sector workers who produce no surplus value in the Marxist sense of that term. These two groups comprise a very large segment of the contemporary society, and yet clearly they have different economic and social situations than manual labour in the private sector. The second group consists of commodity producers who sell goods rather than their labour power. Their numbers have not declined as Marx anticipated, and their relationship to the owners of major industrial plants and financiers requires a class analysis but one which does not rest on a simple labour theory of value.

The third category consists of groups defined by gender, ethnicity, religion, region, or any other condition which is not reducible to class. Nothing in Marxist theory enables us to analyze the numerous social movements spawned by such groups. Historically, groups such as these have far more frequently engaged in active opposition to prevailing social conditions in industrial and industrializing societies than any groups properly defined as class-based. In contemporary society, national liberation movements, civil war between different ethnic groups, the feminist movement, religious strife, and territorially-based conflicts even within a relatively staid nation such as Canada cannot be explained in terms of class struggles.[35]

Even with these caveats, one may still accept the basic argument that there are classes, and that the nexus of class differentiation is control of surplus value by one class and production of it by another.

That much may be conceded to the Marxist theory, but there remains the further assumption contested by liberal theorists: that industrial production could be carried out in another fashion, and specifically in a fashion by which no controlling class exists. At this point the argument is entirely ideological since no industrial society is known in which there is no controlling class. In fact, the argument suddenly extends beyond this because it opens up the question of whether the class structure is specifically a function of capitalism or of industrialism. At the time Marx wrote there were no industrial societies which were not capitalist. If one accepts the description of Soviet society as non-capitalist (debatable) then the continued existence of a controlling class, though the controllers do not own the means of production as private property, leads to the hypothesis that industrialism, with or without capitalism, creates a class structure. At this juncture in history, there is no empirical means of testing that hypothesis.

Marx's theory of history is also subject to debate. The precise mechanisms by which capitalists and industrial society grew out of feudal society are not agreed upon. Marx, for example, argues that the bourgeoisie was an outgrowth of the serfs of the Middle Ages, who became the burghers of the early towns.[36] A contrary interpretation rests the development of the towns on the very early development of monopoly trading companies, and the development of a class of tradesmen who were never actually part of the feudal population. Moreover, the class struggle that ensued and became the bourgeois revolutions was not between the two major classes of the feudal period, the lords and serfs, but between this entirely urban class and the feudal aristocracy. If one projects from history a set of abstract laws, as Marx proposes, then one might suppose that the next revolution would not be between the proletariat and the bourgeoisie, but between the bourgeoisie and some third class to which, dialectically, it has given birth. The evolving class of professional managers in both the very large state bureaucracies of capitalism and the Soviet system may be such a class. Whether such a class would or could develop a society in which production is carried on without alienation and without a division of labour as specialized and compartmentalized as the present system is certainly open to debate.

What was not anticipated by Marx was the astonishing capacity of capitalist society to generate wealth and distribute it within both the imperial centre and in some of the peripheral regions. This has come about in good part by imperialistic growth; the exploitation of labour and the appropriation of resources in the peripheral countries. As a consequence of this, the working classes in the United States, Canada, Australia and New Zealand, Western Europe and parts of the rest of the world have become extremely wealthy compared to any subordinate (and most ruling) classes in history. In addition, the small business sector and professional classes have not disappeared; the total working class and petit bourgeoisie remain stratified not only by income but as well by authority, range of individual choice, and social mobility. While a Marxist might well argue that the process of impoverishment is yet to come, that the apex and reversal of monopoly capitalism has not yet occurred, none the less a century and a half have passed since the predictions of impoverishment were made, and during that time there has been undeniable improvement in the material conditions of life for most workers in the industrial centres. Inequalities have persisted, but the base line, except during the notable periods of depression, has been high enough that workers have been able to do far more than merely replenish their class.

Marx defined alienation as an objective condition of the working class, consisting in part of the internalization of the dominant ideology. Numerous contemporary writers have treated alienation as a subjective condition, consisting of unhappiness or a feeling of powerlessness. When the term is used in the subjective sense, especially when so used in the context of survey questionnaires, the conclusion may be that workers are not alienated if they express satisfaction with their work. The Marxist might argue that in that case they are truly alienated because they cannot see their class situation at all and are completely overwhelmed by the dominant ideology. For the Marxist, the confirmation of the alienation thesis is that the working class reproduces the dominant ideology—explains its own circumstances in terms of the legitimacy of private property and measures itself in terms of wages—rather than that it experiences conscious unhappiness.

The fact that many workers do reproduce the dominant ideology, together with the fact that in many survey studies they are reported to enjoy considerable satisfaction with their work or, if not their work, their wages, and that their wage levels have increased beyond the level of survival and reproduction needs appears to contradict the Marxist prognosis. These facts may be explained partly in terms of imperialism. Workers in the central industrial countries and some satellite regions such as Canada have enjoyed a share of the surplus extracted from the rest of the world. The impoverishment of the working class which Marx predicted has therefore been experienced by the colonial populations rather than by the workers in the industrial centres. Even though this may be the case, however, the affluence and support for the system within the central nations' working classes raise questions about the predictive capability of the Marxist thesis. If maintenance of the imperialist system is in the objective (material) interests of the workers in the industrial centres and if they do not experience any sense of being "miserable commodities" then their ideology is not adequately explained as "false class consciousness." Alienated or not in the Marxist sense, they are unlikely to develop a class consciousness and opposition to the ruling class if they continue to reap considerable benefits from the capitalist system.

The theory of ideology is powerful and persuasive because it locates the source of our beliefs in something tangible: our social relations of production. But if the most persistent divisions in society, the divisions which generate the most heated debate and armed struggles, are actually located in ethnic, religious, sexual, and regional conditions, then we are obliged to seek causes in addition to or in place of production relations. This becomes a central problem of Marxism: its monocausal approach to history, conflict, and ideology. Class relations clearly are important; the problem is that they are among the important relations of human life and not necessarily the central ones. Going beyond Marx, then, involves developing a theory of differences in social conditions within capitalism and asking "under what particular conditions is class conflict generated?"

Marxist theories of ideology have been attacked from another angle as well. Abercrombie et al.[37] have provided a careful empirical study of ideologies in Britain, concluding that the ruling class ideas have been adopted by subordinate classes only at certain periods in history, and even then they have been considerably watered down and filtered through other ideas. The dominant ideology as a model of ruling class idealizations of itself and its importance to the society is not, in their opinion, supported by historical evidence.

Perhaps the most problematic and currently controversial aspect of Marxist theory is its treatment of the capitalist state. To be fair, Marx himself did not produce a theory of the state, and the interpretations offered by Engels,[38] Lenin,[39] and more recently by neo-Marxists such as Poulantzas,[40] Miliband,[41] Gramsci,[42] and O'Connor[43] cover a broad spectrum of differing theories. What they have in common is the assumption that democratic governments are not neutral and impartial umpires within capitalist economies; they are either instrumentally attached to the ruling class or structurally constrained by its behaviour to act in its long-term interests.

One might accept a theory of class and a generally Marxist perspective on the nature of the accumulation process in capitalism yet dispute this view of the capitalist state. To begin with, capitalism has survived for long periods in societies without democratic governments or other "camouflages" for their operations. Secondly, most democratic governments make no pretence of their support for capitalist enterprise, so why make such a fuss about legitimation exercises to fool workers? Third, democracy cannot be reduced to the services governments perform for capitalist enterprises, and it seems unnecessarily cumbersome to reduce all services to the interests of capital.[44]

One may acknowledge that the state is an institution severely constrained by its dependence on the process of capital accumulation for continued existence, yet hesitate in viewing it as but the handmaiden of capitalists. Like the theory of class conflict, the important question may be, not whether the state is closely allied with capital, but under what conditions the state would be obliged to act only with reference to the interests of capital.

Beyond these questions there is a level of reality problem in most existing theories of the state. Both liberal and neo-Marxist theories tend to assume the territorial sovereignty of national states, an assumption that is tenuous at best within the global economy we now inhabit. No state, and certainly not the Canadian state, can control the economy within its borders; many states suffer not from the pressure of capital to act in particular ways but from the exodus of capital from the territory. This problem poses new demands on theory, for now we must explain not the relationship between a national ruling class and the capitalist state but the relationship between international capital, smaller and national capital, and in many ways impotent nation-state governments.

7

Signally missing in Marxist theory is acknowledgement of the nature of bureaucracies. The public sector within governments is an enormous part of industrial societies, and governments or public agencies are major employers of labour. Bureaucracies have momentum, regulated existences, personnel, and objectives which cannot be reduced to class and accumulation of capital. For this reason, many theorists of contemporary states turn to Max Weber for a starting point. As well, noting some of the deficiencies in the Marxist understanding of non-class conflict, one might turn to Weber for the conceptual tools appropriate for studying these.

Weber accepted a theory of class structure and relations similar to that argued by Marx—the propertied and the unpropertied, created and sustained within the market-place—but did not see class relations as the motive force of history.[45] In his opinion there are no historical laws to social evolution. Each society develops in response to numerous conditions, and while the economic level is extremely important it is not determinate. Class struggles, he said, would occur under particular circumstances, but are not necessarily the important struggles in a society and might have very little impact on the development of social interaction. Among the conditions that might affect the probability of class struggles are high visibility of a common enemy, large numbers of people having the same material conditions, an intelligentsia willing to provide leadership, and the conditions of size and communications which would affect the ease of organization. In an aside Weber noted that struggles often take the form of fights with the visible enemy rather than the more important one, as when workers vent their rage at a manager rather than at the financier who actually owns the business.

In addition to classes, which he saw as being objectively defined and therefore independent of subjective evaluations of positions in society, there are status groups. Status groups may be class groups— e.g., the commercial class may also be a status group—but may be independent of class or may cross class lines, e.g. castes, ethnic groups. Status groups involve the subjective evaluations others make of individuals' social positions, the esteem and prestige they hold. Status groups are usually conscious of their common position. Status can affect class relationships through influencing market conditions, e.g., when a religious or ethnic group is prohibited from selling its labour or from buying land.

He identified party as a separate grouping of individuals who work together to gain control of an organization in order to implement specific policies. Parties may be class or status based, but normally are not: normally they are coalitions of interest groups. Thus the contemporary political party would not be best analyzed in class terms from a Weberian perspective.

Weber rejected both the idealist and materialist versions of history; the idealist being associated with Hegel's theory of ideas governing social organization, and the materialist being associated with Marx's theory of social organization governing ideas. His study of the relationship between protestantism and capitalism demonstrated the constant interaction between ideas, or the social psychology behind human action, and material forces. He argued that one could not explain the more rapid and complete rise of capitalism in Protestant countries without recognizing the significance of religious ideas.[46] For different purposes, Durkheim also argued that religious ideas affected group and personal behaviours to such an extent that suicide rates could be predicted through knowledge of religious affiliations.[47]

Weber defined capitalism as a system by which individuals pursue profit through continuous, rational investments and employ and organize a (formally) free labour force to produce goods for a market in order to increase profits. By the term "rational" he meant the calculated linking of means with stated goals. In capitalism, the stated goal is profit, and calculations are rational when they are made specifically for that purpose rather than for purposes of maintaining kin relations, traditional values, or any other non-profit objective. Marx saw capitalism as inherently irrational because it maximized profit at the expense of large numbers of people; it was, for Marx, socially inefficient. Weber is concerned with its inherent efficiency, but recognized that its efficiency was directed entirely toward the making of profits for the propertied class. This is a difference in emphasis and focus rather than substance.

Unlike Marx, Weber was very much concerned with the rise of bureaucracy and its relationship to capitalism. His chief objection to socialism was that, in his opinion, it would inevitably increase bureaucratic controls and ultimately become oppressive for this reason. Its evolution, none the less, was linked not to socialism but to capitalism. Bureaucracy involves fixed rules for management. In its ideal form (which may not be met in particular circumstances), recruitment is based on credentials and qualifications rather than kinship and personal contacts. It rests on the separation of office from domicile, officer from person, business assets from private fortunes. There is, in a bureaucratic organization, a set of rules for the exercise of authority, a definite hierarchy of positions each of which has limited powers. Office holding becomes a vocation, a primary task in life, rather than a secondary role for someone whose powers derive from hereditary or kinship relations.

The capitalist state rests, in Weber's opinion, on the development of public sector bureaucracies. These in turn depend on a fixed and regular taxation system, which can only occur in a fully developed capitalist system where budgeting and calculation of profits ensure taxable yields. Weber noted that if a working class was obliged to pay taxes, the state would have to provide safeguards on its ability to pay, and thus protect workers against uneconomic exploitation. In the capitalist society, the state fully develops as a separate institution.

The technical advantages of bureaucratic organization lie in its impersonality, rationality, predictability, and efficiency. It has two important consequences for social organization: on the one hand it tends to level social differences as it rests more and more on rules, regulations, laws, recruitment procedures all evenly applied; on the other, it tends to permit those at the top of the system to gain too much power because ultimately they make the decisions that affect the distribution of wealth.

Weber did not produce a systematic and comprehensive theory of society, because he rejected the notion that there are laws to development, or some necessary evolution between feudalism, capitalism, and socialism. Thus each society has to be studied separately, and all generalizations tempered with reference to empirical conditions. With this much less deterministic perspective, Weber's work may seem less compelling than Marx's studies of capitalism. But he does provide an alternative starting point for contemporary sociologists who recognize the existence of classes, the need to understand how capitalism operates, and the problem of the capitalist state and ideology.

6 CLASS AND CLASS PROTEST

Marxist theories are not common property in the sense that large numbers of people read and debate them. In Canada, very few people at any time have studied either the original texts or the neo-Marxist literature. But certain ideas derived from Marx have become common property. Sometimes these are taken out of context. Frequently they are unconnected to a general theory of society. Sometimes they are little more than slogans. But in this ideological form, they have had the power to mobilize many people over the past century. This chapter considers how these ideas have influenced the history of trade unions, and social democratic, socialist, and communist movements and parties in Canada. The final sections provide a description of the contemporary Canadian class structure.

1

Three-quarters of a century before the "New Left" emerged in Canada, workers in the mining and logging towns of British Columbia and the Atlantic Provinces phrased their grievances in terms of a class struggle. During the late 1890s and the 1900s, several socialist parties were formed in various provinces, those in British Columbia being the most radical. Here one group demanded "the public ownership of all industries controlled by monopolies, trusts, and combines and ultimately of all the means of production, distribution and exchange."[1] "The Revolutionary Socialist Party of Canada proclaims itself the political exponent of the working class interests. It will deviate neither to the right nor to the left of the line laid down in its platform."[2] It elected two members to the British Columbia Legislature, one of whom had been a Liberal member who declared on leaving the Liberal Party that it did not believe in "class legislation." The peak for the socialists came in the election of 1909 when their party superseded the Liberal Party as the official opposition in British Columbia. The party paper exulted:

Wiping out of the Liberal Party cleared the field for a struggle to the death between the two extremes of capitalist society; capital on the one hand, dominant, aggressive and brutal; on the other, labour awakening from the lethargy of ages and determined to conquer its freedom from class rule and class exploitation.[3]

The success was short-lived. By 1913, the party no longer had representation in parliament, several leading trade union members had been ousted from the party and others had quit, and the movement was split apart by dissension.

What was it that made the miners and loggers of the two coastal regions different from the Toronto tradesmen? Two conditions: isolation and the lack of a middle class. The effect of isolation has been studied in cross-cultural perspective by Clark Kerr and Abraham Siegel. They argue that: "The strike for the isolated mass is a kind of colonial revolt against far removed authority, an outlet for accumulated tensions, and a substitute for occupational and social mobility."[4] They found that workers in typically isolated conditions were very much more likely to engage in frequent and long strikes than workers in urban industries. The conditions of isolation are partly geographical, but they are, as well, social. The workers in strike-prone industries, according to Kerr and Siegel, form a homogeneous mass, undifferentiated in status, wealth, life-style; they share common grievances and are able to communicate these to one another. No other groups intervene, no buffer state exists between these workers and their employers. No likelihood or expectation of mobility compromises individuals and there is no easy exit route.

Nanaimo, on Vancouver Island, was a centre of radical activity at the turn of the century. It was also a two-class town: employers (some representing distant interests) and workers. The workers had all of the characteristics described by Kerr and Siegel. They were also the most vocal, the most violent, and the most likely to speak of their activities as a class struggle. It was these workers who supported the early socialist parties and the radical arm of the early trade union movement.

The conditions of isolation did not long remain for large numbers of these workers. Immigration was constant, new industries were developed, urban centres became established to which these workers could move or where they could spend a few weeks from time to time. Professionals, merchants, skilled tradesmen, and families obscured the class divisions, offset the isolation, and dissipated the class identity of the workers. The two-class nature of Nanaimo and other similar towns disappeared.

These coastal towns at the turn of the century were already dissimilar to the manufacturing areas of central Canada. There the transition from *quasi*-feudal society to liberal capitalism had already occurred. The appeals from British Columbia tradesmen to their

Toronto counterparts to join their brothers in revolt made no impact. The conditions of the isolated towns had no parallel in Ontario, where a stratified society had been in existence for a very long time and where urban conditions and high immigration and emigration rates provided for a heterogeneous mobile work-force.

During the three decades at the end of the 19th century, emigration from Canada was greater than immigration. During the early part of the new century, immigration had its ups and downs while emigration continued steadily. Most of the emigrants left for the United States, where there were more jobs and better salaries. The reasons for this situation go beyond our inquiry. They include the very slow development of manufacturing industries in Canada, a condition in turn developing out of the relatively small and widely dispersed population, the domination of capital markets by a "Family Compact," and the dependence of Canada on staples production for export trade. For present purposes, the immigration-emigration situation is important because it has a bearing on the lack of class consciousness amongst workers in the urban centres.

The new manufacturing industries of the 1870s suffered from a lack of skilled labour. British workers, in high demand, would emigrate to Canada rather than the United States only if the conditions of work were commensurate with those in the United States. The early trade union organizations intended strictly for skilled workers in high-demand trades, took advantage of the shortage and the need. The legislature of 1872 provided the first bill allowing trade union organization after a very explicit recognition that the workers were essential to the growth of manufacturing.[5]

The need for skilled workers in the manufacturing centres was matched by the need for unskilled workers in the outports, and for agricultural workers across the prairies. The unskilled workers were the mainstay of the labour force in the isolated towns; the skilled workers formed a hierarchy of occupational groups in the urban areas. However, the need for the skilled workers steadily increased and that for the unskilled decreased. Thus, in addition to the heterogeneous nature of the population in urban centres, and to the immediate need for particular skills, there was a general need for skilled workers which could absorb immigrants, migrants from rural areas, unskilled workers willing to learn a trade. The opportunities were considerable, and where they failed, emigration to the United States remained a possibility. Under such conditions of high mobility and labour demand, workers are unlikely to view themselves as oppressed even when they do view themselves as deprived. Deprivation can be cured by strikes for shorter hours and larger wages as long as employers are in need of workers.

The workers in British Columbia continued to promote radical unionism throughout the early 20th century, but their appeal was never widespread, and their successes were invariably short-lived.

2

The Winnipeg General Strike of 1919 is sometimes cited as a major class conflict. Kenneth McNaught, for example, has this to say of it:

... the Winnipeg strike was a most significant occurrence in Canadian history, if for no other reason than that it was the first and only time in Canadian history that a majority was split clearly into two opposing classes.[6]

Briefly, the history of the Winnipeg General Strike is this: employees in the building and metal trades in Winnipeg refused to negotiate with the Metal Trades Council, who took their case to the Winnipeg Trades and Labour Council. That body held a vote, and an overwhelming majority indicated their willingness to engage in a general strike. Some 30 000 workers, of whom 12 000 were not union members, walked off their jobs. These were supported by the Army and Navy Veterans' Associations, and sympathizers across Canada joined the strikers. In Vancouver, an equally long and massive strike was mounted.

The Winnipeg Council fired their civic employees and eventually fired as well all but 16 members of the Winnipeg police force who refused to sign an anti-strike agreement. A Winnipeg Citizens' Committee—composed of leading businessmen and professionals—organized a "special police force" and on the 27th day of the strike, clashes between this force and strikers turned into a riot.

Employers in the metal shops offered some conciliatory proposals, and railway workers called for an end to the strike a month after it began, but at the same time strike leaders were arrested by federal authorities. A supporting parade for the strikers was organized, prohibited by civil authorities and interrupted by Mounties and special police. At least one person was killed, some 30 were injured. The *Riot Act* was read. Main Street was patrolled by soldiers with rifles, Mounties, and trucks with machine guns. The union newspaper was banned. On the forty-second day of the strike, the Trades and Labour Council capitulated, and workers returned to their jobs.

Newspapers of the time claimed that the arrested leaders were to be deported without trial. They were, in fact, tried on charges of "conspiracy to bring into hatred and contempt the governments of

the Dominion of Canada and the province of Manitoba and to introduce a Soviet system of government." One was convicted and
imprisoned for six years, five were imprisoned for one year, and one
was freed.[7]

The violence and duration of this strike make it a critical event
in Canadian history, but more important, the workers who engaged
in it included clerks and postal employees, transportation, telephone, electrical, railroad and telegraph employees, bread and milk
delivery workers, restaurant and barber shop employees, firemen,
and finally even policemen. This far-ranging support is what sets
the Winnipeg strike apart from other industrial disputes.

Interpretations of the strike were as opposed as the employers/
government and the workers themselves. The first group, supported
by most Canadian newspapers, declared it to be part of a communist
conspiracy:

*There is no longer any doubt about it. Bolshevism has for certain planted
its tent at Winnipeg.*[8]   *(La Presse)*

*. . . Their avowed purpose is not shorter hours, or better working conditions,
or the recognition of trades unions, but the destruction of the present social
system and the introduction of the Marxian form of political and industrial
organization under which only manual workers would have any share in
the government of the country and the community and in the ownership
of the implements of industry.*[9]   *(The Globe and Mail)*

*. . . they oppose all bargaining, and are out to destroy the whole industrial,
financial and governmental institutions of Canada, including the present
system of labour unions . . .*[10]   *(Morning Leader)*

The strikers had a different interpretation. According to the strike
leader, F.J. Dixon, the strike occurred because:

*. . . the masters refused an eight-hour day and a large hour wage, but chiefly
because of the employers' refusal to recognize their union. . . . Here we
have the two vital causes of the strike: (1) a living wage, and (2) the right
to organize.*[11]

The strikers' interpretation was later supported by the Robson
Commission, appointed to investigate the causes of the strike.

The strike did not happen in a vacuum, and the context is important to our understanding of an event which seems to have no
parallel in Canadian history. Part of the context was economic:
inflation was making life difficult for all wage-earners. Part was
political: conscription was introduced in 1917, and the federal government had developed a pattern of intervention in industrial dis-

putes. Wartime profiteering created a great deal of hostility and brought into question many of the moral arguments that had induced the workers to engage in the war: "Is it patriotism to manufacture implements of war at scandalous profits? . . . Is it patriotism to speculate in the most vital part of the soldier's existence, that of foodstuffs?"[12] Beyond this, two patterns were evolving that greatly affected the trade union movement: (i) the membership was increasing rapidly throughout the closing years of the war and was growing in crafts and industries hitherto unorganized; and (ii) the split between Western radicals and the Trades and Labour Congress was coming to a head. The Congress had supported conscription against the Westerners and had refused to support the formation of "One Big Union": industrial unionism on a broad front as contrasted with many craft unions loosely joined in a federation. The One Big Union organizers kept alive the ideology of class struggle and did this with increasing hostility to the "conservative" craft unionists:

There is no hope for the worker in the arena of politics. The ruling class had coralled [sic] all the political machinery that there is for a democratic government. As they have treated the worker in the past they will treat him in the future. . . . Only by the One Big Union can labour ever realize its solidarity and bring pressure to bear upon the exploiting class that will result in justice and a square deal for the workers.[13]

The union convention expressed in resolutions its acceptance of the principle of "Proletarian Dictatorship" and its support for the revolution in Russia.

The One Big Union was not, in fact, responsible for the Winnipeg General Strike,[14] but it did give rise to fear among employers and to a heightened interest in industrial or at least industry-wide bargaining units among workers. The issue that sparked the strike was precisely this: the refusal of employers to recognize a federated body as the bargaining agent for a number of affiliated unions. Clearly, industry-wide or industrial bargaining appeared as far greater threats to employers and governments alike in 1919 than craft unions acting independently or with little formal alliance. The strike of a craft union, however inconvenient, could not cripple an economy or jeopardize a government; the general strike of all workers in an industry or all workers in several industries could do both as the Winnipeg Strike demonstrated.

Yet the strikers did not take over the Winnipeg city government, let alone the provincial or federal governments; at the height of the strike, the only services they were able to handle were emergency food distributions. The Canadian historian D.C. Masters has argued cogently that government intervention in the Winnipeg Strike was inevitable given the failure of the strikers to assume political control.[15]

Those who share McNaught's interpretation of the strike argue that the failure of the strikers to take control signalled the conclusion of the significant class action: that is, action that unambiguously had a class base and that its protagonists understood in those terms. The difficulty with this argument is that while the employers and newspapers labelled the strike as a class war, it is not at all clear that the workers saw it in those same terms. They claimed to be fighting for the right to organize and to strike and for better working conditions and wages. Such a struggle is not a proletarian revolution: it is rather a demand to be included, as workers, in the capitalist state. There is no evidence apart from the claims of the One Big Union organizers and the fears of the editorial writers and parliamentarians, that the Winnipeg workers intended at any time to overthrow capitalism, take control, or attempt to set up a workers' society. Their failure to take control when it might have been possible (although, of course, that is a slim possibility, given the range of opposition forces across the country) seems to have its origins in a lack of motivation to do so.

Again, an explanation for the acceptance of the political arrangements of capitalism seems to rest with an account of the developments in the labour force, in manufacturing, in wages, and in immigration patterns.

Throughout the first half of the century, including the period of the strike, roughly a quarter of the population in Canada at any one time consisted of immigrants.[16] The proportion of foreign-born was greater in cities than in rural areas. The largest groups of immigrants were British, and these were familiar with trade union activities. They expected the right to organize and to demand better wages, but at the same time, they came to Canada because there was more opportunity here than in their homeland. The opportunity was defined in terms of getting a decent job, being able to purchase a home, sending children to public schools. They were, in short, mobile and desirous of "getting ahead."

These immigrants entered a rapidly changing labour force. In 1901, most workers in Canada were in unskilled occupations or in agriculture. In 1911, the drop in proportions in these areas was marked. Skilled workers were joined by an ever increasing number of workers in white-collar occupations and in service jobs. White-collar workers—managers, professionals, clerks, salespeople—were in high demand at the time of the Winnipeg Strike. "Getting ahead" for many workers, immigrants and native-born, meant moving away from unskilled work and farms and becoming clerks, letter carriers, managers, salespeople. Thus the workers who went on strike were not those described by Marx. They were not losing their occupational status, or becoming ever more alike as unskilled labourers. They were, on the contrary, moving up, becoming more differentiated in skills, status, and authority.

The increase in the number of distinctive skills and statuses within the industrial, urban labour force continued throughout the 1920s up to the Depression. During these years, American capital began to support the development of manufacturing industries such as automobiles, utilities, synthetics, and electrical products. These industries required new skills, and the new skill groups did not have a history of unionization. Some of the old skill distinctions were breaking down, and as they did this, the attention of the workers was directed toward saving the remnants of their own trades rather than organizing others.[17] Contrary to the Marxist prophecy, the skill changes did not bring about a general downgrading of labour.

These facts appear to account for the failure of the socialist ideology to take root amongst Canadian workers. The liberal ideology, in fact, with its emphasis on achievement, getting ahead, and private ownership was entirely congruent with the ambitions of workers and with their opportunities. In explaining the decline of union activity during the 1920s, Stuart Jamieson touches on this:

> . . . the social climate and prevailing ideology of the times, with the idealization of "free enterprise" and competitive individualism, were favourable to employers and hostile to unions. Employers in many industries were able to take advantage of the situation to launch a widespread attack on unionism. A nation-wide campaign for the "open shop" was given the appealing title of the "American Plan." The adoption of company unions was only one of a panoply of anti-union tactics of the more belligerent kind, while a variety of policies classed under the term "welfare capitalism" had primarily the same objectives and similar effects.[18]

Liberal party handouts and official platforms of both parties in the 1920s emphasized the welfare policies designed to "guard the home and protect the good name of Canada."[19] Some legislation was enacted to extend wage reforms to government employees and limit the control of monopolies (e.g., *Combines Investigation Act*). Such Acts were said to "provide protection for the great mass of the consumers against illegal business consolidations."[20]

The government also reiterated a phrase that has since become a central core of the prevailing rhetoric: "Liberalism and the Liberal Party are founded on the principle of consideration for the rights and welfare of ALL people, not the interests of a privileged and powerful few."[21]

In a two-class system, the powerful few are easy to find. In a multi-class system, the spread of privileges obscures the existence of an elite. Even where its existence is recognized, the range of interest groups from top to bottom provides for a range of very different needs, and the elite becomes (from the point of view of those further down) just the most powerful in the hierarchy. The ideology of classlessness and government for the people may smother the cries of those under the heap, but for those in the intermediate and mobile class, it apparently makes more sense than the ideology of class conflict.

3

Up to 1930, there was always employment of some kind. And there was emigration to the United States for those whose skills could bring higher prices there. The Depression brought unemployment to both countries.

Unemployed workers had never been organized. As the Depression set in, there were violent strikes and encounters in several industries but the demands of the workers were only for those conditions from which they themselves could benefit: wages, hours, and union contracts. At the height of the Depression some 20% of the labour force had no work, and in spite of the much talked-about welfare measures, welfare consisted of little more than Salvation Army soup line-ups. No level of government was prepared to cope with the vast numbers of families and homeless unemployed men. When the Communist Party attempted to organize the unemployed, the Conservative government of the day arrested eight Communist Party officials and imprisoned them under Section 98 of the *Criminal Code* with the explanation that the unemployed workers were suffering from low morale and were "very susceptible to the contagion of Communist ideas and to the influence of subversive organizations."[22] The next year they established a system of work relief camps under military administration. The men were paid $1 per day of which they received 20¢, the remainder going for their food and housing in isolated camps.

In the spring of 1935, an estimated 4000 men from the camps in British Columbia gathered in Vancouver to press for higher wages and abolition of military control. Although they had no success in pressing for these reforms, they kept the Vancouver police force busy for several weeks during demonstrations which culminated in the reading of the *Riot Act* and the provision of meal tickets to strikers for six days. But it required federal government action to change the conditions in the camps, and with numbers dwindling and no response from Ottawa politicians, an army of 1000 planned a "trek to Ottawa." Their numbers doubled between Vancouver and Regina where federal officials met them.

The officials met them head on with enforcement from the RCMP and city police. The Regina riot was bloody and ended in serious injuries of rioters, policemen, and civilians. Reports vary as to whether there was one death or several. Seventy-six strikers were arrested, and those who were still able retired to the Exhibition Grounds in Regina under RCMP guard. Some of these were returned to Vancouver by the Saskatchewan government. The riot had brought no better wages, camp conditions, or civilian control. But as it happened, the economy began to regain its health and the number of unemployed declined.

While the unemployed suffered the conditions of the military work camps in British Columbia, the prairies gave birth to a new political movement. In its early years, the Co-operative Commonwealth Federation provided the most consistent counter-ideology and by far the most articulate analysis of Canadian capitalism that any movement in Canada has produced. The CCF did not gain the support of a majority of the population even at its most successful period, but it was the strongest anti-capitalist group to emerge in Canada prior to the 1980s. It is instructive to examine in some detail the ideological development of the party. This begins with a cry of despair at the conditions of the Depression. It softens to a whimper with the onset of the war and becomes a relatively polite request for reform before the war is over. Its development coincides with the improvement in economic conditions due to the growth in war industries and the re-employment of the population.

Its members and leaders were intellectuals, social workers, lawyers, and clerics. Its leading spokesman was a Methodist minister, and his interpretation of Christianity informed and suffused the early programs. As a party, it steadfastly argued for parliamentary democracy and for a reform within the democratic system, an argument that alienated the more radical socialists. Its strategists called themselves The League for Social Reconstruction, and they collectively wrote a long and scholarly analysis of the Canadian economy entitled *Social Planning for Canada*.[23] Such a membership under such a title did not appear as the likely successor to the demagogues of the One Big Union and earlier labour movements, but they spoke in no less compromising tones:

... every CCF member should insist and understand that in no sense is the socialism of the CCF mere reformism, mere gradualism, or compromise

with capitalism of any kind. A CCF government attaining power must proceed promptly, drastically, thoroughly to liquidate the power of capitalist forces and secure for the socialist party in control of the organs of the state the most ample assurance that capitalist interests could not sabotage, weaken or overthrow socialism . . .[24]

In the opening chapter of *Social Planning for Canada*, the authors observed that:

Peculiar to Canada as a new country is the slowness on the part of the majority of her citizens intelligently to diagnose the situation. The middle class optimism even of the disinherited groups, the lack of militancy in the trade union movement, the calm acceptance of the success psychology of individualism by the mass of the people, reveal the absence of a realistic analysis of our social structure. Less naive have been the attitudes and tactics of the privileged group. Behind a carefully controlled and manipulated press, our economic overloads have refurbished the fading illusions of individual independence and democratic freedom while they consolidated the control which completed the negation of these ideals.[25]

The rest of the long book is a scholarly and probing analysis of the Canadian economy, its operation, its control, and its political system.

The founding convention of the CCF in 1933 produced the *Regina Manifesto*. This clearly recognized the existence of a class society and dedicated the movement to its eradication. Twenty-three years later, at the Winnipeg Convention, a second declaration of principles spoke of the domination of an elite, but found that there was much room in the economy for private enterprise. Between the two declarations, the party had moved from a revolutionary to a left-liberal version of how society is structured, and its objectives had shifted from the replacement of capitalism to the reform of capitalism. Following are sections of the two manifestos:

REGINA MANIFESTO: July, 1933

Power has become more and more concentrated into the hands of a small irresponsible minority of financiers and industrialists and to their predatory interests the majority are habitually sacrificed. When private profit is the main stimulus to economic effort, our society oscillates between periods of feverish prosperity in which the main benefits go to speculators and profiteers, and of catastrophic depression, in which the common man's normal state of insecurity and hardship is accentuated. We believe that these evils can be removed only in a planned and socialized economy in which our natural resources and the principal means of production and distribution are owned, controlled and operated by the people.[26]

WINNIPEG DECLARATION OF PRINCIPLES (1956)

. . . The CCF has always recognized public ownership as the most effective means of breaking the stranglehold of private monopolies on the life of the nation and of facilitating the social planning necessary for economic security and advance. The CCF will, therefore, extend public ownership wherever it is necessary for the achievement of these objectives.

At the same time, the CCF also recognizes that in many fields there will be need for private enterprise which can make a useful contribution to the development of our economy. The co-operative commonwealth will, therefore, provide appropriate opportunities for private business as well as publicly owned industry.[27]

While trade unions elsewhere had given birth to socialist labour alliances, the Canadian unionists, like their American brothers, did not support the CCF. The unions were affiliated with the American Federation of Labor (AFL) and tended to share its view that they should not take direct political action but should instead support whichever candidates were "friends to labour."

The Trades and Labour Congress kept busy throughout the 1930s with its internecine fights over the status within the AFL of the Canadian Committee for Industrial Organization (CIO). The initial constitution of the CCF did not provide for the affiliation of unions, but a 1938 revision did not succeed in bringing in any enthusiastic response from organized labour. Nor was the lack of enthusiasm undirectional. The unionists were widely regarded as "right-wing" conservatives, and the 1938 motion was bitterly contested by the teachers, church and social workers who led the movement.

The movement was generally intolerant of "mere reformers" in these early days. Its public statements bristled with condemnations of compromise with the capitalists. But if it was intolerant, so too was the general public, who, like many trade unionists, condemned its proselytizers as Bolsheviks and crackpots.[28]

The first and possibly the most remarkable reversal in the stance of the socialist movement was the adoption of support measures for Canada's participation in the second war. From an unambiguous condemnation—"We stand resolutely against all participation in imperialist wars. Canada must refuse to be entangled in any more wars fought to make the world safe for capitalism"[29]—the National Council came to support Canada's entry when the vote was put forward to the 1939 parliament. "Our opposition to the war was not on the ground that we are Socialists, but that we are Canadian Socialists. . . . To brand the war as purely imperialist would imply that all the Socialists of Great Britain, France and Poland were completely wrong. . . ."[30] These were among the ambiguous explanations as the party shifted policy.

Of this shift, Leo Zakuta in his analysis of CCF policies, argued that:

. . . the abandonment of pacifism was unquestionably a major turning point for the CCF. In so doing, it removed the largest barrier to its association with the world and for the first time, aligned itself with the over-whelming majority of Canadians against a common enemy.[31]

Zakuta examines the national party statements to show a move from "conscription of wealth rather than manpower" to "no conscription of manpower without the conscription of wealth as well as manpower." He suggests that as the war progressed, providing as it did an external enemy as well as an upswing in the economy, the appeal of class conflict diminished.[32]

The second major shift in ideology for the CCF marked the upswing of its political fortunes and the transformation of a revolutionary movement into a reform party. In 1944, with the support now of trade unions and a large share of the electorate, and against a background that included the Liberal and Conservative parties championing welfare measures and a planned economy, the National Convention announced:

The socialization of large-scale enterprise . . . does not mean taking over every private business. Where private business shows no signs of becoming a monopoly, operates efficiently under decent working conditions, and does not operate to the detriment of the Canadian people, it will be given every opportunity to function, to earn a fair rate of return and make its contribution to the nation's wealth.[33]

With the end of the war, the party's fortunes declined. The Liberal Party, having reached its low point in popularity in the early stages of the war, hastened to adopt the reforms pressed on it from a popular Left including an unemployment insurance program. Unlike earlier political parties of the Left, the CCF, and later the New Democratic Party (an alliance of the CCF with the Trade Unions of 1961), became a permanent and significant political organization in Canada. But it did this as a reform party, not as a revolutionary movement.

4

Following the Winnipeg General Strike in 1919, and in spite of the finding of the Royal Commission that it was not organized by foreign agitators nor for the purpose of overthrowing the government, the federal government added a clause to the *Immigration Act* which allowed for the deportation of foreign-born citizens. It also added Section 98 to the *Criminal Code*, defining an "unlawful association" as:

... *any association, organization, society or corporation whose professed purpose or one of whose purposes is to bring about any governmental, industrial or economic change within Canada by use of force, violence or physical injury to person or property, or by threats of such injury, or which teaches, advocates, advises or defends by the use of force, violence, terrorism or physical injury to person or property, or threats of such injury, or for any other purpose, or which shall by any means prosecute or pursue such purpose or professed purpose, or shall so teach, advocate, advise or defend, shall be an unlawful association.*[34]

The threat of deportation and this definition of illegal organization were added to prohibitions already existing under wartime measures which had not been lifted by 1920 against organizations which opposed the existing social order. Numerous socialist organizations which had emerged throughout the first two decades of the century had been banned or lost membership under these conditions, and the establishment of the Communist Party of Canada in 1921 occurred as an illegal act.

Although several of the leaders of the party in the 1920s were of Anglo-Saxon origin, membership consisted mainly of Finnish and Eastern European immigrants, resident mainly in northern Ontario, Montreal, Toronto, and Winnipeg. Throughout that first decade, attempts were made to organize workers in the trade unions, and some gains were made for the party amongst miners in Nova Scotia and British Columbia, amongst workers in the needle trades and amongst forestry workers. According to Ivan Avakumovic, historian of the party's development:

The ethnic composition of the CPC affected the communist movement in several ways. First and foremost, it strengthened the impression of those Anglo-Saxons who came into contact with Communists that the CPC was an alien growth on Canadian soil, a foreign outpost of a great power, an organization with little or nothing to offer in a North American setting. This belief was and is still widely held, in spite of repeated attempts to identify the CPC with Canadian interests, traditions, and aspirations. To a native Canadian a Communist was someone who spoke English with an accent, used jargon incomprehensible to most Canadians, read newspapers in what seemed to be exotic languages, and who lived in parts of the town that go-ahead Canadians were only too eager to leave.[35]

As the Depression deepened in the early 1930s the party attempted to organize the unemployed. In this they were hampered by Canadian laws against "unlawful assembly," infiltration by RCMP officers, and surveillance. In 1931, the secretary-general of the party, Tim Buck, together with several other leading communists, was imprisoned. Foreign-born communists were deported or threatened with deportation. In spite of this, and perhaps aided by the publicity of Buck's trial, membership in the party increased to about 5000 throughout the Depression. Real support was always greater than membership in the party, because much of the party's activities had to be carried on through "front" organizations under other names, and some of the party's objectives—such as repeal of Section 98 of the *Criminal Code*, relief for the unemployed, unemployment insurance and welfare measures—were shared by other groups. Among these other groups by the mid-1930s was the CCF, but in the early history of the CCF the Communist Party denounced it as "a twin of fascism" and a "traitor to the working class." It was one of the persistent characteristics of the party that it was unable to avoid factionalism on the left and that it regarded the socialist party as a threat rather than as an ally.[36]

The major ideological slogan of the Communist Party was (and is) "Dictatorship of the Proletariat." This implies the overthrow of the bourgeoisie, the end of capitalism, and revolution if necessary. However, the party itself never took action that would have led in this direction, and the chief reason, apart from its small membership and organizational difficulties, was that its policy was to follow the directives of the Communist International, led by the Russian party. The stance of the Comintern was, following Lenin and Stalin, to "subordinate theory to tactics" by which was meant that all national parties would take whatever action was deemed most advantageous for the moment by the central organization relative to very long-term objectives of world revolution. In Canada this policy led the party to take positions that, from one year to the next, were contradictory. In the early 1930s, the party denounced the craft unions and American international trade union organization. It established its own trade union central organization and was moderately successful until, abruptly in 1935, it disbanded this organization and embraced the American trade union organization in the interests of a "common front against fascism." In 1929, it called J.S. Woodsworth, later leader of the CCF, "one of the most dangerous elements in the working class,"[37] and in 1934 called the CCF program "liberal-laborism and the bourgeois revision of Marxism."[38] Yet in 1936, the party was attempting to form a united front with the CCF, and unilaterally announced that they shared a common interest in fighting Fascism.

Even more curious than the changing policies vis-à-vis the Socialist Party, was the Communist Party's attitude toward the Liberal Party. From 1936 to 1938, and again, from 1943 to 1945, the Communist Party advocated a policy of "liberal-labourism" (the same term used to denounce the CCF earlier). In 1944, the party publicly supported Mackenzie King with the statement: "The Liberals have worked to maintain the unity of Canada. They represent those of the Capitalists who understand that they can and must co-operate with Labor and farmers for Victory and great post-war advances."[39] By this time the Communist Party was again rejecting the CCF.

In 1940, the Communist Party along with the Fascist Party was banned under the federal government's proclamation of an Order in Council under the *War Measures Act*. As well, several communist newspapers were closed, property belonging to communist organizations was confiscated, and communist activists were arrested. One hundred and ten communists were interned, together with Fascists and citizens, including especially Quebecois, who opposed Canada's involvement in the war.[40] This ban remained in force until Germany invaded the USSR, Russia became an ally of the West, and it became embarrassing to the Liberal government to have a banned Communist Party in Canada. The party re-emerged under a new name, the Labour Progressive Party in 1943.[41]

At its height the party never had more than 8000 members. Throughout most of its history before the end of the Second War, it was either an illegal organization or subject to the repressive measures of the *Criminal Code*. Its leaders were frequently under arrest, in jail, or in hiding. Its membership fluctuated according to the degree of repression being exerted by federal and provincial authorities. Since a large part of its membership consisted of immigrants, and these were always subject to deportation orders, many supporters were passive or silent when the party attempted to organize workers and the unemployed. Because its strongest supporters in the 1920s were Eastern Europeans and Finns, in a country that was dominated by Anglo-Saxons, and, in Quebec, populated largely by Francophones, the party was culturally alien to the majority of the population. These many conditions prevented the party from becoming a major political force in Canada, and its adherence to the Comintern directives added a further dissuasive influence.

What is most significant about this party is not so much the party itself as the fear of it generated by federal and provincial governments. The amount of attention devoted to its activities by the RCMP, the number of times the party was blamed for labour strife or protests by the unemployed, and the paranoia expressed by authorities about the party's capacity to take over Canada can hardly be explained in terms of any real power possessed by the party. This paranoia, extreme enough in the 1920s, 1930s, and 1940s, reached its zenith in the 1950s, with the cultivation of "the cold war."

The chief reasons for the weakness of socialist ideology in Canada lie outside the socialist movements themselves. They are, particularly, the persistent attacks by established powers against any form of socialist thought, and the general prosperity enjoyed by the middle working class throughout the post-war period. The first of these created obstacles to both knowledge and thought, and social punishments for those who critically assessed the nature of capitalism. The second provided positive rewards for those who accepted and worked within the system. Between the two, there was no economic or political reason for members of the working and middle class to consider alternative perspectives. Understood in terms of Marxist theory, the failure of socialism was a manifestation of the success of the liberal ideology. The "free world" may have been a nonsensical description, but it was a successful abstraction of what the ruling class believed itself to stand for.

Not all of the weaknesses were due to these external causes. Neither socialism as an ideology nor Marxism as an intellectual analysis provides a means of explaining some of the significant inequalities, injustices, and problems that are due to causes other than class. The analysis of imperialism does not explain the relationship between the working class of the imperialist nation and that of the subject nation; on the contrary, as ideology it denies the legitimacy of nationalism and insists on the similarity of situation for all workers regardless of national residence. The difficulty of expressing a national protest within the framework of a Marxist analysis is evident in the Waffle Manifesto and in much else that is written in both Quebec and Anglophone Canada.

Essentially the same problem arises with sex and ethnicity: neither is well analysed if the central terms of reference are restricted to class differences. Women qua women do not comprise a class; neither do Francophones or immigrants from any particular region. Yet for all of these dimensions there are real situations: people live in particular territories, and even if those territories are artificially defined by political history, they are essential components of the identity of their residents. People are born either men or women, and that basic fact of life determines a very great deal of what subsequently happens to them. All women do have some characteristics in common, even when they are divided by class, just as all Francophones in Canada have some things in common despite their class divisions.

There is another problem in socialist ideology which dissuades many Canadians from pursuing socialist objectives: self-righteousness. One notes this in much of the Communist Party reactions to social democratic movements. The Communist Party was convinced that it held a monopoly on truth; it alone fully understood the enemy and only it could be the vanguard to the proletarian revolution. That self-righteousness pops up again in post-war history especially in left-wing sectarian literatures. An illuminating experience is to read fundamentalist Christian magazines alternately with sectarian socialist magazines, transposing certain words from one to the other. If "Satan" becomes "capitalists" and "archangels" become "agents of the ruling class," if "satanic forces" become "capitalist accumulation processes" or "capitalist relations of production," then it is remarkable how similar the literatures become. Both are absolutely sure they tell the truth, and that virtually every other institution in the society is telling lies. Both know precisely what the world should be like, and both know absolutely that a revolution must occur before nirvana can be achieved.

Canadians shy away from such self-righteousness, and there is little doubt that social democratic parties in Canada have been harmed by the slogans, and sometimes the actions, of sectarian left movements outside the democratic spectrum. They have also been harmed by the totalitarianism of the self-proclaimed "communist" states of Eastern Europe.

The Soviet societies did not go through the historical sequences of capitalism before establishing what they declared to be communist states. One might, with generosity, argue that it is for this reason that their communism has turned out to involve such an extensive use of force against both internal dissidents and satellite neighbours. Because it was not well developed industrially, Russia used the age-old methods of political and military intervention, policy coercion and the expulsion of minorities where American capitalism could rely on economic intervention and economic incentives to achieve the same ends. There is little doubt that the claim to personal freedom in North America and Western Europe has a basis in fact, and has a comparative truth to it when one views the relative lack of personal freedom in the Eastern European countries. However, there is no way of knowing whether, had Russia conformed to Marx's prophecies and gone through the anticipated sequence before developing a communist ideology, or any of the means and modes of production that might attend a communist society as envisaged by Marx, it would have created an entirely new social organization.

With less generosity, one might argue that by its nature communism must sacrifice personal liberties to collective interests, and that a population must be forced to act in the interests of the social whole. If one takes that interpretation, then communism is inherently totalitarian, and Russia is a genuine example rather than an historical aberration.

Yet a third view is possible. It is that industrial production, whether directed by state managers or corporate directors, establishes its own demands and limitations on the relations of production. Mechanization involves workers in a series of repetitive tasks whether or not their surplus product is appropriated by private capital. A chain of authority is created, and a hierarchy of power and privilege evolves in similar measure to that of the capitalist societies. Marx believed, but never demonstrated, that his version of communism would bring both industrial development and equality to human society. His communist society was a capitalist one, somehow transformed at the level of relations of production and ideology, yet still productive of industrial goods. How this could be achieved is still a mystery. In the capitalist society the inequality, authority hierarchy, and regulation of labour are explained in terms of liberal ideology, as the results of differential human capital based on equality of condition. In the communist society there is no easy ideological explanation for essentially the same problems, and force may be more readily applied in its absence.

If it is industrialism rather than capitalism which gives rise to or at least sustains a class structure, then the prolonged ideological battle between communism and capitalism may be seen as a war of words, and sometimes of arms, between the captains of industry and political leaders of two systems similar except in one respect: that in one, the leaders own the capital they invest, and in the other, they control public capital.

In both the real problem, yet to be addressed, is how the process of accumulation and technological change could be redirected toward peaceful ends, toward goals more beneficial to the whole populations in both countries and in the impoverished countries that make up the larger part of the world economy. The capitalist countries have yet to find ways of curbing private greed; the communist, of curbing private power exerted in the name of the collectivity.

5

Whether or not one adopts a Marxist approach to the Canadian economy, there are divisions within the society attached to positions

within the economic organizations. Following sociological convention, these would be recognized as classes and sub-class divisions.
Where the divisions within a class are hierarchically organized so
that one group has power over the next, they are known as strata.
Where they are different but roughly equal in power, they are known
as class fractions. Where they are different and unequal in some
significant way but one has no direct power over the other, they are
known as class segments. Canadian sociologists have used these
terms to describe the class which owns the means of production and
major financial institutions (dominant class or elite class fractions);
a working class stratified by authority and income differentials; and
segments where men and women experience entirely different
opportunities and rewards within the labour force.

The Canadian class structure is complex because, to begin with,
so much of Canadian industry is owned outside the country. This
means that the ultimate owners are not resident in Canada, and thus
much of the "ruling class" is not inside the territory. A class of
owners does reside in Canada (at least formally), their assets located
primarily in the financial, utilities, and resources sectors.

It is a matter of relative unimportance whether the members of
this class personally own large blocks of shares in industrial or financial companies. That phase of capitalism in which industrial
companies were wholly or largely owned by single private families
is passing though not yet past: some of the largest world industrial
companies are still held by private families and clearly controlled
by them. However, a large number of these companies are formally
owned by a combination of private families, groups of private investors, and finance companies which themselves are owned by families
and groups of private investors. All such companies are controlled
by combinations of their formal owners or their representatives, the
top executives of the management staff (who may or may not own
shares in the organization), and representatives from other corporations. In subsidiary firms, the board normally includes primarily
the representatives of the parent firm plus the top executives of the
subsidiary. The term "capitalist class" refers to this range of individuals, regardless of their ownership shares in the organizations
they direct, for the reason that this class has control of the surplus
value generated in the corporations and invests this surplus according to its interests.

The corporation labour force is not sharply divided between the
owners and the workers because at the top there is a large sub-class
of employed workers who, though they earn a wage in the form of
a salary and they can be dismissed by the executives or directors,
enjoy a limited authority within the organization. This authority is

delegated by the board of directors, and may include considerable decision-making powers to manage the affairs of the corporation. The qualifications for holding this authority may involve personal family relationships, in which case the incumbents in office are unambiguously still part of the capitalist class, but they may also involve technical expertise which is not restricted to the children of that class. This sub-class consists normally of professional administrators, accountants, engineers, lawyers, and other technically trained persons who provide the effective daily professional and management services to the organization. Since they do this as delegated representatives of the directors and could function only if they managed the business affairs such that the accumulation of capital and reinvestment continued to increase the size and scope of activities of the organization, they occupy a class position ancillary to that of the capitalist class.

The ladder of managerial success is from middle management to top management of relatively small organizations, to middle and to top management of the giants. Executives are paid enormous salaries and obtain dividends from shares, but their private wealth does not confer on them their status and power. These are functions of their position both within an organization and within the inter-corporate hierarchy. The larger their corporation, the higher their status and the greater their power. The larger their corporation, the more likely they are to be recruited to other, still larger corporations and higher status positions. Thus the managerial-professional strata within the corporate economy shares the interests of the directors and owners.

Since the head offices of large corporations are geographically centred in their home country, the larger part of both the owning-directing class and the managerial-professional sub-class reside there; those who reside outside that country, as, for example, the subsidiary managers, tend to be citizens of the original country. The indigenous capitalist class connected to industrial corporations in dependent countries is therefore relatively small.

In Canada there is a second fraction of the capitalist class consisting of those who control financial establishments.[42] While Canadian banks and investment companies such as Canadian Pacific, Argus, and Power Corporation, are closely connected to the major Canadian industrial companies (most of which are in the resource sectors, including, for example, Noranda, MacMillan Bloedel, and Inco), they are not major direct investors or owners in American industrial companies. Their role vis-à-vis the American companies is to provide portfolio investment funds. They provide extremely large quantities of these funds to American companies, which are used for, among other things, expansion of facilities in Canada, but they do not, in return, obtain controlling shares similar to the share they have in Canadian companies.

At the turn of the century and for some period thereafter, the financial class in Canada was the dominant class, though there was an industrial fraction to the capitalist class, and its power is a matter of debate amongst political economists today. As American corporations came to dominate industrial production in Canada, their directors became the major fraction of the ruling class even when they did not actually reside within the country. At the managerial level, one section of the sub-class represents foreign capital; another, indigenous capital.

A further division of the capitalist class in Canada involves a regional dimension. Up to 1930, the three prairie provinces did not have control of their own land as was true of the other provinces; the federal government had legal jurisdiction over all resources. The federal governments of that period took it as their task to develop the West in such a fashion as to increase the wealth of the financial and industrial concerns in Ontario and Quebec.[43] As a consequence, no industrial capacity was developed on the prairies, and the wheat trade was carried on by merchants and milling companies located in central Canada. The prairie population was entirely dependent on central Canadian merchants, banks, and the CPR, for their imported consumer goods and agricultural implements. The legacy of this situation was intense resentment against central Canada. Toward the end of the 1940s, with the oil discoveries and development of the oil industry, Alberta began to develop its own oil companies and service sector. The larger oil companies were American, and over the next two decades American interests became more dominant as Alberta companies, unable to obtain sufficient funding from central Canadian financial institutions, sold out their holdings to the multinationals. The service sector and some substantial Alberta companies remained, however, and these became the nexus for the development of a regional bourgeoisie directly related to and dependent on American capital.[44] In addition, there grew out of the American companies a regional managerial class, also dependent on foreign capital for their wealth and positions.

In addition to these fractions of the capitalist class and the subclass of managers-professionals tied to corporations, there is a class at both the federal and provincial government levels which is engaged in the management and direction of crown corporations or *quasi*-crown corporations. In several of the provinces, and particularly in Alberta, Quebec, and Saskatchewan, the "technocratic" class, as it has been called, represents both the provincial state as an entrepreneurial organization and private capital. The private capital is frequently represented as a partner in government-private sector consortiums, but is also often the "silent partner" insofar as the state corporations exist largely to facilitate the industrial expansion of the private sector.

Overriding all of these divisions within Canadian capitalism is another between those corporations, privately or state-owned, which mainly serve a domestic market and are concentrated entirely or primarily in Canada or even in a particular part of Canada, and those which are essentially international. For the latter, the Canadian market, Canadian labour force, and Canadian resources are only part of a total world empire, and whether these are owned in Canada or are foreign-owned their growth depends not on Canada alone but on the balance they achieve by maximizing the gains from investments in many countries. Thus they may choose to move production facilities out of Canada into a Third World country where they can obtain a cheaper labour force or better taxation advantages. By contrast, a company dependent on the Canadian market is primarily concerned with taxes, capital costs, labour costs, and production incentives within Canada. The capitalist class attached to these two kinds of corporations has somewhat different interests to protect when dealing with the Canadian government. In general, the largest companies in Canada are foreign-owned and it is these which most frequently have world-wide interests.

At various points in Canadian history and with respect to particular issues, these various fractions of the capitalist class may have divergent interests. For example, during the 1970s the regional bourgeoisie in Alberta was in conflict with the Ontario bourgeoisie over energy prices. In each case the provincial elite represented as well the interests of American capital, oil companies in Alberta, and manufacturing and mining corporations in Ontario. The federal government attempted to advance an energy policy, but could not simultaneously satisfy both groups.

This example will indicate how the fraction of the capitalist class can have divergent interests; it should not be thought, however, that their differences exceed their common interest. In the long run, all fractions of this class have an interest in the maintenance of the capitalist system.

6

The corporate class system includes many strata of workers. They have in common their situation relative to the means of production that is, all sell their labour power in return for wages. Beyond that, however, their differences are considerable.

At the top of the working class in terms of status and income, and often as well in terms of authority within the corporate structures, are technical advisors and professional managers who are distinguished from the corporate elite more in terms of degree than of kind. They do not have policy-making functions, are not the directing executives of the organizations, but their functions, none the less, include a wide range of discretionary powers.

It can happen that professionals have interests beyond those of the executives and directors because their expertise and professional identity may be more vital to them than their corporate office. It is not unknown for such persons to subvert corporate goals in their pursuit of technical excellence or respect for professional ethics. The overall objectives of the organization as seen by the directors may require less perfect technical inventions or organization than an expert is capable of providing, technical inventions that are profitable rather than socially useful, or inventions that are known to the expert to be socially harmful. Sometimes this conflict leads very simply to dismissal or resignation; socially conscious professionals are frequently ill-suited to corporate bureaucracies. Perhaps a simple analogy will make the point. The objective of a restaurant manager is to make profits. The objective of the cook, the expert, is to make excellent meals, perhaps because he wishes to enhance his reputation as a master chef or because his self-respect is tied to his carefully nurtured skill. The making of excellent meals and the making of profits may quite easily conflict. Meanwhile, the customer becomes impatient waiting for service because the waiter has defined his immediate task as the clean-up of the dining-room.

Professional experts are, like managers, dependent on the continued growth of the corporation, and this growth is reflected in increments to their income as the corporation grows. It may be expected that they will adopt the ideological perspectives of private enterprise, since otherwise they would be in persistent conflict with higher management, suffer internal anguish, and lose their own motivating force. In the first edition of this book this author accepted the argument (and no longer does) that these technicians might be expected to be relatively indifferent to the nature of ownership of their organization. That argument was based on the (correct) observation that they already work within a highly planned economy. Whether that planning is done in the name of public governments or private governments is not crucial to their performance provided it does not affect their job security. What is missing in that perspective is an appreciation of the impact of the corporate ideology on its professional workers. They are surrounded by shibboleths about free enterprise, the evils of big government, the inventiveness of the corporate organization. They are part of "a management team" at the forefront of technological development, and leaders of humanity toward ever higher goals. Very few would choose to imagine a less comfortable world for themselves.

There are three major groups of workers who rank lower on corporate scales in income, status, and decision-making authority or personal discretionary powers. One of these consists of administrative, sales, supervisory, clerical, and technical workers, none of whom actually produce industrial products. These workers are employed in the offices of industrial corporations and in the corporations that deal exclusively in the circulation of money or in the merchandising of goods. Traditionally, these workers have enjoyed higher incomes and status than production workers, and at an earlier stage of capitalism it was they who comprised the middle class. Over the postwar decades, their numbers have increased greatly, to such an extent that they make up the largest single portion of the labour force, giving the appearance of a greatly expanded middle class. Their actual incomes and status have declined relative to unionized workers in some of the production sectors. As well, computerized technology has begun to displace some of the job security of many "white-collar" workers. None the less, the traditional distinction between "white-collar" and "blue-collar" workers, plus steady employment and salaries, continues to provide these workers with a sense of belonging to corporate organizations and a reason for supporting corporate enterprise.

The second group consists of production workers in industrial enterprises. These workers are divided into skill groups, with gradations of income between the groups, and by industrial sector. Workers in the manufacturing sector, which, in Canada, is primarily located in Ontario, have been for most of this century organized in craft unions. A craft union bargains on behalf of workers with the same general skills, e.g., carpenters, or electrical workers. Some of the largest unions since the 1930s, however, have been industrial, that is, bargaining units on behalf of all the workers in an industry regardless of skill. These include the steelworkers and the automobile workers. All of these unions are international, that is, affiliated with American parent unions. The "international" union bargains with the "multinational" company to protect workers employed in subsidiary plants.

Although there is an official relationship between the international union movement and the social democratic NDP party in Canada, many union workers do not vote for the NDP and the international unions have always maintained the position of "business unionism." By this is meant restriction of bargaining to the immediate material conditions of workers such as wages, fringe benefits, retirement plans, holidays, and hours of work. Considerations of class, class consciousness, or the relationship between the employed unionized workers and the rest of the labour force or the unemployed are not components of business unionism.

Workers in the resource industries have generally been more militant than those in the manufacturing sectors. Since the resource industries are located particularly in the West, in parts of Nova Scotia, northern Quebec and northern Ontario, these regions have supported higher levels of militant unionism than the central-southern region. This may be due to a higher level of class consciousness, though that is simply a hypothesis and has not been demonstrated to be true. It is the case that workers in resource industries experience higher levels of isolation from the middle class, greater cohesion because of constant interaction within their own restricted class, and a higher exposure to the gulf between managers and workers. Many of these workers live in resource towns which still have a very small "middle" population. Their unions are also predominantly international, just as their employers are predominantly multinationals.

Both the manufacturing and the resource sector workers who are unionized have been fairly successful over the past half century in advancing their relative incomes and improving their working conditions. In the resource sectors, however, they continue to be subject to extreme fluctuations in employment levels because of market fluctuations. For example, when there is a slow-down in housing construction in the United States, due to increases in interest rates or an energy crisis, the forestry industries in Ontario, Quebec, and British Columbia are severely hit. In British Columbia, up to 30% of the forestry labour force can be put out of work for many months by such adverse market conditions, a fact which emphasizes the vulnerability of an economy dependent on the export of raw or semi-processed materials.[45]

The bottom level of the corporate structure consists of service workers who maintain, clean, and do the menial tasks of the organization. These workers are also organized into unions, though their wages and working conditions are considerably less beneficial than those of production and administrative workers. Both production and service workers are normally paid by the hour and can be dismissed or laid off on short notice and without severance pay. Provided they have worked for a stipulated period of time (eight weeks in most cases, but the provision may change from year to year), they are eligible for unemployment insurance. Unemployment insurance for production workers is a means for the worker to support his or her family while the industry is "shut down," but more significantly, and often overlooked, it is a means for the industry to keep a reserve labour force resident and ready for work without actually paying wages.

All of these workers belong to corporate organizations. As long as the organizations maintain their growth rate, they have relative job security. Technological advances pose a threat to some jobs, but typically such advances affect new recruitment rather than incumbent employees, that is, old jobs are phased out so that new entrants to the labour force are not employed, but employees on staff at the time are provided with other tasks until their retirement. Thus workers once in the corporate sector have a material interest in sustaining their employer. Failing the actual breakdown of the system, they are not likely to rebel against it.

7

Corporate organizations are not the major employers within the capitalist system. They extract by far the larger part of the surplus value, control industrial output and markets, and have the greatest economic power, but they are capital-intensive organizations which actually employ not more than a quarter of the labour force.

The major employers are the state, service organizations, and small businesses. The state employs thousands of workers to staff its educational institutions, health and welfare agencies, juridical systems, government departments, crown corporations, and public works undertakings. The majority of these workers are engaged in tasks that do not produce industrial goods and thus do not generate new wealth, but which service the private businesses and maintain the labour force. These workers, like their counterparts in private business, are (or perceive themselves to be) members of the middle class. In general they support the capitalist system because, like other workers in private businesses, they perceive their incomes to be dependent on the stability and expansion of the system. Further, many are engaged in tasks that are essentially maintenance tasks: socializing the young, retraining workers, propping up the poor, or, at another level, establishing trading relations with other countries, negotiating treaties that would permit capitalism to expand, or providing security forces within the country and armies outside it.

Within the state sector, there are groups of employees, some portion of which are antagonistic to capitalism. These are found, particularly, in universities and schools. This may be because their work demands that they think about the nature of the system. In social service agencies, it is because the victims of the system are encountered. Intellectuals, journalists, and social workers often provide a disproportionate share of the socialist and reformist movements' support. While this is the case, it is also the case that the vast majority of workers in these sectors support the system just as do unionized production workers.

There is another sector to the population which is defined neither as corporate owners nor as employed workers. It is the petit bourgeoisie in Marxist language, or small business owners and other self-employed persons in liberal language. The economic power of this class is not great, since it has a small share of industrial markets, is dependent on outside financing, and depends on the large corporations for supplies and sometimes as well for markets. However, it is a class that operates in a limited free enterprise economy, unlike the planned economies of the corporate sector. Because of this, it is often the most staunchly supportive class for private capitalism.

Its most important function is that it employs a significant share of the total labour force. Since small businesses must cope with costs and supplies which are determined by the corporate sector, they are not usually competitive with respect to wages. They use labour rather than machines which they cannot afford, and employ many workers on part-time and temporary bases. The net effect is a segment of the labour force that is not affluent, generally not unionized, and not permanently employed; but which, none the less, is maintained while the corporate economy advances technologically and reduces its overall labour requirements.

The lower levels of the working class generally have lower levels of education and less marketable skills. The difference in education between the top and the bottom of the working force is such that J.K. Galbraith has suggested that education, rather than wealth or authority, is now the main distinction between the classes.[46] By this he means education that is useful to the corporations. As the skill hierarchy becomes more complex and those at the top increase their value, those without special skills and education lose ground. Their incomes do not rise at the same rate so that their income position is lower than it was a decade ago. As automation continues to erode jobs once done by unskilled workers, the bottom of the labour force becomes unemployed.

However, education is valuable only as long as the demand for bureaucratic workers increases. In an expanding economy that is the case. If the economy contracts, and especially where, simultaneously, automation begins to erode clerical as well as manual jobs, the room at the top shrinks. Then education provides no automatic entry. Even professional skills and graduate degrees lose their marketability.

While, in general, manual jobs have been most affected by technological development, other skilled jobs have been similarly affected. Mechanization and automation frequently reduce the need for specialized skills, so that an increasing proportion of the labour force, especially in the production sectors, performs machine-tending tasks which are neither purely menial labour nor skilled work.

These changes are occurring today. But over the past three decades there has been growth in the economy, and jobs for workers in most skill areas have been available. For many, these jobs have provided security, high wages, and better life conditions than were available for their parents. The children of immigrants have been able to move up through educational channels to relatively secure positions, and for them and others on the road upward the liberal ideology has been a satisfactory explanation for the good life.

7 NATION AND NATIONAL PROTEST

In 1947 United States President Truman announced that the United States was prepared to lead the struggle of "all free peoples" in the "free world" against oppression and in the cause of "freedom." This struggle would take the form of military intervention against imperialist aggression, if necessary, and otherwise economic aid. The instrument of the aid was to be the Marshall Plan. Marshall Plan aid would be directed entirely to private enterprise in recipient countries, and would consist of credits to purchase goods from the United States and Canada.

The definition of the free world was not given. However, since aid and military alliances under its terms were extended to Western Europe, Turkey, Greece, Taiwan, Spain, Portugal, Iran, and numerous right-wing dictatorships in Asia and Latin America, and since the only characteristic all of these countries had in common with the United States and Canada was that all were engaged in the economic system known as capitalism, one must conclude that it was the free flow of capital across borders which defined the free world. It could not be democracy since these countries did not have liberal democracy in common. Several were Fascist or near-Fascist dictatorships.

The military alliances that buttressed this "free world" included the Organization of American States (OAS, transformed into a military alliance in 1947); the North Atlantic Treaty Organization (NATO, agreements concluded in 1949); a series of agreements with Canada that effectively integrated North American defence, including the North American Air Defence agreements (NORAD, 1957). The stated objective of these alliances was "to contain communism." Containing communism was further defined as protecting democratic peoples (but as well all those in the free world, not all of whom were democratic) against external aggression and against indirect aggression. Indirect aggression consisted of propaganda and possible seizure of power by communists within a country, that is, indigenous communism.

This announcement, and the cold war that it ushered in, was probably the single most important event in Canadian history. Shocking as that statement may seem, it is a fact that the American declaration of its intent to contain communism, and the underlying reasons for that declaration, had a greater long-term impact on Canadian development than any single action taken by Canadian leaders up to that time and possibly since then. For Canada, the cold war meant an immediate boost to national prosperity, the dramatic growth of an affluent middle class, the growth of corporate organizations with American parents, the vast growth of industries producing arms and other war materials, the demise of national sovereignty over Canadian defence, and the full integration of the Canadian economy with the American economy. It was also a period in which left-wing ideologies and parties were aggressively attacked by governments, atheism as a position on religion was condemned, and public debate of the political issues affecting Canada was virtually stopped. The cold war lasted into the mid-1960s, after which it thawed slightly only to re-emerge as the 1980s began.

1

There are two very different interpretations of the causes of the cold war from 1947, when the Truman doctrine was stated, to about the mid-1960s. Though in 1947, Canadian political leaders and journalists expressed some skepticism about the wisdom of American policy, by 1949 and with increasing insistence through the 1950s, they accepted the explanation provided by the United States State Department. Their acceptance of this explanation rested on a basic premise that the United States was a friend and ally, and that Canada's interests were coincident with those of the United States.

Accepting that premise, the basic argument was that Russia posed a military threat to what was defined as "the free world." The second argument was that communism posed a political and social threat to liberal democracies, and that all forms of communism were directed by Russia. The third was that communists were atheists, and that atheists posed a social and spiritual threat to predominantly Christian countries. The world was divided into two irreconcilable camps, and one of these, the Russian communist camp, was bent on destroying the other. In the rhetoric of the time, the "other" was not called capitalism. It was called "the democracies," "the free world," and "the non-communist world."

Russia was viewed as a likely aggressor, for the reason that it was, or was believed to be, imperialistic. The evidence for Russia's aggressive imperialism included the many statements on the desirability of a world revolution issued over the previous two decades by the Comintern, Russia's bargaining postures at the Potsdam and Yalta Conferences, its take-over of neighbouring countries at the conclusion of World War II, and, in 1948, her intervention in the communist take-over in Czechoslovakia and the Berlin crisis.

While in general the argument was not advanced that Canada itself was a prime target for Russian military force, Canada's situation was viewed as vulnerable because of its proximity to the United States, its close and friendly ties with that country, and its resource reservoir as a supplier to American defence.

If Russia did not pose an immediate military threat to the United States, then in any case its potential military intervention in Western Europe was believed to threaten United States' interests to which Canada's interests were attached. This would be so because the Soviet sphere would, it was believed, close the borders of communist countries. Thus the United States, and Canada, would be excluded from major trading areas.

This might also be the case if Russia became dominant in Third World areas. Further, if Russia dominated either or both of Western Europe and some strategic areas of the Third World (e.g., the Middle East), it might use these areas as launching positions for a military invasion of North America.

Combined with these considerations was a belief that Russia was involved in the development and encouragement of communist parties in other countries. These parties, particularly in Italy and France, were seen as potential "fifth columns" in the overthrow of democratic governments. Communist parties in North America were likewise viewed as potential saboteurs, aided by Russia. A year after the Truman doctrine, the Czechoslovakian government fell to a communist coup, and it was believed that this was the first of a series of aggressive acts of imperialism by Russia. The Berlin crisis a year later, and the repression of the Hungarian revolution in 1956 increased the conviction in the West that Russia would suppress all internal dissident movements and was preparing for a world take-over.

The second argument in this general framework was that communism posed a threat to liberal democracy. In order to understand this argument, one must accept the proposition that Russia was the embodiment of communism, in the same way that North America was the embodiment of free enterprise. Communism, of course, was the official political ideology of the Soviet countries. In theory it implied that the system within which it was espoused was, or would gradually become, a classless society. All industrial property would be publicly owned, and would be managed on behalf of the working class (the entire population) by elected or appointed managers who themselves could not privately own any means of production or become otherwise personally enriched by their service to the state.

The production system would thus be managed in the interests of the citizens rather than in the interests of profit. As well, the distribution system would be so ordered as to avoid wasteful competition, gross inequalities in consumer opportunities and wealth, and pockets of unemployment and poverty.

The theory, like that of free enterprise in North America, was not well meshed with the reality of Soviet Russia either in 1945 or at the present time. The ownership of private industrial property was not permitted, but the managers of the system became a directing class within the state apparatus somewhat similar to the directors of private enterprise in the West. The distribution system, lacking a well organized market, was frequently inefficient in the vital tasks of feeding and maintaining the population, with the result that not only poverty but considerable inequalities were engendered. A black market in consumer goods has continued to characterize the system and has become a major feature of Soviet life.

Our concern is not with whether the Soviet system has succeeded in achieving the theoretical state of communism, but with the fact that the capitalist countries believed Russia to be the embodiment of communism. This belief led to the supposition that anything which happened in Russia was a necessary aspect of communism. One of the features of the Russian system which became, for North Americans, the paramount feature, was the growth of concentration camps and other punishments for dissidents, and the general silencing of internal critics. It was said that communism was responsible for the loss of freedom in Eastern Europe. Since the major attraction of liberal democracy was believed to be its encouragement of individual freedom, this constituted a direct contrast with the western political system. If Russia, therefore, posed a threat to Canada, the threat extended not only to military intervention but as well to individual freedom. If Russia and communism were the same thing, then communism as such was a threat to the people of liberal democracies. But if this were the case, then communism in any form, including the form of indigenous communist or socialist parties, posed such a threat.

The third argument in this framework was that communists are atheists, and atheists posed a threat to Christianity. In the 1920s, many European communist parties as well as the Russian Party disavowed the Church, and Marx had viewed religion as one of the ideological tools of the ruling class. The reason for this had less to do with religion than with power politics. Like Quebec, much of Europe and Russia had been subjected to a conservative and hierarchical church structure which dissidents identified as one of the major obstacles to social change. Their version of Utopia therefore included the overthrow of the conservative Church and its institutional capacities for obstruction of change. Conservatism and communism actually have one feature in common, namely, their emphasis on the collective good as opposed to individual material greed. This may be the important explanatory variable for why Russia in 1917, rather than liberal and capitalist Britain, experienced a class war and a revolution in the name of communism. The transition for a feudal society from Catholic conservatism to collective communism may be less extreme than for a liberal and capitalist society. In any event, the Church was overthrown in Russia insofar as it was a major institution upholding the Czarist regime; Christianity was not overthrown as a system of belief. As the political and economic power of the church decreased, it ceased to be a threat to the state bureaucrats, and hostility to religion declined.

In North America, where an understanding of the role of the Church in Russia was absent, and where, outside of Quebec, no parallel history existed, the argument was advanced that communism (rather than the Russian state) was opposed to religion, specifically to Christianity (rather than the Catholic Church). Communists were atheists.

In 1945, liberal democrats were not atheists. Atheism was not held in high regard in Canada, and it was a way of thought to which only curious intellectuals admitted. The particular form of Christianity prevalent throughout Anglophone Canada and the United States in the 1940s was Protestantism. In that form, popular Christianity had much in common with popular liberalism. It espoused egalitarian values with respect to opportunity structures, it was individualistic with respect to salvation and the means of achieving it, and it was optimistic with respect to the capacities of the society to overcome obstacles. The egalitarian themes were stressed by those Canadians who became supporters of the early socialist movements on the prairies; they saw their Christianity as consistent with socialism. The individualistic themes were stressed by other Canadians who became supporters of the social movements on the prairies; they saw their Christianity as consistent with socialism. The individualistic themes were stressed by other Canadians who became supporters of the Social Credit movement and Fascism; they saw their Christianity as consistent with these political positions. Neither group divorced their Christian principles from their political philosophy, and for most Canadians, the Christian principles—however diverse their interpretation of these—were significant components of their overall ideology. In Quebec, though Christianity took a different form, it was, as we discussed earlier, extremely antagonistic to a political theory that made no room for the supremacy of

God. Since it was believed that communists were atheists, and since atheism was not widely espoused by sections of the population who were clearly and unambiguously non-communists, there was a linking of these two belief systems which worked backwards, i.e., atheists were communists as well as the reverse.

Popular magazines were a major form for expression of the cold war beliefs. *Maclean's Magazine*, for example, published numerous editorials and articles purporting to analyze the conflict between the "western democracies" and communist Russia. On January 1, 1949, an editorial expressed this opinion:

Western democracies need to be strong—but not because a violent clash is inevitable. We need strength and are building strength not because we are resigned to a mutually suicidal war but because that seems the best way of establishing a feasible way of getting on with the Russians. Democracy must demonstrate that it's the better system and in 1948 we did pretty well with that demonstration. The European Recovery Program is an operating reality, the revival of Europe is a perceptible fact.[1]

Two weeks later Matthew Halton reported in *Maclean's*:

It's plainly a spectacular distance that the democratic world has come since it reluctantly realized a year or so ago that there was no peace on earth, that its nations must live in a state of continuous crisis and that it had no hope of bargaining with Russia or of stopping the Communist technique of aggression in country after country unless it was economically rejuvenated and militarily strong.[2]

The most persistent belief was that the United States did not pose a threat to Canadian sovereignty and would never become a military threat to Canada. Critics who questioned this view were accused of giving "ammunition to the Soviet press for its barrage of propaganda to its own people and to the world,"[3] by a professor of international relations in an article on Canadian foreign policy. International embarrassment could be caused by Canadians asserting national independence or weakening the continental defence system against the communists.

The liberal version of the cold war, then, was a political interpretation, i.e., that Russia posed a political threat to liberal democracy. This was a somewhat tenuous thesis when the "free world" had been defined so that it included non-liberal, non-democratic, and non-Christian regimes. None the less, this thesis was and still is widely accepted. It was so widely accepted in the United States that nearly a decade of persecution and prosecution of suspected communists took place under the aegis of the "Un-American activities" committee headed by Joseph McCarthy. Similar trials did not take place in Canada and during the 1950s, the Communist and CCF parties were not banned as were their counterparts in the United States, but dissidents and critics of Canada's participation in the American crusade against communism were frequently labelled "communist sympathizers" and "fellow travellers" by the press, politicians, and general population. When the NATO treaty was being discussed in parliament, for example, a CCF member from Vancouver Centre, Rodney Young, pointed out that Portugal was not governed by the principles of democracy and was, in fact, the oldest Fascist dictatorship in Europe. He was denounced as "apologizing for Russia" by the Liberal Minister of Labour.[4] One of the very few institutions in Canada to speak against the treaty was the United Church of Canada. The majority of the CCF accepted it, and the academic establishment and media provided no serious opposition.

The media and academics also remained silent when, as NATO developed further and the Korean War involved Canadian military personnel, it became clear that, to quote Lester Pearson:

> ... The field of our foreign interests and the extent of our military commitments have in recent months been almost visibly stretched; and such a process can never be accomplished without discomfort. This will be eased and Canada's participation made more effective only if Canadians can be made to feel that their share in the vital decisions which must be made is proportionate to their contribution. But that is a necessity for many other countries besides Canada. Indeed, it is a requirement to which great importance is attached by all countries which, like my own, have voluntarily and wholeheartedly accepted the leadership of the United States.[5]

This statement makes it clear that American leadership and control were accepted; junior partnership was what Canada was to have in this league, proportionate to Canada's contribution rather than equal as might have been expected for a sovereign nation.

Canadian students of international relations and history in the 1950s were normally given American textbooks for study of world affairs. One of the most popular of these was *International Relations* by Palmer and Perkins, published in 1953. This was viewed as an objective and scholarly study, though its references to Russia and communism were frequently attached to such adjectives as "aggressive," and "hostile," and the other Soviet states were referred to as "faithful satellites," and "henchmen."

In a section on "the balance of power," Palmer and Perkins report that the United States:

. . . has developed a strong anti-balance of power tradition. She is saddled with historical, constitutional, and psychological handicaps—one might call them glorious handicaps—which seem to rule out the overt and covert manipulations that an active pursuit of a balancing role would require.

By contrast, they report: " . . . Soviet Russia is not interested in regulating the balance of power; she is interested in destroying the present balance and perhaps the society out of which it has developed."[6]

The various military alliances of the United States are described in this text as friendly and reasonable agreements by peaceful countries. The foreign policy of the Soviet Union is described as: " . . . characterized by growing hostility to the West, by increasing tendencies toward non-cooperation and isolation, by consolidation of the Soviet orbit, and by general intransigence."[7]

In a description of how Russia took over neighbouring countries, Palmer and Perkins explained that:

They were clever in their propaganda appeals, especially in exploiting the weaknesses of other parties and institutions, in disguising their real motives, and in posing as champions of needed economic and political reforms and as enemies of exploitation whether by favored groups within the countries or by foreign nations.[8] . . . Along with persuasion went ruthless terrorism. The opposition was intimidated and gradually liquidated, and opposition leaders were imprisoned or executed unless they had fled for their lives. . .[9]

With respect to the coup in Czechoslovakia in 1948, which is called "a tragedy which cast lengthening shadows over the entire free world," Palmer and Perkins state that it:

. . . came as a particular shock and surprise to the non-Communist world and helped to dispel many illusions about the nature of the new "people's democracies," the extent of their popular support, and the implications of the Communist consolidation of Eastern Europe.[10]

A Canadian student, studying this text, was exposed to the assumption that American interests were identical to Canadian interests. Canada was not viewed in the text as an important country, and throughout the text the assumption was made that it was an appendage to the United States. The United States was pursuing a peaceful and co-operative foreign policy. Compared to Russia, for example, "in the months following V.J. Day the United States was primarily concerned with such matters as peacemaking, occupation policies, economic rehabilitation and recovery, and cooperation with the United Nations."[11] The American people (and by implication the Canadian people as well), were extremely tolerant of Russia's peculiarities at this point in history. In fact,

Soviet intransigence and non-cooperation came as a particular shock to the American people, who were not aware of the wartime friction until the real story was released with the lifting of censorship. They clung to the belief that all the major powers would cooperate for the common good; and they also clung to their illusions about the nature of communism, even though Soviet words and deeds had made it clear that the leaders of Communist Russia had deliberately reverted to doctrinaire Marxism-Leninism.[12]

By 1957 there were criticisms of Canada's foreign policy as an American satellite. Some of these were raised in a *Maclean's* interview with the Secretary of State for External Affairs, Lester Pearson.

Referring to the case of the External Affairs Officer, Herbert Norman, who had committed suicide because of a persistent barrage of criticism from the United States which insinuated that because Norman had been a member of a left-wing group at university 10 years earlier he was a threat to internal security and should be removed from the Canadian service, Pearson admitted:

*Well, we're vulnerable in more ways than one. We're vulnerable because we want to cooperate with them [the United States] and we're willing to make some sacrifices to co-operate with them, even some sacrifice of national interest, and so should other countries, because without the United States we're vulnerable before Communist imperialism in a military sense. So we have to take that into consideration when we differ with the United States. The price of disunity is high. Any weakening of the coalition is serious. The Russians fear our unity more, almost, than they do our strength.
. . . We're vulnerable economically, we're vulnerable geographically, we're vulnerable strategically because our defenses are interlocked, and we're vulnerable in other ways because we're so close together in so many ways.*[13]

Still, Pearson denied that Canadian foreign policy was slavishly following American directives.

2

The second version of the cold war was held by skeptics who were not necessarily also socialists or communists (though during the period they were generally assumed to be of these political persuasions) and by some but by no means all socialists in Canada. The CCF did not, as a political party, espouse this second version.

Essentially this rests on an economic interpretation of American actions. One need not argue that Soviet Russia was an innocent bystander in the global power game in order to interpret events in this way. The general thesis is not that one of the powers was evil and the other good, but that both were imperialistic and that they were rivals for the economic and political control of the world's resources and markets.

The counter-argument begins with the observation that North America would have fallen into a depression following the war if no strong and aggressive expansionist policies had been pursued. Expansion of American industry (including American industry in Canada) depended on the preservation of a capitalist economy in Europe, the Middle East, and other countries from which resources could be obtained and markets secured. This would be blocked if these countries created publicly-owned industries, internal market systems, and obstacles to the free flow of capital across borders. The political dimension then becomes an appendage, and has nothing to do with democratic government but rather with the existence of a block of countries into which capital could not flow nor goods be exported. The indigenous communist parties of Western European and other nations, in this interpretation, become a problem for the capitalist countries if they are successful in developing systems of public ownership of the means of production, public planning of internal economies, alliances with the Soviet Union, and non-capitalist markets.

This view is supported by an argument to the effect that the Soviet Union did not have the industrial or military capacity to launch an offensive after the second war. It is not communist propaganda which is quoted in this context, but the military and civilian leaders of the United States. For example, in 1948 General Eisenhower stated that in his view ". . . the Soviet Union simply does not have the smoothly functioning industry and mountains of supplies of all kinds which any country would need to start a big war."[14] This view was seconded by John Foster Dulles in 1949, then a senator and subsequently the United States Secretary of State under Eisenhower, who said he did not know " . . . any responsible high official, military or civilian in this government, or any government, who believes that the Soviet state now plans conquest by open military aggression."[15]

These and similar though not frequent statements indicate that high officials in United States government and military circles were not of the opinion that Russia posed an actual and immediate threat to North America and Western Europe. When the Truman doctrine was enunciated, only the United States had atomic technology. The Soviets did not obtain this until 1949, by which time NATO was already organized. At that stage Russia still did not have a very well developed industrial capacity, and it appears doubtful that she could have maintained a war economy. This information would have been available to business and political leaders in North America. Indeed, it was available to the general reading public. Journalist Max Werner wrote a long article for *Maclean's* early in 1949 outlining the extent of Russian military strength compared to American reserves and argued that:

The Soviet Union is strong enough to defeat any aggression; it is not strong enough to make aggressive war. . . . Everything the Soviet leaders are doing in long-range economic planning indicates that they do not intend to expose the unfinished industrial structure of the country to the risk and dangers of war. . . . This military realism of the Soviet leadership implies strong self-restraint.[16]

Similar articles appeared in other popular journals of the period.

The situations of Czechoslovakia and Berlin are also controversial. Skeptics of the American version of Russian aggression against a democratic state point out that in the elections of 1946, two years before the communist coup, 38% of the Czech population had voted communist. In other words, there was a very substantial body of support for communism in that country. The Berlin blockade was preceded by several aggressive actions by the United States and Britain and the general tone of hostility after the Truman speech. Indeed, the Truman speech, the nature of the Marshall Plan, and the general tenor of American foreign policy between 1947 and 1950 are regarded by some critics as the major cause of the Soviet Union's participation in the cold war. Russia may have been engaged in a largely defensive action. With respect to the take-over of Eastern European countries, critics point out that this was essentially the same process of expansion and carving-up of the world into spheres of influence being practised by the United States. The United States' "spheres" were Western Europe, Mexico, Canada, Australia, and New Zealand, India, the Caribbean, and Latin America. The contested areas were the Mediterranean and Middle East, where the United States had extensive oil interests, Asia, and Africa. The Korean and Vietnam wars were outcomes of the contest between the super-powers, in each case, according to this view of history, the manipulation of small countries undergoing what would otherwise have been civil wars.

With respect to Canadian participation, the skeptic emphasizes the consequences of the military agreements under NATO, NORAD, the Defence Production Agreements (discussed in Chapter 3), the New Hyde Park Agreements of 1950, and numerous other agreements between the two countries. Among the consequences are the standardization of arms, equipment, organization, and methods of training, which, together with American command of NATO and NORAD forces effectively deprives Canada of an independent defence capability. Since Canada is blessed with resources essential to American military and industrial growth, these agreements mean that she could not defend her right to use these resources against American claims on them should a conflict of objectives ever arise. C.D. Howe announced in Washington in 1950 that "Canada and the United States march side by side in time of war,"[17] but critics point out that this requires Canada to have no disagreements with the United States in time of peace. In addition to these integrative mechanisms, the United States controls parts of the Canadian north through the various northern radar stations, and bases in Newfoundland under 1941 agreements which will be in force until 2040.

The Marshall Plan required the recipients to purchase goods, on credits provided by the U.S. government, from American and Canadian companies. This fact alone suggests why Canada was a willing partner in American expansion. The argument of the critics, then, is that the Marshall Plan, backed by the labelling of the major postwar rival of the United States as a ruthless enemy, was a means of securing "tied" markets in Western Europe and the Middle East and of ensuring Canada's support and thus the continuing availability of Canada's resources.

With respect to the argument that the "free world" was threatened, critics point to the fact that the "free world" as defined by American foreign policy was not free. Iran, reconstituted by American aid as a monarchy, Portugal, Greece, Turkey, Spain, Taiwan, and many other dictatorships were included. Only by substituting the word "capitalism" for the words "liberal democracy" could the statements in defence of these alliances make factual sense. The Truman doctrine and the military alliances that followed it were designed to protect capitalism, not an abstraction called "the free world."

This interpretation is somewhat strengthened by some of the attacks on critics of the NATO alliance, which stressed the economic implications of the cold war in their defence of America's foreign policy. In Canada, for example, the liberal magazine, *Saturday Night*, editorialized:

It is probably not a bad thing that the North Atlantic Treaty is having the effect of sorting out the sheep from the goats in the socialist pasture. The test for distinguishing between them is not difficult. He who believes that private profit is itself immoral is fundamentally on the side of the com-

munists; and anyone who believes that the pursuit of private profit inevitably leads to war and that the universal abolition of private profit will prevent war, must clearly believe that private profit is immoral. He who believes that private profit is not in itself immoral is not a communist nor on the side of the communists.[18]

Finally it may be observed that North American hostility to both Russia and communism did not begin with Russia's actions following the second war. It began, rather, in 1917, with the Bolshevik revolution and the closure of Russia to capitalist expansion. One may observe this antagonism in the view held in 1919 during the Winnipeg Strike by business and media leaders in Canada; as indicated in the quotations of the previous chapter, they argued that an industrial conflict in Canada must be caused by outside agitators from Russia. That was a quarter of a century before the official beginning of the cold war.

This second interpretation is not necessarily a Marxist one. It need not involve a theory of the class structure of capitalist countries, nor even a theory of imperialism as an integral component of capitalism. It is not, however, consistent with the liberal version of capitalist societies. As the cold war proceeded, and merged with both the Korean and the Vietnam wars, an increasing proportion of the population began to question the shibboleths of liberalism. The inconsistencies between the American posture of "defence of freedom" and the emerging facts of American involvement in the maintenance of various dictatorships in Latin America, Asia, and the Middle East created a gulf between public faith and private knowledge. American involvement in the Vietnam war greatly increased that gulf, but between the mid-1940s and the mid-1960s, the vast majority of the Canadian population, together with the American public, accepted the liberal version of the cold war and regarded critics within their countries as communists, fellow travellers, dupes, atheists (*ipso facto*, communists) and saboteurs. The question we pose in this book is, why? A second question, for which the answer is largely self-evident, is how did this situation affect indigenous socialist and communist parties?

3

The argument has been advanced throughout this text that a dominant ideology has two functions: it legitimates the status quo, and it provides a satisfactory explanation for private realities.

It legitimates the status quo by selectively informing people what the status quo is. It may omit what is not apparent. It provides positive judgements on that status quo, shows why it is good, makes people feel protective of it. Since any social organization includes a power distribution, it is successful to the extent that it makes that power appear beneficial. It can do this in a variety of ways depending on what would be consistent with the rest of the ideology and with apparent reality. If people hold strongly to a religious view of the world, then the power distribution might be explained, as it was in Quebec through the first three decades of this century, as a manifestation of God's will. If people believe in a collective enemy, then the power distribution may be explained as a necessary means of opposing the enemy.

The status quo can be made to seem legitimate, however, only if what can be seen by people can also be recognized as consistent with private realities and private knowledge. While societies can hold ideologies that are manifestly untrue as descriptions of society, none the less there are limits to the degree of discontinuity between beliefs and realities. For example, great differences in material wealth can be explained as differences in achievement only if there actually is a substantial class which experiences some congruence between its efforts and its rewards. One citizen may not be personally successful but may none the less believe that success does follow from effort if he or she can see that others do succeed as a consequence of their own efforts. If it were apparent that the only people who succeeded were those who are born into a particular class or caste, an ideology which linked achievement with effort would not be widely believed. A liberal ideology would not be successful in an economy characterized by extremes of wealth and poverty with little middle ground between them, or in a social climate which provided no mobility for children of the working class.

The liberal ideology was probably at its height in the 1950s in Canada. It was so widely believed that few thought to question it, even fewer dared to express skepticism of its central tenets. That aspect of it which explained the cold war and Canada's unquestioning alliance with the United States came under no serious attack from the institutionalized Left or any other sources during that decade. Thus the analyst must assume that the public presentation of "the facts" and the internal realities of private life for most citizens were congruent; there was no compelling reason to disbelieve the public ideology.

The explanation for this appears to be that a very substantial portion of the Canadian population benefited materially from the cold war, and that they, or their children, were upwardly mobile in an expanding economy; their mobility was entirely consistent with a belief in achievement, private freedom, and the general goodness of democracy and private enterprise.

American industries were expanding in Canada, especially in the resource sectors where vital minerals, oil, and wood products fed the American manufacturing industries. Manufacturing companies also developed in central Canada, especially in the sectors connected to production of goods for the Korean war, subsequently for the Vietnam war, and overall for the American defence build-up. As these industries grew, employment became available for Canadians in these corporate subsidiaries.

The new employment channels included a vast increase in skilled and professional jobs. Workers whose parents had suffered through the Depression, second-generation Canadians whose parents were peasant immigrants from Eastern and Southern Europe, and young people from working-class homes who, with the new wealth, could obtain university educations were all entering the mobile middle class. This was not, perhaps, the upper strata of the middle class as defined by Porter in the late 1950s. A little more modest and defined more broadly as the skilled to managerial strata with secure jobs and steady incomes, it was a class that was growing and sensing its own expanded opportunities.

A growing middle class with what appears to be unlimited mobility quite reasonably develops a firm faith not only in the "goodness" of an egalitarian philosophy but as well in its existence. Regardless of their family origins, they are, and it is apparent in the results that they are, the equal of any other members of the population; if they can achieve, then all can achieve. Hard work, attention to studies and obtainment of the necessary academic and technical degrees: these are the criteria of success in an economic boom.

The economic boom was accompanied by new and increasingly complex technologies for production. The acquisition of new technical skills created a middle class that was not only mobile and optimistic, but as well technically sophisticated and dependent on a sophisticated technology for their employment. This gave rise to a welcoming attitude toward technical change, toward the further conquest of nature and exploitation of natural resources, to faith in the capacities of technology to solve the world's problems. It obstructed opposition to exploitation and blinkered recognition of the possibility that some of the world's problems were actually caused by the same technology.

Following Marx's insight into the nature of a ruling class ideology, one may note the idealization of what that class was doing during the post-war decades. The magical words were "the free world," "the democracies" and "the Western world," combined with their

opposites, "the dictatorships," and "the imperialistic communists."
It was behind this screen that the great private corporate empires
grew across the national borders of all the countries that would agree
to foreign investment, but one need not "blame" the directors of
those empires for propagating a deliberate mystification of the world
political and economic situation. If Marx was right, they are likely
to have believed their own idealized version of their activities. The
interview with Lester Pearson quoted earlier gives some idea of the
way in which the cold war was understood by the political leaders
of the "free world." On the one hand, there was a persistent defence
of Canadian foreign policy in terms of the need to oppose the communists; on the other, an acknowledgement that the United States
was too powerful to offend. Pearson, in the same interview, referred
several times to public opinion in Canada, to the many letters he
received from Canadians and other indices of opinion, arguing that
Canada should never give in to the communists. There is every
reason to suppose that this was the case: that the majority of Canadians accepted the dichotomy between good and evil as manifested in the political balance of terror between the "free world" and
"the communists."

If capitalism could produce jobs, affluence, steady employment,
mobility and such a sense of optimism and well-being, then capitalism could be seen as a positive good. It was thus not so difficult
to suppose that any movement away from or in opposition to capitalism must in like fashion be viewed as a potential or positive evil.
If communism was such a force, then it should be prevented from
expanding.

Few members of the society were, in the 1950s, obliged to consider
the causes of poverty *outside* North America; few who were not
experiencing it to consider the nature of poverty *inside* North America. During the 1950s there was a general belief in the possibility
for eradicating poverty and hunger by extending both North American technical know-how and North American democracy. The United
States, aided by Canada, sent out missionaries in the form of technical advisors, teachers, military advisors, and salespeople, all with
the message that if the poor of the world would educate themselves
they would emerge from their miserable conditions. North America
(a conceit on Canada's part) could become the world's saviour.

Through the 1950s and most of the 1960s, politics in Canada
consisted of periodic elections which provided either a Conservative
or a Liberal Party government. The CCF, having reached its highest
popular support before the end of the war, went into a steady decline.
By 1958 it could muster only 9% of the popular vote. With the cold
war in full flower, the Labour Progressive Party remained only a

name and a handful of "the faithful." After the Hungarian uprising of 1956, even this handful declined. The regenerated CCF, having allied itself with the unions (most by now American-dominated internationals), remained in politics as the New Democratic Party but through the 1960s it continued as a small reformist liberal party. Students in Canada were not involved in politics. Those who studied economics, political science, and sociology were concerned with such questions as why individuals voted for Liberals rather than Conservatives, why individuals chose product A rather than product B, and a "stratification" rather than a "class" system of social organization. Capitalism was taken for granted rather than examined, and the role of the state was rarely seriously questioned from other than a liberal point of view.

As the 1960s advanced, the expanded middle class began to take up new consumer interests. Where the 1950s generation had been intent on obtaining better jobs than their parents had, and in buying new houses and new furniture and clothes, the 1960s generation was interested in expanding its spiritual horizons. This involved everything from batik, astrology, novel forms of psychotherapy, and manipulated sexual encounters to experiments with drugs. It was the decade of the "do your own thing—you're the only one who counts" philosophy; the logical extension but as well the mockery of the liberal ideology of individualism. There was no room in this culture for an examination of the class structure, a critique of the sources of prosperity, or a skeptical interpretation of American capitalism.

It was not until the late 1960s that serious challenges to this belief were expressed outside of the Marxist circles in the Third World. Within North America, studies of internal poverty which were more searching than liberal ideology would permit began to be published in the same late 1960s. By that time, the economic boom was past its peak.

The first in a series of little recessions hit Canada in 1957, coincident with the election of a new government but not due to that circumstance. The Korean war boom had passed, and it was some time before the benefits of the United States waging war on Vietnam were felt by Canadian workers. Though these benefits offset the recessions and kept the economy buoyant through the 1960s, the war economy had economic as well as ideological repercussions in North America in the form of inflation. By the late 1960s, with the "baby boom" population entering the labour force, the expansion of the economy could no longer be maintained. Europe had recovered and was challenging American dominance of world markets. Japan had become a modern technical giant and produced high quality goods at prices lower than the United States' export prices because labour costs in Japan were lower. OPEC had been organized and was beginning to exert pressure towards higher oil prices for American industries. The Third World, for many reasons that go beyond this text's coverage but which included the very success of American technology and ideology, was beginning to demand entry into world markets on better terms for its resources. The expansion of the United States' economy, and thus of the Canadian economy, began to slow down; the great job market began to contract; the mobile middle class began to lose its security and endless horizons.

Perhaps more critical than the economic slowdown—which was just beginning in the late 1960s and didn't reach its first public recognition until the "oil crisis" of 1973–74, nor its official depression predictions until the late 1970s and early 1980s—was the effect on ideology of the "hot" war in Vietnam. The generation of young people who had been reared on the liberal ideology took it seriously; they believed it, and that meant that they believed in the essential equality of human beings, in the relativity of culture, and in the goodness of democracy. Even with a blind faith in the evil of communism, many of them found it impossible to believe that the dropping of napalm bombs on Asian villages would make the world safe for democracy. Some began to ask whether democracy could be made safe for the world, a cynicism that was very much in contrast with the ideology of liberalism in North America. It was a cynicism in the United States, the imperial centre of an inherited liberalism in the 1970s, that provided the opportunity to Canadians to reconsider their allegiance to that imperial centre.

4

Canada emerged from the cold war with an economy fully integrated into the American economy. The multinational corporations were the major economic actors in the capitalist world by the late 1960s. In Canada they controlled every vital sector, including the minerals essential to a war economy. The American economy was geared to war production: its large defence sector was its means of maintaining economic momentum. Canada had no option but to remain within the American orbit as a junior partner; no military independence if it had attempted to remove itself from it.

Canada may not have had the option of changing its fate by the late 1960s, but by that time there were Canadians who were both able and willing to publicly criticize the alliance. Disillusioned by the United States as the Vietnam war dragged on, increasingly aware of the effects of American expansion in the Third World, and re-cognizing that the great threat from Russia had failed to materialize, these intellectuals and journalists began first to criticize the foreign dominance of Canadian industry and culture, then to engage in a more sustained critique of capitalism. Their voices were first heard within the ranks of the New Democratic Party, as they attempted to move the liberal-left party to a more nationalist stance with what came to be known as the "Waffle Resolution" in 1969:

RESOLUTION 133

... The major threat to Canadian survival today is American control of the Canadian economy. The major issue of our times is not national unity but national survival, and the fundamental threat is external, not internal. . . .

... American corporate capitalism is the dominant factor shaping Ca-nadian society. In Canada American economic control operates through the formidable medium of the multi-national corporation. The Canadian corporate elite has opted for a junior partnership with these American enterprises. Canada has been reduced to a resource base and consumer market within the American empire. . . .

... The American empire is held together through world-wide military alliances and by giant corporations. Canada's membership in the American alliance system and the ownership of the Canadian economy by American corporations precluded Canada's playing an independent role in the world. These bonds must be cut if corporate capitalism and the social priorities it creates is to be effectively challenged.

Canadian development is distorted by a corporate capitalist econ-omy. . . . The problem of regional disparities is rooted in the profit orien-tation of capitalism. . . . An independence movement based on substituting Canadian capitalists for American capitalists, or on public policy to make foreign corporations behave as if they were Canadian corporations, cannot be our final objective. . . . Without a strong national capitalist class behind them, Canadian governments, Liberal and Conservative, have functioned in the interests of international and particularly American capitalism, and have lacked the will to pursue even a modest strategy of economic independence.

Capitalism must be replaced by socialism, by national planning of in-vestment and by the public ownership of the means of production in the interests of the Canadian people as a whole. Canadian nationalism is a relevant force on which to build to the extent that it is anti-imperialist. . . .

English Canada and Quebec can share common institutions to the ex-tent that they share common purposes. So long as the federal government refuses to protect the country from American economic and cultural dom-ination, English Canada is bound to appear to French Canadians simply as part of the United States. An English Canada concerned with its own national survival would create common aspirations that would help to tie the two nations together once more. . . .[13]

The Waffle Manifesto was rejected by the NDP. In its place the Marshmallow Resolution was adopted. This decried American foreign domination but omitted the analysis of capitalism. Said David Lewis, the leader of the party:

We have made that decision . . . not for any narrow chauvinism, not for any arid nationalism, not for any ideological nonsense. We made that decision because of our conviction that unless Canada is free economically, it will not be free politically. . . .[20]

With this statement, the differing conceptions of Canada as well as of its future were underlined. The revolutionary definition was still not that of the majority, not even of the majority of socialists in Canada.

5

The defeat of the Waffle Resolution in the NDP split not only the Left in Canada, but also the Francophone and Anglophone groups within the Left. Up to this point, the NDP, being an organized political party, was viewed as the most likely vehicle for reform on the scale necessary to overcome American control. Though it had never had a significant following in Quebec, young socialists in that province were prepared to support it if it gathered sufficient momentum to move in the nationalist direction. At the same time, many other groups were growing in Quebec, differing amongst themselves on the degree of national independence they wanted for their province but agreeing at least that they were no longer willing to support the kind of Canadian nation that had developed under American control. Some of these groups were militant and doctrinaire Marxist-Leninists. Some were moderate socialists. The majority were neither of these: they wanted a separate Quebec in which they were "masters" of their own house, but the house was to have essentially the same kind of capitalist economy as the rest of North America. These groups provided the initial support for the Parti Quebecois, a party of the moderate left, with a platform of separatist sympathies and welfare capitalism.

Parti Quebecois sentiments are not the stuff of the Marxist critique. A non-liberal interpretation of what happened in Quebec with the Quiet Revolution was provided in the early 1970s by a popular author in Quebec, Léandré Bergeron. He argued that the "industrial revolution" in that province occurred because the American corporations no longer required merely raw materials and cheap labour.[21] They began to need a new population of consumers. Their labour needs had shifted from illiterate and unskilled workers to educated bureaucrats capable of staffing the middle administrative ranks of industries, providing the engineering skills at the lower levels, and selling the goods in Quebec.

In his view, the Anglo-American industrial interests maintained the Church as long as it was useful in maintaining a cheap labour force. With the new capital-intensive industries, they no longer needed a regime based on moral and physical coercion.

The American managers, argued Bergeron, were a conscious elite. They could and did manipulate conditions to their interests. In an age of mass-produced and ready-made goods and services, they camouflaged their real interests, bought a labour force, disguised power. As long as the front was successful, the elite enjoyed unchallenged power. If they were seriously challenged, if their ownership of social and natural resources were questioned, they would have to use force just as their predecessors used force.

The role played by the former Negro-Kings, Duplessis and the Clergy, was not useful enough to our colonizers, American and English-Canadian capitalists, in the modern system of exploitation. The requirement was no longer a Negro-King preaching hard work and an austere existence, but a Negro-King who could make the Quebecois people believe that they had to work hard to live extravagantly. That is, that they had to consume, and consume. Therefore, a new elite was needed, a liberal lay elite who would adopt and preach the American way of life, gradually Anglicizing the Quebecois to make them into "real" Canadians—in other words, second-rate Americans who are submissive producers and servile consumers for American imperialism.[22]

Among the tools used by such an elite, in Bergeron's opinion were social insurance funds to appease popular discontent, ensure that the population would act as consumers, and prevent different sectors from recognizing their common slavery to the American system. Another tool was the nationalization of electricity, not to give ownership to the people of Quebec, but to ensure that American industries had a secure source of energy. "Electricity is another service the state offers to industry, just like the roads it builds."

In addition, they used democracy. Says Bergeron of the 1970 election in which the Liberals were returned after a four-year interlude with the final gasps of the Union Nationale: "The Quebecois were slowly learning that bourgeois democracy is bourgeois dictatorship; and that any contest for power that follows the rules of those who will not relinquish it is as predictable as a stacked deck of cards."[23] This view was shared by many students, writers, and trade unionists.

Their analyses, based on the imperialist theme, ran through the pages of many monographs published by the numerous radical movements of the late 1960s and shibboleths and slogans of the street-fighters. The common theme was that the Anglo-Canadian elite in Quebec and in the rest of Canada was a puppet show manipulated by and shielding American monopoly capitalist power. Separation only from Canada would therefore be no solution; rather, complete separation from the American orbit, from capitalism would be needed. The proponents of this revolutionary ideology were particularly opposed to the Parti Quebecois. It, too, represented the interests of bourgeois democrats, and it deflected the anger and awareness of the workers.

When the FLQ, representing the desperate arm of the working class, proclaimed in its Manifesto of the October Crisis that it wanted a complete change, it meant the overthrow of capitalism in Quebec:

The FLQ wants the total independence of Quebecers, reunited in a free society forever purged of its clique of voracious sharks, the patronizing big bosses and the lackeys who make Quebec their protected domain of cheap labour and unscrupulous exploitation.[24]

The FLQ, however, did not represent the wishes of a majority of Quebecois, even, apparently, of the growing numbers who wanted some kind of separation from Canada. Although there were Quebecois who wanted both complete separation from Canada and a break with capitalism, the majority wanted neither of these. A gradually emerging group of business owners and new financiers wanted greater integration with continental capitalism, but with the aid of a stronger provincial government. A technocratic group, employed largely within the public sector, wanted greater autonomy for the provincial government, and a more liberal, possibly social democratic government in Quebec. A third group, which possibly straddled the middle and working classes, wanted complete separation of Quebec from Canada, but envisioned no dramatic break with continental capitalism in the process.

These different positions were explained by Quebec social scientists in class terms. Following the analyses of Guindon and Taylor in the early 1960s (quoted in Chapter 4), two French sociologists, Bourque and Laurin-Frenette[25] argued in the 1970s that there were two fractions of the French bourgeoisie: the "technocrats" who were French-speaking, well educated, and technically competent managers who were concentrated in the public sector; and the "neo-capitalists" who were entrepreneurs, financiers, and executives engaged in private corporations and in tasks connected with property ownership and control.

These two groups combined, in the view of these authors, to push through the reforms of the early 1960s, but their interests were not identical. One fraction sought state intervention in the economy, and greater national (Quebec) control of the economy. The liberal slogan of 1970, "Maîtres chez nous," was their slogan, and it represented their interests. The enemy was the English-speaking elite. The neo-capitalist fraction, while supporting the technocrats in such areas as educational reform, economic planning councils, the creation of new industries, the development of a bureaucratic class, reforms in the federal civil service and government, stopped short of repatriation. Nationalism is not in the interests of international capitalism.

These authors argued that the rural class was reactionary in the sense that it did not identify with the interests of the majority middle class and did not benefit from most of the reforms that had been implemented. On the contrary, it lost its social institutions, its security, and was not sharing in the new prosperity. It voted Creditiste, Parti Quebecois, or Liberal almost indifferently, according to whichever party properly exploited its discontent and promised solutions.

The working class remained divided. While some segments of the trade unionists were militant (as represented in the "Common Front" tactics of the CNTU in a strike against La Presse in 1971, and the CNTU document "There is No Future for Us in the Present Economic System"),[26] many were trying to find a way of fitting into the capitalist state and sharing in the distribution of goods and services. Voting for the Parti Quebecois was one such response and voting Liberal was another. Since both parties represented liberal interpretations of the Quebec situation, the difference was one of popular appeal, leadership, and varying positions on the proper degree of Quebec control of her economy.

The changing class structure was an important component of the Quiet Revolution in Quebec; another and equally important feature was the changing economic underpinning as Toronto rather than Montreal became the metropolitan financial centre of Canada (see discussion of Jacob's arguments in Chapter 4). There is yet a third dimension to the separatist movement, and ultimately this may have been the most significant contributor to the defeat of separatism in the referendum of 1980 and during the post-1980 period. It is language rights.

One of the chief complaints of Franco-Canadians had been their disadvantages in obtaining jobs because of their language. The numerous language bills that passed through the Quebec legislature from 1960 to the late 1970s attest to the salience of the issue. Gradually the notion that Quebec should be a French language province, and that children residing there should learn French rather than English in public schools became accepted. The acceptance came after numerous and bitter battles over language rights, particularly involving immigrants to Quebec and their desire to have children instructed in English. By the late 1970s, the battle seemed to be over. As well, the federal government under Pierre Trudeau had systematically reconstructed the federal civil service so that bilingual applicants and employees enjoyed greater promotional opportunities. The effect of this was both greater mobility for Francophone civil servants and greater commitment to federalism for these and other educated Francophones who chose to leave Quebec.

By 1980, much of the steam had evaporated from the complaints over language. In fact, another kind of problem emerged in the process: a growing difference in status and opportunity between educated and bilingual Francophones, and less educated, unilingual Francophones within Quebec. For many of the first group, the appeal of separatism had vanished; indeed, a national Quebec appeared as a parochial and unattractive alternative to full participation in the larger Canadian and continental economy. The referendum of 1980 was only narrowly defeated, but events following it and finally the defeat of the Parti Quebecois and return of the Liberals again under Robert Bourassa strongly suggested that separatism was a lost cause for this generation of Quebecois.

6

Like the French-Canadian protest against its dual domination, the English-Canadian protest in the 1970s was carried by intellectuals, professionals, particularly in the media and universities, and a very few trade unionists. Like the French technocrats, these were the people whose mobility was blocked by American academics in universities, by the American stranglehold on publication distribution and sale, and by American international trade union control of the labour movement. Like French nationalism, this had two different characters: one, a simple anti-American response, enhanced by the Vietnam opposition and ridicule of the Nixon-Watergate scandal; two, an attack on monopoly capitalism.

It may be argued, as for the French-Canadian separatists, that this was mainly an upper middle-class nationalism, an ideology born of blocked aspirations and over-sized expectations. As in Quebec, it did not represent the aspiring working class nor what was left of the rural class. Furthermore, it was contrary to the interests of the English "neo-capitalists"—the Anglo elite—in exactly the same way as it was contrary to the interests of the French elite.

The differences between the two populations were (i) that the French had two colonial masters, the English-speaking population had only one; (ii) the French could identify their masters all the more easily because they had a distinctive culture and language. These had been nurtured, perversely enough, by the same forces that were overthrown with the Quiet Revolution of the early 1960s. And (iii) the corporate society from which the French had so recently emerged defined the world in class terms. They did not have the century of forgetfulness against which the class analysts of English-Canada struggled. Their nationalism, their class analyses, their awareness of the situation were all the more acute for these differences, but the society they analysed and the class version of it that the militant arm proclaimed was essentially the same as that proposed by "the New Left" in the rest of Canada.

It was in the writings of the revolutionaries that French- and English-speaking Canadians were of one voice. English-speaking political analysts began with Quebec and quickly recognized the extension of the problem to the rest of Canada. Stanley Ryerson spoke for two cultures in his study of Quebec:

Trudeau by his insecure intransigence ensures the deepening crisis, not of liberalism only, but of Canada. One might add—of Canada constructed on the rickety base of the colonial BNA Act, and on the corrupt and corroded fundament of private-corporate capital, and on the irremediably "unequal union" of two nations, embedded in a social matrix that is obsolete.[27]

However, as was true of the Quebecois protest, the Anglophone criticism of American imperialism gained its greatest support when it was couched in strictly ethnic terms. Walter Gordon, a former Liberal Member of Parliament and Finance Minister, was one of the early voices for a reform movement which attacked foreign domination but did not attack capitalism. "More and more of us are realizing that we have become free of the British only to become a satellite of the United States."[28] In this sentiment he was supported by many Anglophone Canadians, including many members of the NDP and some of the Liberal and Conservative parties. This was the Anglophone version of "Maîtres chez nous." It was a version that attracted the students, workers, journalists, and office workers.

It was not a rejection of government, state, or business, and it was not an appeal to class consciousness. It was nationalist, not socialist.

This movement was unwelcome to some Liberals, especially those who dominated the business world and led the Liberal Party, as is evident in the rift between Gordon and his colleagues, and in the defeat of Gordon's policies at the Liberal Conference of 1966 in Alberta. As reform movements go, this one had some short-term success. One of its manifestations was the election of liberal-left governments in several of the provinces, and growing pressure on the federal government to alter some of its policies on foreign investment. Another was the formation of various independence movements across the country. The common theme was an independent Canada, but a liberal one, and one still safe for capitalism. The theme found its way into such non-revolutionary appeals as this, by the former leader of the British Columbia Liberal Party:

The Columbia River Treaty represents too much of what has been wrong with Canada for it to be dismissed today with a federal shrug. It was one of Canada's greatest negotiating disasters and represents what a continental energy policy should not be. That is a policy where Canada provides the resource, commits the land, suffers the ecological damage, and in the end finds that politicians have allowed it to be sold for a fraction of its true value. The real test of new political values is the determination to seek renegotiation of one-sided arrangements of which the Columbia River Treaty is a prime example.[29]

The statements of the New Left did not persuade the population, but they did influence its thinking. Though the more radical often expressed contempt for piecemeal reforms, their strongly worded attacks created reformers. Those who did not share their views sought ways of overcoming their complaints. Here is an analysis of both the situation presented by the separatists in Quebec, and the reforms required to modify it, given by a liberal social scientist to the House of Commons in 1971:

. . . We have witnessed a rising tide of dissent against the established order. Indeed, it would be inconceivable to speak of the crisis of Canadian federalism without mentioning that other crisis which, perhaps more radically, is shaking the very foundations of Canada's socio-political order. . . . The challenge is no longer directed against federalism alone: the socio-political system itself is being questioned. . . . It is therefore necessary, in the attempt to reform the structure and operation of the Canadian political system, to strive for a fairer socio-political order for all sectors of the population and all regions, and for the pre-conditions of genuine participatory

democracy, as well as for a new modus operandi between the two main
cultural groups, and between Quebec and the rest of the country. . . .[30]

The nationalist movement of the early 1970s received a boost
from an unexpected source in 1973. The Organization of Petroleum
Exporting Countries (OPEC) managed to become sufficiently cohesive to mount a battle for greater revenues from the multinational
oil companies. This obliged the industrial countries to pay more for
their vital energy source and to seek ways of avoiding continued oil-
dependence and of tapping new supplies. Alberta had large unused
supplies, but most of these were under the effective control of a few
large American oil companies. New reserves of gas and oil were
known to exist in the Beaufort Sea, and exploration for new sources
was occurring in the Atlantic, offshore from Nova Scotia and Newfoundland. The question was, would Canada benefit from these resource supplies, or would they be exploited by American companies
for the benefit of the United States? The nationalists argued strongly
for national protection of our energy supplies.

The "oil crisis" controversy in Canada was complicated by two
additional conditions. Resources are under provincial jurisdiction,
though international and interprovincial trade, taxing, transportation, and communication links are all under federal jurisdiction.
This complication underlay a continuing battle between the province of Alberta and the federal government after 1973, over which
government and territory had the right to benefit most from the oil
boom.

The second condition was the unresolved native land claims in
northern Canada. The Dene of the Mackenzie Valley and the Inuit
of the circumpolar north stood to lose a great deal if their cultures
and the northern wildlife were subjected to an influx of non-natives
attached to oil exploration and transportation, and without guarantees they would not gain from the added wealth of oil and gas
sales. The Berger Commission was appointed to investigate the native claims, and this Commission became a major public event
throughout Canada as Commissioner Tom Berger set out to make
the natives and their needs known to southerners. His final recommendations were that no pipeline be built through the Mackenzie
Valley, that a 10-year moratorium on an alternative route be instituted so that the natives could prepare themselves for the changes
and ultimately benefit from the boom, and that numerous protections be instituted for the environment and wildlife.[31] In stirring
language, he said:

We are now at our last frontier. It is a frontier that all of us have read about, but few of us have seen. Profound issues, touching our deepest concerns as a nation, await us there.

The North is a frontier, but it is a homeland too, the homeland of the Dene, Inuit and Metis, as it is also the home of the white people who live there. And it is a heritage, a unique environment that we are called upon to preserve for all Canadians.

The decisions we have to make are not, therefore, simply about northern pipelines. They are decisions about the protection of the northern environment and the future of northern peoples.[32]

What happens in the North, moreover, will be of great importance to the future of our country; it will tell us what kind of a country Canada is; it will tell us what kind of a people we are.[33]

The Mackenzie Valley was saved on that round, but an alternative route was advanced and the Canadian government indicated its intention to push ahead with the Alcan route. It also indicated an intention to increase Canadian ownership and participation in oil exploration and development, instituting the controversial *National Energy Policy* (NEP) in 1980. This was partly in response to nationalist sentiment, partly a strategy to offset Alberta's claims, and partly an attempt to allay the fears of the industrial interests in Ontario and Quebec. These groups would have had to pay world prices for oil if Alberta had its way. Ironically, of course, many of these industrial interests were under American ownership. Behind the Alberta government, pushing for world oil prices against central Canadian demands for lower prices, were the American oil companies. Thus even in the process of apparently defending Canadian national interests on the one hand, and Alberta's provincial interests on the other, these governments were tied to economic concerns outside Canada.

The *National Energy Policy* was controversial, but it was also short-lived. After the "oil crisis" of the mid-1970s, every country became involved in seeking out new supplies and reducing oil-dependence. No sooner was the NEP in place than the world price for oil began its steep descent. Within a year, Alberta was feeling the pinch of oil-glutted markets and low prices, and in the north, plans for proceeding with the pipeline were on the skids. A new federal government in 1985 dismantled the NEP. This symbol of Canadian nationhood was now history.

At the same time, the new Conservative government dismantled much else that was distinctively national or publicly-owned, and effectively dismantled the *Foreign Investment Review Agency*. It began negotiations with the American government for what was called "Free Trade," meaning the complete removal of all tariffs on goods going across the border. Since 85% of all goods traded bilaterally were already tariff-free, the thrust of this was ambiguous. Many nationalists observed that it appeared to have more to do with the Canadian government's desire to obtain more American investment in Canada than with trade.[34]

The issues were complicated when the United States, in a highly protectionist mood, began putting countervailing duties (tariffs by another name) on goods which had been freely traded with Canada for many decades, such as agricultural products and lumber. These countervailing duties were imposed when the United States declared that Canadian producers were being subsidized by Canadian governments (either provincial or federal). It became clear that Canadian government policies, both with respect to subsidies or other financial incentives to companies, and with respect to social services, could become components of the "free trade" negotiations. Clearly if this occurred, Canadian sovereignty would be that much further eroded.

By the middle of the 1980s, Canada was still an independent country in name. In the course of the previous few years, there were some indications of greater independence than in the 1970s. For example, several important unions had disengaged themselves from their American parents and established national organizations, including the United Auto Workers and the International Woodworkers of America (name to be changed when the move is finalized). With the immediate threat of Quebec separation past, and with Alberta suffering from the loss of oil revenues, it appeared that all regions of the country were again united. Formal American ownership of Canadian industries was declining, particularly in the western regions and in the resource industries. Their properties were being purchased by central Canadian financial companies, particularly the Bronfman family holdings, the Reichmann family holdings, and Power Corporation, headed by Paul Desmarais of Quebec.

But beneath these changes were events that did not support the thesis that Canada was coming of age. The unions were suffering severe setbacks as American capital moved out not only from Canada but as well, in important sectors, from the United States. Capital was moving to newly industrializing countries and into new technologies. The resource industries and some of the traditional steel-based industries in North America were in deep trouble, and parts of Canada, which had failed to develop an industrial strategy and diversify their industries during the affluent period, were reeling from the shocks. By the mid-1980s, the resource regions were suffering extremely high unemployment rates, small business bankruptcies, and depression, while central Canada—Ontario and southern Quebec—were experiencing growth and considerable affluence. This was a country divided, not united: the surface indicators were not telling the whole story.

8 THE NEW RIGHT

The popular way of thinking about political ideologies is to classify them as "right," "centre," and "left." The positions correspond roughly to positions on the equality-elitism continuum, with "left" closer to egalitarian beliefs and "right" closer to elitist beliefs. But if we use these terms, we have a problem in classifying what has come to be known as "the new right" because part of its message is neo-conservative, and part, libertarian. Referring again to the chart and descriptions in Chapter 1, we may note that conservatism and libertarianism have very different stances on the continuum from individualism to collectivism, even though both are on the "right" side of the equality-elitism continuum.

There are also quite different interest groups involved in the creation and nourishment of new right ideology. One is the international corporations, including those involved in the Trilateral Commission whose message is that the world requires more international planning and less democratic government. The second consists of assorted smaller forms of capital which favour a libertarian, ultra-free enterprise version of the new right. The third is the fundamentalist religion stream, featuring a combination of personal salvation and neo-conservative morality together with a persistent attack on communism defined with great latitude. These sources and messages differ enormously and are internally contradictory, but they come together in their attacks on democracy, equality, unions, many social services, and nationalism.

In this chapter, we will consider some of the statements made by libertarians, the publications of the Trilateral Commission, and the viewpoint of a major Canadian magazine, *The Plain Truth*. In the concluding chapter, we will consider how the rapid growth of the new right might be explained within the context of the changing global economy and Canadian society. It should be noted here that Canada is not the birthplace or central location for the new right, though one government (British Columbia under the Social Credit party between the early 1980s and 1986) took the new right as a guide for legislation, and other governments have introduced measures consistent with new right arguments. The new right is an international movement, with its central location in the United States but with institutes and publications in all the industrialized, capitalist countries.

The arguments that are propounded in the 1980s by libertarians are not new. Various insights are gleaned from such precursors as Say, Adam Smith, Hume, Locke, J.S. Mill, and deTocqueville. Hayek, the elder statesman of the movement, wrote his major work in the 1940s (*Road to Serfdom*, 1944) though he won his Nobel prize in 1974. But since the mid-1970s new scribes and prophets have emerged, and their ideas have been acclaimed by some governments and prominent individuals. As well, since the mid-1970s, a number of institutions have been established which actively propagate libertarianism through publications, conferences, and news releases to the press. The statements included in this study are primarily from the works of scribes elsewhere, who are quoted by Canadian adherents. The major exceptions are *The Plain Truth* magazine and the work of the Fraser Institute, both located in Vancouver, British Columbia.

1

The new right addresses some outstanding complaints and fears held by many people in the industrial countries. It provides simple answers to these. It argues, for example, that economic decline in these countries is caused by greedy unions and overgrown governments. The solution: attack unions and dismantle governments. It argues that there are too many freeloaders on the welfare system. The simple solution: get rid of welfare systems. It argues that children are not properly cared for, and that uncared-for children are the cause of juvenile delinquency and social problems. The simple solution: oblige women to stay home and care for children. Women are also responsible for broken families, high divorce rates, and numerous other social evils. The simple solution: prevent women from leaving husbands by cutting off all alternative sources of income. It argues that there are too many chiefs and not enough followers. The solution for this is to limit higher education to a few and decrease offerings that do not obviously lead to increased wealth, such as the social sciences and the arts.

Where social democratic parties enjoyed a certain prestige as moral consciences for their nations in the 1945–75 period, the new right has undermined that by frontal attacks on them. For example, where most citizens in that period would have agreed that "equality is a good thing," even if they would not support a social democratic party because "maybe they go too far with equality," (in other words, taking the liberal position), the new right advocates now argue that "equality is a bad thing," and argue that social democrats, even liberals, have misdirected the society by defending the rights of women, minorities, unions, the unemployed, and the handicapped.

The new right is radically opposed to equality and to all forms of state aid to the disadvantaged in our society.

The argument in defence of this anti-egalitarian stance is that there are "born leaders" who create the survival conditions for all others; hindered by regulations, high taxes, obligations, and other measures which are inconsistent with a totally free market, they are unable to lead. Ultimately, according to new right spokespersons, this is the cause of decline in the industrial economies and social fabric of the capitalist countries.

In libertarian arguments, individuals are motivated exclusively by wealth. Creative individuals will not produce unless adequately rewarded and uncreative individuals will not produce at all if they can obtain rewards without working. Society must provide special incentives to those with talent if it wants to receive returns on these: the talented owe nothing to society. The word "talent" refers to entrepreneurial skills.[1] Being musical, for example, is insufficient: one becomes talented only if one can persuade others to pay for one's musical performance. Thus everything people do can be measured by one yardstick: does it sell? An application of this idea was made by a senior vice-president of a major Canadian financial institution in November, 1986:

I believe that all professors should be obliged to develop revenue-generating projects as part of their responsibilities . . . a professor's ability to generate funds should be one of the conditions of tenure.[2]

The obvious objection to this is that entrepreneurial talent is but one dimension of human beings; to oblige everyone to be a salesperson above all else would be to deny society the aesthetic, intellectual, scientific, athletic, and numerous others gifts that its members possess. It would also deprive society of internal sources of dissent, and thus of visions of alternatives. This yardstick turns every talent into a commodity and values nothing which is not marketable.

The libertarians argue quite a reverse case. They say that the benefits of gifted individuals with something to sell are denied the society in which equality takes precedence over liberty, and the rewards of talent are taxed in order to sustain the "untalented." They say that this is what has happened in the Western world. Governments have so taxed the talented that they, along with Ayn Rand's fictional heroes,[3] have gone on strike. Taxation is a form of theft and it deprives society of the spontaneous innovations that only the talented can create. The ungifted in the democratic society receive benefits to which they are not entitled, and they demand equality which they do not deserve. Democracy equalizes unequals.

Says George Gilder: economic equality "tends to promote greed over giving." Democracy is flawed when it reverses "the appropriate direction of influence."[4]

In their opinion, the appropriate direction of influence would be achieved only if those who successfully sell their skills on the market-place obtain whatever rewards they can negotiate. These people would then establish businesses which would employ others, and thus everyone would become gainfully employed and society would benefit. They would employ others at the price others are actually worth, that is, according to how much profit they can make out of employing those others. Thus if someone does not work hard, the employer would dismiss them or pay them less, and if they produce a great deal, they would receive more.

The market-place, says Milton Friedman, is an information system: as prices rise, it informs people that they have to produce more in order to purchase goods; if prices are artificially maintained, they do not receive the message. If incomes bear no relationship to product prices then people become indifferent to prices; they then have no incentive to improve the quality and nature of their work because it will make no difference to their earnings or purchasing power. From this he deduces a wide range of applications, including the negative effects of rent controls, minimum wage requirements, unemployment insurance, and welfare. All of these are, in his view, unwarranted interference in the information system.[5]

"Supply creates demand" is a central slogan in new right theories. Demand is the artifact of successful management. The phrase refers as much to ideas as to commodities. Not only does supply create demand in the production of goods and services, but as well, and even most especially, in the sphere of beliefs and human desires.

Thus, Keynesian economics and the welfare state were imposed on the world after the Second World War not because these were essential to the prolonged prosperity of the industrial, capitalist societies, but because governments induced people to become dependent on them. From this framework advocates of new right ideology can deduce that welfare creates welfare recipients, minimum wage laws "penalize those with limited talents—the young and old, unskilled and handicapped," and "unemployment insurance creates unemployment."[6]

Said an Australian libertarian senator: "If you subsidize single parents you get more single parents. If you subsidize sickness benefits you get more sickness."[7] Said both the Fraser Institute and a British Columbia cabinet minister at almost the same moment: "Having programs in support of single mothers causes mothers to be single and need support."[8]

Libertarians are not persuaded that discrimination occurs, or that, in a free market-place discriminatory employment practices would survive. Says the Fraser Institute:

The market tests of profit and loss . . . tend to eliminate from the private sector (through bankruptcy) those who indulge in discriminatory practices. . . . Laws which control rent, set minimum wage floors, compel equal pay for equal work, enforce union wage levels, all retard market forces which tend to reduce discrimination.[9]

Following this logic, there is no need for a Human Rights Commission, a Status of Women Advisory Office, or special civil rights protections.

There should be, say libertarians, one test only for all social policies: do they sustain the absolute right of individuals to do whatever they please short only of physical violence to others or violence to property rights? This test ignores inequality of opportunity for individuals who have no property. For libertarians, individuals who begin in disadvantaged positions simply have to fend for themselves in an open market-place.

At the same time the new right, both in libertarian and religious forms, decries the disintegration of the family unit and generally blames women in the work-force for this. Women have proper roles in families, including the care of the elderly and sick as well as children. These roles have been usurped by the state. Women now demand state services because the state provides them, rather than because they originally wanted or needed them. In fact, they develop dependency on the state because families are so overtaxed that women are obliged to seek employment. Taxation, therefore, prevents women from meeting their family responsibilities.[10]

The cause of society's ills, in this view, is the growth of a middle class which has its foundations in the universities, colleges, mass media, and the public sector. This class depends on the welfare state for its employment, and it creates the climate of discontent with commercial activity. By turning on the intellectuals, media, and public sector, the new right implies—and some of its proponents explicitly state—that the working class is the natural ally of the ruling class. They share common enemies in the educated, urban middle class. Irving Kristol, in *Two Cheers for Capitalism*, says, for example, that the unusual feature of capitalism is that "its aim is the satisfaction of the 'common' appetites and aspirations," and the most persistent opposition comes not from industrial workers whose interests it serves but from the upper middle class which strives to usurp corporate power. The problem of American capitalism is not class inequality: it is, in his view, the lack of ideological legitimacy for the class hierarchy of a well functioning capitalist society.[11] It is at this point that libertarianism shades into neo-conservatism.

The Fraser Institute and other think-tanks established throughout North America, Europe, and Australia disseminate libertarian ideology. But it and others are financed by very large corporations. The Fraser Institute has an annual budget of $800 000 provided by the largest corporations in North America, some of which are not located in British Columbia, though the majority are the forest, mining, transportation, and insurance corporations with branches there.[12] Thus though the corporate and libertarian views differ especially with respect to the value of an unplanned free market, they clearly have some common interests and we need to enquire what these may be.

2

The initial and in many ways most important contributions to the neo-conservative strands of the "new right" came from the Trilateral Commission Reports in the early 1970s. The Trilateral Commission was a private organization established by David Rockefeller, originally including selected representatives of business, academe, politics, and unions from the United States, Western Europe, and Japan. It has since expanded its membership to other capitalist countries, but continues to be concerned with the need to include the emergent giant, Japan, in alliances with the previously dominant capitalist nations.[13]

One of the first reports written for the Commission was concerned with what its authors called "the distemper of democracy":

The heart of the problem lies in the inherent contradictions involved in the very phrase "governability of democracy." For, in some measure, governability and democracy are warring concepts. An excess of democracy means a deficit in governability: easy governability suggests faulty democracy.[14]

This is a radically different view of liberal democracy than that provided within liberalism, social democracy, or socialism. Essentially this is saying that the more the average citizen participates in democratic government, the less acceptable the outcome. Other features of the report support this contention, persistently attacking democratic governments and calling for more centralized, more hierarchical, and less open governments in nation states together with more co-ordinated action at the international level by all national governments.

Like the libertarians, the trilateralists blame intellectuals in universities and the mass media for the problems of democratic governments. They argue that this class has sabotaged capitalism and has taught the young to distrust corporations and businessmen. They say there is an "overproduction of people with university education in relation to the jobs available for them," and claim that this is unfair to "the lower class" who "pay for the free public education of the children of the middle and upper classes."[15] Similarly, the trilateralists attack the press for being critical toward government and public officials when they support corporate activities.[16] Again, there is an appeal to "ordinary" citizens who are subjected to the undermining of their own society by a force that has failed to perform its social obligations.

But the trilateralists do not entirely agree with libertarians. They are not opposed to all government. In fact they call for greater powers to government, and more power to specialists in government. There is, they argue:

... a need to restore a more equitable relationship between governmental authority and popular control. The steadily rising need for government to manage the interrelations of a complex society is likely to require an increase in the material resources and political authority available to government.[17]

They warn against "the internal dynamics of democracy itself in a highly educated, mobilized, and participant society,"[18] but not against government as such. They consider the democracies unable to "share a common purpose in combining, coordinating and developing internationally"[19] but none the less argue that certain changes should ensure that governments develop the capacity.[20]

The corporate world is not a world of individualists, not anti-government; but it is a world that requires governments to plan with reference to transnational corporate interests rather than the interests of ordinary citizens. One of the remarkable features of the trilateralist reports is frankness on this score. With reference to an apparent crisis in democratic states, for example, the major report says:

This crisis involves the problem of representation and the problem of expertise. Modern parliaments do not have the necessary expertise to maintain an effective check on the executive and their members cannot represent citizens adequately in policy-making debates since they have to rely on earlier, now meaningless cleavages to be elected.[21]

Entirely diverging from the libertarian message, the trilateralist report notes that:

The market economy, though far preferable to the state-run economy, does need some degree of modification if it is to be successful in providing all its citizens with a reasonable standard of living and the opportunity to work.[22]

In line with these observations, it warns against the devolution of power where this could conflict "with macroeconomic commitments to a better international economic order."

The message of trilateralism is not liberalism, but it is also not traditional conservatism. It does posit the existence of a ruling class and the legitimacy of that class's prerogatives, but has little to say about the mutual obligations between that class and workers. To fully understand where the trilateralists stand, we need to know more about the reshaping of the world economy, and the role of transnationals in it. We will examine this in the last chapter.

3

Libertarians and trilateralists provide economic and political messages which pull on assumptions about human nature, the family, "good" human values, and morality. Some of these assumptions are widely held amongst Canadians of every political persuasion, and some of the values are common to "the left" as much as to "the right." These common values become more apparent when we examine the overtly religious literature associated with the new right.

Here we discover, for example, considerable anxiety about the super-powers and the prospect of nuclear war; condemnation of extreme materialism, selfishness, and greed; urgings to readers to live moral lives in harmony with God's intentions and the bounty of nature; a longing for stable homes, families, communities, and societies. Some writers emphasize the need for world government in order to establish peace on earth; others stress the virtues of small and simple societies. Where socialists blame capitalism and capitalists for the evils of modern society, fundamentalist Christians blame Satan and the satanic influences on humanity. This is an important difference of course, but what is more striking to the reader of both literatures is how similar they are in identifying the problems. Their different explanations, even so, lead to very different proposals for solutions.

The Plain Truth is published by the Worldwide Church of God in Vancouver, and distributed free to news-stands throughout Canada and numerous other countries. One of its major services is to inform readers about books and radio and television broadcasts interpreting world events in terms of the Christian Bible and fundamentalist Christian beliefs. As well, it provides short interpretative articles. The basic themes throughout these are that Satan, God, Jesus Christ, angels and archangels exist, struggle for human souls, and ultimately determine the history of the world. This magazine is typical of a genre, and the ideas are similar to those of many other magazines and Christian groups. It is of interest to us here because its messages intersect with those of the political new right.

Among the concerns of this publication is the breakdown of the traditional family and, linked to this, the breakdown of traditional sexual morality. Citing biblical warnings against fornication and adultery, the writers admonish parents to keep their home in good order, forbid teenage promiscuity, and teach children to obey God rather than Satan. The same message permeates articles on various historical subjects, showing how good parents raise their children. The September, 1986 edition, for example, contains articles on pregnant teenagers and the importance of the Queen Mother in saving the British monarchy. In this concern, these writers are not alone. But the emphasis on family leads to other convictions that sharply depart from much of contemporary ideas about gender. For example, in an article about Bhutan, the author notes in passing that "men can be men. Women are happy to be women."[23] Thus the same basic concerns that motivate other social and political reformers are linked to versions of proper sex and age roles which diverge from both liberal and socialist versions. This emphasis appears in another setting: the ghetto. One writer argues that the ghetto could be erased if mothers changed their "unfortunate life-styles."

These mothers need to repent of complacency and instill in themselves, by seeking God's help and neighbors', a desire to achieve. To rise from public assistance to self-assistance.[24]

The writer explains how mothers should change their habits, and how governments should stop giving them handouts. Another article has a similar message to the unemployed.[25]

Another concern is the growth and expense of government. Quoting the Bible, Ronald Reagan, and Adam Smith, one article argues that all people should pay the same 10% rate in taxes:

Everyone would be in the same bracket. Those who have enough initiative

and resourcefulness to become prosperous would not be penalized for their
industriousness. (God doesn't penalize the prosperous tither. But people
often penalize those who honestly prosper).[26]

Many issues throughout 1985 and 1986 included chapters from
Herbert W. Armstrong's last book, *Mystery of the Ages*. The mystery
to which Mr. Armstrong refers is humanity's willful ignorance of
man's relationship to God. He argues that this has occurred because:

All nations have been deceived! (Rev. 12:9.) And the fact of this universal
deception makes certain the fact of a super DECEIVER! [sic][27]

Although ultimately the super deceiver is Satan, Armstrong argues
that Satan's message is carried through modern institutions, and
particularly the educational system which injects ideology into "the
unsuspecting minds" of the young; in particular, it teaches the "fable
of evolution."[28]

As these few examples suggest, the new right has considerable
support from Christian fundamentalism. Some politicians speak in
religious terms when they explain their political solutions. Others
use less religiously charged words, but argue their case against big
government, modern educational systems, and welfare systems in
terms that coincide with these.

4

We may examine the statements of the new right advocates in light
of class and corporate interests. The libertarian version is coincident
with the realities of small business enterprises. These businesses
must compete in the market-place, and they are not in a position
to hand on the costs of union-negotiated settlements to customers.
They are shouldering an increasing proportion of the costs of social
services as transnationals move out or shift investments and evade
taxes. The libertarian message might be expected to appeal to these
self-employed entrepreneurs for these reasons.

The corporate critique of democracy may be understood in terms
of the new international order within which the trilateralist member
corporations are the chief beneficiaries. They have an overriding
need to create new rules for a game that now has Japanese, united
European, and some newly industrializing nations competing with
American capital. They are inhibited from constructing these rules
to their mutual benefit by democratic national governments, each
of which is primarily concerned with the problems of their territories

and which have to be accountable to citizens of these territories. At the same time, such corporations are not seeking a completely free market-place. They, themselves, do not operate in such a market-place: they have and could be expected to want to continue to have preferred, low-risk conditions for their global investments. The attacks on democracy and unions via libertarianism provide some ammunition for reducing the constraints imposed by national governments, indeed for reducing the independent powers of national governments.

There are obvious sources of opposition to this version of Canadian realities: the unionized working class in the private sector, unorganized workers and especially those who are disadvantaged by gender discrimination, poverty in childhood homes, and handicaps of many kinds. But perhaps the strongest opponents of this ideology are the middle-class state-employed workers. This class is the chief beneficiary and proponent of expanded state services within democratic governments. Its employment is tied to the continuation of a large and expanding public sector. Thus it is not only the cost of the public sector to which the new right objects: it is a much deeper antagonism between two fundamentally divergent principles of social organization and the classes which support them.

5

But surely this is not a complete explanation. Without doubt, the economic dimension is closely related to the emergence of the new ideology. Yet the new right is not simply an expression of economic interests for business owners; it appeals to and has gained many adherents within the working class and amongst the same middle class which it attacks. What are the other realities?

One of the realities is the growth of unemployment and the increasing load of taxation borne by workers still employed. There may be genuine resentment of that burden and willingness to agree to a public philosophy which blames the victims and removes the sense of responsibility from others. There is also anger at organized groups—perhaps especially labour unions and civil servants, teachers, and hospital workers—which appear to be obstructing prosperity through demands that many unorganized workers see as excessive. The working class has always been divided by the numerous differences in occupational situations, income, opportunities, and stability of employment. At a time when unemployment dramatically increases, these differences grow, and resentments are fanned by explanations for the slump which cast the blame on other workers.

A generation raised on the assumption that people must earn their keep through paid labour now finds its children unemployed. Some parents blame "the system." Many blame their children, perceiving laziness in a generation that cannot find work. Amongst those who do have work, there is a sense of achievement and a sense that somehow those without work are lacking in initiative and willingness to work.

Another reality is a profound sense of anomie in Western societies. The 1960s and 1970s provided what many people felt was an overdose of personal freedom, and many people were hurt by this at a very personal level. For some part of the population, especially in the upper middle class, these two decades brought affluence but also personal dislocations and sometimes tragedies as women experimented with liberating options, and permissive childrearing turned out to have impermissible results. The success of "remake yourself" cults, of the authoritarian substitutes for religion such as AMWAY and EST appealing most particularly to the mobile middle class, attest to the unease with affluence too easily achieved, and the personal costs. Perhaps there is a strong undercurrent of guilt, and it leads to puritanism rediscovered. If these feelings underlie support for the new right, then it is surely paradoxical that what the new right is actually calling for is absolute liberty. It appears that what may be heard is the neo-conservative underpinning more than the libertarian overlay: the appeal to traditional family virtues, to closure of freedoms for women, to the end of sexual permissiveness.

The paradox is apparent in the actual policies promoted by new right advocates when in government. While calling for individual freedoms and the iron law of the market-place, the catchword of the new right has been "restraint." The word—not the budgets and financial implications, but the emotional connotation of the word—catches that sentiment. Restraint seems to mean discipline and the curbing of excesses. It can mean a more puritanical sexual code: it can mean women playing traditional motherly and wifely roles and men being unchallenged heads of families. It can mean obedience by children to adults, by workers to employers, by students to teachers, in short a more authoritarian society. It can mean the establishment of rules for everyday behaviour: rules that all are expected to observe so that everyone knows what to expect and how to behave. And while it can mean obedience, it also suggests courage, willpower, bravely taking control of one's life and accepting responsibility for one's own success—or other people taking responsibility for their own failure. These meanings may well be imputed to the new right message. For those with wealth, there is a happy joining of the sense of being courageous members of a revolutionary force in history and simultaneously keeping jobs and paying lower taxes. They have the chance to be born again without any serious inconvenience.

Not all adherents are upper middle class. Union members and the unemployed have responded to new right messages, whether in their economic attire or in religious forms. This sense of a society that has somehow gone sour and a growing fear of its diseases—nuclear war, AIDS, drugs, and tobacco—have led to disenchantment with the existing order. The vast majority of people in any society have limited access to information about the full nature of economic and social changes. It is not obvious to all laid-off geologists that the oil economy is in a slump because there was over-investment in the 1970s and a technological change away from oil-based energy: more obvious that there are governments which do not seem to know how to reverse the changes. It is not self-evident to the logger in British Columbia that eucalyptus trees grown in seven years in Brazil and Spain are about to replace softwoods in the processing of pulp: more self-evident that governments are failing to get him back to work.

The realities of the economic changes discussed in the concluding chapter, and most particularly the movement of capital from the industrialized countries and away from the resource industries, are not well understood. Few people have the time or the prior knowledge to study the changes as they are happening. But governments, unions, and taxes are obvious targets for frustrations. And it is these that the new right targets as the enemies of prosperity.

Ironically, though Canadians have never experienced a federal social democratic (let alone socialist or communist) government, and though it is capitalism, not socialism, which has reigned as the dominant ideology of the past 40 years, much that people appear to fear in the 1980s is blamed on "the left." The left has championed women's rights (and thus the breakup of traditional families); the left has spoken up for greater equality in the distribution of income (and thus dissuaded corporations from investing); the left has argued for national sovereignty (and thus inhibited foreign investment); the left has supported collective bargaining rights (and thus upped the price of labour). Social democrats find themselves on the defensive against a market ideology which would turn all goods, services, and people into commodities, and reduce the democratic constraints on corporate behaviour. A population seeking social change and moral renewal is tempted by an ideology which calls them to restrain their instincts, curb their demands for equality, and obey "natural leaders." This is not quite the same as the fascist appeals of the 1930s, but it does indeed have a resemblance.

There are serious deficiencies in the new right appeals. The market-place may be a suitable vehicle for exchange of many goods and services, but the history of industrial countries is filled with the struggles of the unprivileged to gain access to many goods and services which have otherwise belonged exclusively to the rich and powerful. These include parks, clean water, fresh air, and the right to use public roads and transportation, public hospitals, and public schools. Private ownership of everything leaves out of account the numerous services from which no one can make money but which are vital to a healthy society, such as institutions to care for the elderly, and care services for the handicapped and for children of working parents. Governments have grown largely in response to the demands of corporations for numerous services they provide, but as well they have provided social services to those who could not privately purchase them. These numerous services have aided the poor and less privileged, but they have equally aided the society as a whole: it is not by accident that Canada has enjoyed a long history of civil peace, nor that her citizens are able to walk city streets unmolested and enter public places without fear.

Much is made in this literature of the natural inequality of people, but that misplaces the argument. The question is not whether people are genetically equal in all respects (the simple division by sex makes it obvious that they are not). The question is whether some kinds of genetic combinations have an inherent right to more rewards from the social pool than others. For the social democrat, the socialist, and the communist, there is no acceptable reason for granting privileges on the basis of genes. For the conservative, corporatist, fascist, and those of the libertarian new right, genes together with inherited privileges constitute adequate reason for receipt of social privilege. But the conservative departs from the company of others on the elitist side of the political spectrum by arguing that the privileged have obligations toward others, and the new right denies all obligations.

In addition to this set of arguments there is the reality of inherited privilege: there is no evidence that those "at the top" are genetically different (let alone superior) from those "at the bottom." There is a great deal of evidence that with relatively few exceptions even during the expansionary period of American capitalism, those at the top have had unequal head starts. The family situation is the single most important condition for providing the next generation with the tools for climbing up social and economic ladders. If that is the case, then the entire argument about genetic endowments becomes irrelevant, and the question of opportunity structures must again be entertained.

The argument is made that if the privileged are given absolute freedom they will enable others to survive simply by pursuing their own interests. There is nothing in human history to suggest that this actually occurs: those with privilege and no obligations tend to protect their privileges and ignore the costs to others. In fact, the flight of capital and its relocation in cheap labour regions provides evidence of the tendency: the corporations, having such power, have chosen to ignore their obligations to the communities and labour force from whom they extracted their wealth in the past. As well, they do not enter the newly industrializing countries with the intent of enabling others to improve their conditions but rather with the intent of profiting from cheap labour. It is possible that their activity will enable some citizens in some previously underdeveloped countries to improve their situations, but the limits on that development are inherent in the form: the corporations engage in this activity only on condition that their shareholders are enriched.

The call for world government is appealing in a time of great fear of nuclear war. But it is not actually world government which is being advanced by private institutions whose members are transnational corporations. It is a world order in which these corporations establish the rules, and national governments are reduced to housekeeping systems for regional populations. The inherent contradiction between a completely free market-place and global corporations establishing rules for their expansion and competition is yet to be confronted. For the transnational corporations, the confrontation will be eased by the eradication of current impediments to their growth in what they once called "the free world." These include unions, liberation movements, and democratic national governments. That is the message of "the new right."

9 IDEOLOGY AND SOCIAL CHANGE

Human history seems to be a repetitious story about the rise and fall of empires. The Greek, the Roman, the Spanish, the Portuguese, the Dutch, the Austro-Hungarian, Pax Britannica, and finally Pax Americana—each imperial system in its turn exercised power over regions beyond the cultural group at its core; each was finally challenged, either from outside or from inside; each eventually declined, no longer able to dominate the world of its time. With each rise and fall of empires, human ideas about the social world, and about history, too, shift to encompass the new events.

In the 1980s, we are hearing a great deal about "the new economic reality" and similar phrases—"the new international division of labour" and "the new international order." These are imprecise ways of talking about a substantial change in the distribution of economic and political power, and associated changes in the way we produce goods and what we produce to maintain human subsistence. From some perspectives the events we are experiencing constitute a "crisis" in American capitalism. We are in the process of inventing new words and euphemisms to explain changes of a magnitude too vast for comfort.

1

We may be witnessing the beginning of the end for the American empire. If so, this empire had a shorter duration of uncontested world dominance than many of its predecessors. The foundations for dominance by America were established in the early 20th century and sealed during the inter-war period. When the contending European powers exhausted themselves in the second "world" war, the only power left with military and industrial plant intact was the United States. Uncontested, the United States fashioned the post-war world to its liking. Its statespeople created the institutions necessary for American control: the *General Agreement on Tariffs and Trade* (GATT); the *Bretton Woods Agreement* on the gold/dollar standard; the World Bank; the International Monetary Fund, and many others. Its military leaders created alliances and defence systems throughout the world, NATO and NORAD among them.

The affluence generated by the expansion of American companies and experienced in North America was unparalleled in history. Ordinary workers had life-styles and possessions beyond the dreams of many landed aristocrats of previous eras. By contrast, there was great poverty in much of the rest of the world, including many regions where American, and later, European and Japanese, companies extracted resources or produced goods.

This era began to pass in the mid-1960s, though it was 1980 before most of North America felt a real chill in economic conditions.

Many blame the "oil crisis" for the decline. In popular imagination, a few oil-producing countries (collectively dubbed "the Arabs" though Venezuela was a leading member of OPEC) "ganged up" and forced the industrialized nations to pay unforgivably high prices for energy. There is no doubt that the increasing cost of oil after the first OPEC price-rise was a contributor to what is now understood as the "crisis" of American capitalism. But it was only one of many contributors, and there is substantial evidence that the drop in United States economic growth began in the mid-1960s, a good eight years before OPEC mounted its opposition to American oil companies.[1] Besides that, if the cost of fuel was the major cause of America's decline, there would be no explanation for Japan's meteoric rise since Japan was far more dependent on imported oil than the United States, and overall fuel costs in Japan were very much greater.

The most obvious cause of decline was the re-emergence of competing centres: a reconstituted Europe in the form of the European Economic Community (EEC), and Japan. But this renaissance was combined with two important other conditions: one, the movement of capital from North America to newly developing countries for production of goods later exported to North America and its markets; and two, the technological revolution encompassing the integrated circuit.

First, we will examine the reconstitution of competing centres. Without doubt, American foreign aid made it possible for Europe and Japan to re-emerge as industrial centres. But as is usually the case with foreign aid, the aid worked in both directions. American expansion could only occur if other nations had purchasing power, and it was predicated on military alliances in Europe and Japan.

Individually, European nations would not likely have gained sufficient economic capacity to threaten American dominance. But combined as the European Economic Community, also known as the Common Market, Europe has become a formidable competitor. The formation of this unified Europe began in 1957 with the *Treaty of Rome*, encompassing a few European countries. Since then, gradually, most of Western Europe has become affiliated with the EEC. Sharing its internal resources and reducing internal barriers to trade, the EEC has a sufficiently great domestic market to sustain its production and provide it with the base for expanding abroad. Inevitably, European investors began to challenge American hegemony on international money markets, and contributed considerably to the monetary crises in the late 1960s. This culminated in the United States abandoning the gold standard and *Bretton Woods Agreement* (which established the dollar as the chief world currency) in 1971. From this time forward, the American dollar ceased to be the base measure for all other currencies.

Japan, used as a safe base during the Korean war and strategically important to the United States for maintaining hegemony in Asia, emerged as a major industrial power finally able to invade American domestic and foreign markets by the mid-1960s. The Japanese strategy included very close alliances between the reconstituted *zaibatsu* (pre-war ruling elite) and the Japanese state, with transnational operations closely monitored and co-ordinated, especially in the procurement of raw materials from places such as Canada and Australia, and in the production of computers and electronic consumer goods.

Japan now has favourable trade balances with almost every other country, and is the world's chief creditor nation. Trade flows have dramatically shifted from the Atlantic to the Pacific, much of these reflecting the internal movements of goods made by Japanese-owned companies in free trade zones throughout the Pacific to either Japan or third countries by Japan. In 1981, Japan's leading exports to the United States were cars, iron and steel plates, radios, motorbikes, and tape recorders. The United States leading exports to Japan were soybeans, corn, logs, coal, wheat, and cotton.[2]

In 1951 the United States' economy accounted for 30% of the world trade of the 16 leading industrial nations. By 1971, when Nixon dropped the gold standard, its share had dropped to 18%. Its share of the world's manufactured exports fell from 25% to under 17% between the early 1960s and late 1970s.[3] American economist Robert Reich cites these statistics:

By 1981 America was importing almost 26 percent of its cars, 25 percent of its steel, 60 percent of its televisions, radios, tape recorders, and phonographs, 43 percent of its calculators, 27 percent of its metal-forming machine tools, 35 percent of its textile machinery, and 53 percent of its numerically controlled machine tools. Twenty years before, imports had accounted for less than 10 percent of the U.S. market for each of these products. Between 1970 and 1980 imports from developing nations increased almost tenfold.[4]

As these figures indicate, the EEC, Japan, and other countries not only compete with American companies abroad, they also compete for the domestic North American market. Taking advantage of trade rules under GATT which were designed by American negotiators for their benefit, other nationals have penetrated American borders the same way Americans previously penetrated theirs.

Competition, then, is a major factor in the decline of American power. But in itself this doesn't explain the new economic reality. One must then ask, why were the EEC and Japan able to out-compete the United States? And one also has to ask whether the assumption on which such a question is based is reasonable any more: is it reasonable to talk about countries competing with one another? When we look at the new ownership patterns, the investment arrangements behind new companies, we discover that many of the transnationals belong no more to the United States or the EEC than to Kuala Lumpur and Singapore where they produce goods. They are global pools of capital without clear domestic links to any single country. We are still trying to understand the long-term implications of this development.

American corporations began their trek to other countries before the second war. With post-war expansion, this movement of capital abroad became much more significant. In 1950, foreign earnings of United States' corporations were about 10% of total after-tax profits. There were advantages to be gained from off-shore sourcing, as production elsewhere was called. An American company could establish a plant in a cheap labour region, often with financial and military aid from the governments of underdeveloped countries. Then, with the aid of constantly improving transportation and communications systems, they could import the goods to the United States and sell them at prices below the prices of competing goods manufactured by the same company in the United States. This process dovetailed with the microchip revolution: much of the production of the microchips themselves was done in underdeveloped countries, and the chips (lightweight and easily air-transported) were then returned to manufacturing units inside North America and Europe.

By the end of the 1960s, foreign earnings of United States' corporations had doubled from the 1950 figure. Bluestone and Harrison estimated that by 1978, taking into account all kinds of overseas co-production, licensing, and subcontracting arrangements, one-third of the overall profits of the top 100 American corporations and banks came from overseas investments.[5]

In effect, American companies, often now in joint ventures with Japanese and European companies, have created their own competition, producing goods in the newly industrialized regions and exporting them to the industrial countries. Some, after closing factories in North America, eventually reopen them but under new auspices without previous union commitments and with new technologies which have displaced labour. In the interim, the regions put on hold have suffered a sufficiently severe depression that local governments, unions, and communities praise the Lord and pass the ammunition for the return of employers at any cost. "Excessive" expectations have been shelved.

For example, the *Globe and Mail* reported in 1985 that Westinghouse Electric Corporation of Pittsburgh and Japan's Toshiba Corporation would establish a joint venture in New York State to produce the electronic tubes in colour television sets and computer display monitors. The new firm would employ about 700 people in a plant closed by Westinghouse in 1977.[6]

The *Globe and Mail* did not report, but others have, that the largest single block of off-shore shares in Toshiba is controlled by General Electric. As well, General Electric has over 60 licensing arrangements with Japanese firms, and 40% of a major subsidiary of Toshiba. These firms are licensed to make GE products for export, and since a 1969 strike against GE in the United States, Toshiba has provided electronic parts to American plants. Westinghouse, now linked with Toshiba and General Electric, began purchasing shares in Mitsubishi of Japan in 1923. Mitsubishi and its affiliated companies, together with Toshiba and its affiliated companies, sold electrical products in such increasing volume to the United States that as early as 1968 American imports of these from Japan exceeded exports.[7]

In such information lies a substantial part of the "new reality" which Canada, along with the United States and Western Europe, is now experiencing. It is the component of the "new international order" which is signally omitted from the new right's analysis of our economic woes.

The off-shore sourcing for American companies occurs primarily, but not exclusively, in industrial sectors that are labour intensive, and the primary, but not the only motivation, is cheap labour. The electronics and garment industries were the forerunners in relocation of their production systems in the Philippines and Southeast Asian free trade zones.[8] In effect, the free trade zones have become integrated spatial components in global production systems, under the control of transnational corporations rather than the countries in which they are located.

These developments raise doubts about the meaning of international trade. Countries are no longer the trading units. What we have now are transnational production systems which include portions of countries and which determine the comparative advantages of regions to their own interests. Australian economists recently estimated that about 40% of all world trade in the early 1980s was conducted entirely within transnational systems, between parents and subsidiaries.[9]

2

Simultaneous with these massive changes in the structure of capital, there has occurred a technological revolution based on the microchip. Every phase of industrial production has been affected by the new technology, and the transformation process is far from complete. The steel era (the era of cars and machinery based on steel) appears to be passing, as the telematics, or "information-intensive" technologies, fundamentally alter the way products are produced as well as the nature of the products themselves.

The early applications of automation technologies occurred in factories where the manufacture of discrete items (automobiles, electrical tubes, etc.) and continuous process items (chemicals, pulp, and the like) was gradually transformed. Many jobs at the bottom of the skill hierarchy were phased out, and many traditionally skilled jobs further up the ladder were so altered that the occupants were obliged to relearn their trades or seek other employment. The automated machinery provides its own check on productivity and quality of work, so that supervisory jobs also changed.

The later applications were even more profound, because they affected every kind of job. Design of machinery could be computerized, displacing many traditional engineering jobs, for example. Offices, banks, supermarkets, and many other "white collar" areas were computerized, phasing out numerous clerical and sales positions. With computers, the "hands on" management level of branch plants and regional offices became unnecessary: top management could supervise, control, and effectively co-ordinate work processes without middle level management. Many service jobs also became redundant as self-service banking stations and automobile gas stations were introduced. The professions are the next area to be computerized, and no doubt such traditionally labour-intensive areas as teaching, nursing, librarianship, various kinds of research, and professional services will undergo changes similar to those in offices.

These later applications have particularly affected women, because it was in clerical, sales, and these professional areas that women obtained employment in the post-war era. Any decrease in public sector services would also affect women, since the public sector has been a major employer for them.[10]

With computerization, mass production is no longer cost-efficient. Small runs of specialized products can be produced efficiently, and small factories or mills could be much more cost-efficient than large ones.

If a few organizations were able to control the technology, they could effectively control the global market. But the technology would be difficult to control, precisely because it is easily adapted to new uses and knowledge of its processes is already widely diffused. Its size makes it suitable for use in homes, so that one possibility is the gradual phasing out of large, centralized offices where all workers are brought together in a single place at the same work times.

The microchip revolution is thus not merely a technical change: it carries with it the capacity to fundamentally alter work, the composition of the labour force, skills, the income distribution, economic opportunities for women, and how we think about employment as well as whether we are able to find employment. It has the potential to create a very small elite with control of vast global empires, and it has the potential to do the exact opposite: destroy highly centralized bureaucracies and provide opportunities for small, technically sophisticated organizations and groups to create new goods and services for small and local markets. At this stage, we do not know which direction the society will take, nor whether the existing large corporations will be able to gain greater control of global markets using this technology. We have many questions about the future, and because it is so unclear, we have many speculations and considerable fear.

For the moment, corporations are concerned with the cost of introducing the new technologies. Changes are expensive. For those who initially created new production systems and products based on the new technologies, there were high marginal profits which offset the cost of the new plant. But as industries become tied to the new technologies, these marginal profits decline. Follower firms do not gain profits from investments in the technology; all they can do is try to stay in the game. All investors in a time of such transition seek ways of reducing their other costs, and also of reducing their commitments based on previous technological conditions. Their outstanding commitments, of course, are to labour.

Contracts with labour undertaken within previous technological conditions cannot be broken unless there are dramatic changes in labour's bargaining power. Those changes can be induced by closures of plants, shifting production off-shore, importing manufactured goods from cheap-labour regions while obliging higher-cost labour to suffer unemployment and, inevitably, declines in union membership and effectiveness.

Not all companies benefit through this process. Some fail in the attempt, and many which produce primarily for domestic markets are shoved aside by the "new" global competition. Some small firms are given life, however, because they become the contractors of a remarkable range of corporate services now "farmed out" rather than integrated into the corporate hierarchy, and they are highly competitive with one another for these contracts. For the time of transition this is a flexible way of employing labour without long-term commitments.

Overall, however, there is pretty solid evidence that employment is decreasing; that employment for women is decreasing at a particularly rapid rate; and that while small firms are staying alive, many firms, both small and fairly large, are not surviving the changes. Some writers call this a crisis. Some call it a "crisis of capitalism," others call it a "crisis of the democratic state." It is certainly a crisis for people who have been permanently disemployed in the process, for young people who cannot find an entry point to the job market, and for people who live in regions that have been "de-industrialized" through the departure of employing organizations.

3

For Canada the effects of these changes are as intense in an opposite direction as the effects of post-war expansion. Living in America's attic, a beneficiary of the American empire in its expansionary period, Canada has tended to accept American ideological leadership, to share the world view as well as the commodities and technology of the dominant empire.

Canada is in many respects an undeveloped country, dependent on the sale of raw or semi-processed mineral, forest, and oil products to the American giant. It has developed little by way of independent momentum, and now experiences the depression caused by the restructuring of transnational capital even more severely than the United States itself.

The impact was felt by Canada in the early 1970s when initial decreases in American ownership shares in Canadian industries occurred. At the time and until the mid-1980s this was interpreted as evidence that Canadian business was developing independent strength. The example of forestry shows how this surface appearance belies another reality: the exit of American capital.[11] Major American companies, including International Paper, Columbia Cellulose,

Rayonier (International Telephone and Telegraph is the parent company), Crown Zellerbach, and Mead have sold Canadian properties to Noranda, Brascan, Canadian Pacific, and two major investment companies. These Canadian companies have not pushed out the American companies, however, they have simply picked up properties as the forest companies have moved elsewhere or gone out of the forestry business altogether. Beneath the surface is a forest no longer plentiful, no longer unique. New technologies for production of faster-growing pulp logs in southern climates, a reduced demand for mass-produced lumber, electronic media displacing newspapers as advertising media, and several other factors make further long-term investments in Canada and also in the northern United States less profitable than investments elsewhere in forestry or in other industries altogether.

Specialty lumber made from softwoods may become an important commodity in time, but its profitable production will require smaller, highly automated mills, and investors are likely to hold back in building these until they are sure of the market, and they will likely seek a new labour force without the conditions that would be imposed now by existing forestry unions. Small automated mills would not require large numbers of workers. In diverse forms, this same general pattern affects other resource industries across Canada. It is as if Canadian resource industries were "on hold" while global changes in resource procurement strategies, and the nature of resources themselves, are worked out by investors beyond Canadian national boundaries.

Most of Canada is affected by changes in the resource industries. Southern Ontario and Quebec, being the central manufacturing regions of Canada, are more affected by changes in the automobile and electronics industries.

The penetration of American markets by Japanese auto-makers undercut the *Auto Pact* agreements by which Canadian parts producers and subsidiaries of American companies in Canada could ship specified products duty-free to the American market (or parent companies in the United States). Imported vehicles accounted for about 25% of North American sales in 1981, up 15% from the late 1970s, and some 80% of these imports were from Japan.[12]

The United States negotiated agreements with Japanese auto-makers to reduce exports but at the same time American auto companies linked up with Japanese manufacturers in numerous new ventures outside and inside the United States during the 1980s. The high price of the American dollar (which increased the relative cost of American labour) and the duty-free trade agreement between the United States and Canada briefly made Canada a useful location for parts and car assembly for American markets. At the time of writing (beginning of 1987), this advantage is a crucial condition of economic recovery in Ontario. And at this moment American companies are urging their legislators to renegotiate the *Auto Pact* in the course of the bilateral trade discussions with Canada. As well, the exchange value of the American dollar is rapidly declining. In this industry, then, the immediate consequences of global changes are somewhat contradictory. Canadians are not able to project far into the future, to plan their manufacturing economy; nor will that situation change as long as the major decision-makers about this and similar industries are located outside Canada.

In sum, Canada is suffering considerable economic decline as global capitalism shifts investments from northern to southern climates, from steel-based to information-intensive industries, from high-wage to low-wage regions, from countries with strong democratic traditions to those ruled by dictators and military juntas. We cannot predict, in 1987, how the overall restructuring will affect Canada in the long run. At the time of writing, the prospects are not favourable, but the technological and financial changes are of such great magnitude that the end results cannot now be foreseen. Possibly the west coast of Canada and the United States will become more integrally related to Japan and China; possibly central Canada will lose control of the western regions; possibly central Canadian provinces will regain industrial momentum but leave the rest of the country behind; possibly Canada as whole will join the underdeveloped part of the world, while Southeast Asia becomes a major centre of industrialism in the 21st century. All of these possibilities have been suggested by prophets (and economists in their more speculative moods). We will not attempt here to choose between them; what we are concerned with is how Canadians are responding to these changes.

───

4

Canadian federal government responses to the economic decline in the late 1970s and early 1980s included the introduction of monetarism, reductions in corporate taxation rates, and increased incentives to American and other foreign investors. The Foreign Investment Review Agency was turned into a foreign investment invitation agency. The *National Energy Policy* was dropped. There were moves toward deregulation of industries and privatization of crown corporations. Defence manufacturing was promoted. By the mid-1980s, the Conservative government had been engaged for many months in attempts to create a "free trade" union with the United States. Social services came under review, and some were dropped or decreased.

The Canadian government response shares with the new right some definitions of Canada's malaise: that the causes lie in excessive expectations, union demands, public sector growth, and an inability to compete in the global market. It does not explicitly recognize the actions of international or national capital. The government seems to assume that Canada could not possibly create its own industrial strategy, develop new products for new markets, or develop greater self-sufficiency in consumer and machinery goods for its own industries.

The federal government has not, however, taken a verbal offensive against democracy, civil rights, welfare, or education. There have been cutbacks, but to date these have been accompanied by apologetic statements about financial restraint. In this respect, then, the government continues to express its commitment to essentially liberal values even while taking actions that counteract liberal outcomes.

This is not the path taken by the United States federal government. Under Reagan, the American government did take a strong verbal position on democratic processes, civil rights, and welfare. The position taken was clearly consonant with the new right ideology. Similarly in Britain, under Thatcher's government, a new right rhetoric accompanied cutbacks in public spending on welfare and education.

In Canada, provincial governments have formal jurisdiction over welfare and education services. These governments differed in their responses to the fiscal squeeze they all experienced. Most notable in the early 1980s was the British Columbia (Social Credit) government, the only one to take a strong new right position and defend massive cutbacks in ideological terms.[13]

British Columbia has a long history of polarized politics. The proportion of the labour force in unions has been greater in British Columbia than in other provinces throughout the entire post-war period. British Columbia has been extremely reliant on a single resource industry, which was clearly in grave trouble by 1983. This was the province selected for the establishment of a new right institute 10 years before the confrontations of 1983. So the confrontation, when it came, was anticipated, though the vehemence of the opposition may have exceeded expectations.

Having announced enormous government cutbacks in the public sector, and legislation designed to centralize decision-making in the Cabinet, the government was faced with massive street demonstrations and the formation of a popular front coalition which came very close to calling a general strike.

The street fighters, under the banner of the Solidarity Coalition, were defeated by the government in negotiations; they called off a projected general strike only to learn, too late, that nothing was being offered by the government in return for their restraint. On the other hand, the government lost such credibility in the process that it limped along for the next two years, and its leader (Bill Bennett) was finally obliged to step aside so that the party could renew itself under a new leader. Parts of the new right program had been implemented—there were severe cuts in education and welfare expenditures, and decreases in public sector employment. But much that had been planned never became fact, and by 1987 the rhetoric of the new right had been greatly softened.

Governments do represent populations, if only in the sense that, when popular, they express what many people believe to be true. The fact that B.C. voters re-elected the Social Credit party does suggest that many, apparently a majority, had sufficient sympathy for new right perspectives that they preferred such initiatives to alternative policies of the NDP. At the same time, there were clearly limits to their tolerance for these policies: they voted for "restraint" in government spending, but not for decimation of public education, public welfare, or civil rights. This distinction was made in the B.C. election of 1986, and at the federal level during the 1980s.

In a time of such change, and especially when the changes are creating unemployment and economic dislocation, people search for explanations which carry with them possible solutions. The great difficulty for Canadians at this moment in history is that the dominant ideology, liberalism, cannot offer either explanations or solutions. It is an ideology that grows out of economic expansion, individual mobility, widespread affluence; it gave rise to the welfare state and expanded educational services. It has nothing in it which "automatically" explains a prolonged and apparently irreversible economic decline.

Those who describe themselves as liberals have argued contrary cases on the economic front—some supporting continentalism, others rejecting it. Some have agreed with new right attacks on the democratic state and welfare system; others have strongly rejected these. In short, there seems to be no clear line of defence for liberals: the ideology has failed to provide the "appropriate" responses to this new economic situation and the new right's definition of it.

At the level of scholarly inquiry, the liberal framework has addressed such questions as why individuals choose one product over another, one political party over another, one religion over another—

in short, questions about consumer choices and the marketing of products. It has informed us about human perception and cognition processes, provided manipulative tools such as IQ tests and job placement studies. It has led to concern with turnover rates in industry, with successful management techniques. But intellectually interesting as such subjects may be, they do not constitute a theory of society to which one might now turn with hopes of understanding the profound economic changes now occurring.

If liberalism does not constitute a theory of society at the level of scholarly inquiry, it does so even less at the level of popular ideology. The individual is given a barrage of daily news, but none of it explains how the society is organized or why the various powers are acting as they do. From every side there are terrors: pollution, climatic changes, nuclear war, Russian aggression, Muslim fanaticism, Third World terrorists, increasing crime rates, inflation, depression, unemployment; all are documented, but none are explained.

The individual is thrown back on himself or herself, required to explain genuine frustrations, tensions, and failures in a social vacuum. The "middle class" in particular faces a dilemma. Its members have denied the existence of a class structure, and thus perceive no relationship between themselves and the rest of the working class. Their existence and identities rest on the expansion of capitalism. Yet their children cannot be guaranteed positions on the same level as the parents. Their job opportunities are declining and they cannot assume further personal mobility. In a depression, they cannot be assured of employment; their nurtured expectations exceed present realities. The previous upward mobility has been achieved at the cost of an extensive kinship network or genuine community, so there is no personal anchor in a social group that might soften the anxieties of downward mobility.

Some people react to this dilemma with anger against obvious scapegoats: the organized workers who demand higher wages, some of whom are earning wages exceeding those of professionals and the lower corporate officers contrary to the belief in the congruence between education and income; and the recipients of welfare on whom high taxes can be blamed. The cure to such social "evils" may be seen to be a stronger state that can "curb" the inflationary demands of the greedy workers and oblige the parasites to stop being a burden on the taxpayers.

Some react by submitting themselves to one or more of the vast range of leadership cults which at one and the same time provide a social group and recreate the illusion that only the individual matters. On the promise that their personal horizons will be expanded, they agree to metaphorically strip themselves before others, remove their own "face" and demand of others that they also deprive themselves of all the traditional means by which human beings maintain dignity, self-respect, and distance. It is apparently believed by such cult members that the total loss of privacy and reserve will somehow allow them to "find" themselves. "Tell me, God, who am I?" seems to be the quest of the society that has no theory of society, no social cohesion, and no social goals. It is the submission of a society to whichever powers will play God, strip its members of their fears and sense of isolation, and tell them, at last, how to behave.

By way of example, one of the popular middle-class cults, a multi-million dollar invention of a successful encyclopaedia salesman, induces thousands of affluent individuals to subject themselves to many hours of harangues during which they are repeatedly told they are "assholes." The objective of this exercise, sponsored by the Erhard Seminars Training business, is to "give" these disciples something imaginatively called "it." "It" turns out to be themselves, but a transformed self who believes that he or she is responsible for everything that happens in his or her own life and is therefore doing and being whomever he or she actually wants to do or be. These students emerge, apparently pleased with the results. Some American businesses are reported to prefer "EST" graduates as workers, and advertise for them.[14]

The voluntary submission to such cults by the middle class is somewhat similar to the submission of members of the working class to various religious sects, except that what the middle class seeks through these immersions is personal identity and assurance that they are acceptable human beings. The working class, in its support of many fundamentalist Christian sects over the past century and more, has sought solace for its material deprivation. One may be reminded, but now with a sense of historical irony, of the warning of the early Christians: "For what is a man profited, if he shall gain the whole world but lose his own soul?"[15] The middle class has grown, contrary to the Marxist prediction, and has become materially affluent; its impoverishment has been of a different kind.

The message of EST and of many other middle-class cults has the function of assuaging the fears of its adherents; but as well it uses a liberal rhetoric to justify an inequality that is not liberal. If I "choose my own parents" as the EST graduates are encouraged to believe, and I am exactly whomever I myself create, then this must be true as well for everyone else. I—and they—have only ourselves to blame: there is no class structure, no state, no corporate power. Politics is an illusion, the economy exists in the imagination. Poverty is the fault of those who are poor.

These escape mechanisms appeal to rootless people. Fortunately, not everyone is rootless; not everyone is a willing prey to cult sharks. As large portions of Canada remain in a prolonged depression, many members of the middle class are expressing concern with the growth of poverty in their midst, with the persistent attacks on welfare and unions, and with the erosion of civil democratic forms. Food banks are no substitute for full employment and decent standards of living for all, and as the line-ups continue, many who are still employed become increasingly distressed by this evident failure in their society. Whether as socialists seeing this in class terms, or as liberals seeing this as an inexplicable weakness in the system, a substantial number of middle-class Canadians are aware that poverty is the forerunner to a disintegrating society.

It is perhaps a measure of the fundamental decency of Canadians bred in a liberal tradition that the new right appeal has not found more fertile ground in this country. It reached the zenith of its popular appeal early in the 1980s, and by 1986 criticism had mounted. At the time of writing, at least, one does not fear that Canada is plunging into neo-facism, its many problems notwithstanding. But evident in the confused responses to the new right and the economic changes are basic weaknesses in liberal ideology; among these, a failure to clearly specify the role of the democratic state in a capitalist economy.

The democratic government is easy prey to the new right when citizens themselves are unsure what precisely they can expect from democracy, what exactly it means, and how much it depends on the consent not only of the population at large, but as well and most particularly, the owners of large amounts of capital.

Some fractions of international capital clearly have little respect for democracy. A Canadian executive of a large corporation expressed his view of this several years ago in a most revealing way:

If what we really need is a free and responsible society, corporate power is the desirable counter-force to the excessive power of government. Modern government is unresponsible [sic] to the taxpayer because of the way the franchise has been extended. It responds mostly to the demands of people with no stake in society. The corporation represents those who do have a stake in society—the stockholders. The fact that developing nations must tailor their policies to big corporations is all to the good. It makes rather irresponsible government more responsible. They have to compete for favours from the more responsible elements in society. The multi-national corporation is a great force for internationalism.[16]

This is a long way from the version of society offered by the liberal democrats. It has, in fact, overtones of the Family Compact ideology as expressed by Sir Francis Bond Head in the 1830s. The difference is in the unit envisioned as the ruling class: no longer discrete families, but rather corporations. There is no pretence here that democracy is to be honoured. Democracy is that "radical reversion of the pyramid of society" to which Sir Bond Head referred.[17]

Who are the people with no stake in society? Apparently they are the opposite of stockholders, yet people to whom the franchise has been extended: voters who are unemployed, peasants who are marginal to the corporate economy, people who are not convenient to, or needed by, the corporations. Their numbers have steadily increased as the need for labour in the industrial countries has diminished. This is a view of society congruent with the sentiments of the new right.

The central thrust of this sentiment is to demean democratic government. When we turn to the neo-Marxist literature on democratic government, we also find it demeaned. Both identify the incompatibility of capitalism and democracy. The new right argues for the dismissal of democracy so that capitalism might flourish. The neo-Marxist left argues for the overthrow of capitalism so that a more extensive form of democracy might be introduced. In much of the neo-Marxist literature, the forms of democracy now in place in industrialized countries are "bourgeois" facades, serving only to "legitimate" the capitalist state. A forerunner to this view, Engels expressed the argument this way:

... in order that these antagonisms, classes with conflicting economic interests, shall not consume themselves and society in a fruitless struggle, a power, apparently standing above society, has become necessary to moderate the conflict and keep it within the bounds of "order"; and this power, arisen out of society, but placing itself above it and increasingly alienating itself from it, is the state. ... the modern representative state is the instrument for exploiting wage labor by capital.[18]

One of many contemporary phrasings along the same line comes from American neo-Marxist theorist, James O'Connor:

The State must involve itself in the accumulation process, but it must either mystify its policies by calling them something that they are not, or it must try to conceal them.[19]

Thus the new right and the neo-Marxist left both treat contemporary forms of democracy with disdain, the one because it fails to fully look after the interests of the dominant class, the other because it enables that class to exploit wage labour. Democracy, in the second view, is an ideology which masks the reality of state support for corporate accumulation.

When both extremes argue against the democratic state, one might conclude that neither view is accurate. The democratic state apparently has some independence, and is neither the captive of big business nor the champion of workers. Another way of thinking about the state is to recognize that it exists within and has no final control over the capitalist economy. If the process of accumulation falters or fails, there is no economic base for the process of government. This defines the constraints on democratic governments, rather than their behaviour inside those constraints. They may undertake activities which do benefit workers, or benefit workers as well as corporations, but cannot extend beyond the limits imposed by the accumulating activities of corporations. When those corporations are not domiciled within the national economy, the national democratic state is severely constrained in the scope of independent activity it can undertake. This does not make democracy a sham; it indicates, however, the severe limits for democratic governments.

Under the barrage of criticism from both the left and the new right, democratic governments may lose their credibility with the population at large. Where citizens are still immersed in a liberal ideology, still cherishing expectations that are no longer realistic in a depression economy, still expecting government to care for them even if they are not stockholders, there is shock when governments support corporations while reducing welfare provisions. As lamented by the Task Force on Canadian Unity: "The rather rough-and-ready consensus which once ensured the reasonably effective governing of the country is at the point of breaking down."[20]

Fifteen years ago, it (the central government) stood high in the minds of a large number of Canadians, and was widely regarded with respect and a feeling of loyalty. . . . Today that is much less true.[21]

The solutions proposed by the task force were in no way related to such possible causes as the magnitude of corporate power, foreign ownership, lack of community control over local resources, the rigidities of the class structure, the persistence of poverty, or the threats to the security of the middle class. Instead the task force proposed a division of powers between the federal state and provinces similar to that which presently exists, and a renewed commitment to democracy, federalism, human rights, the law, equality of opportunity, and cultural diversity: all the noble sentiments embedded in liberalism, together with the conventional refusal to acknowledge grave economic problems and real inequalities that have grown with the global economic restructuring. The task force managed to demonstrate the basic flaws of liberal ideology in its blindness to economic realities.

Even so, there is no evidence that Canadian voters have abandoned democracy. Unlike the United States, the Canadian participation rates in elections have remained high over this decade of change. This is small but not insignificant evidence that democracy, whether as ideology or as a form of government, is still dear to many Canadians. It is also a small but not insignificant indication that neither the Marxist left nor the new right has persuaded voters to give up on a cherished institution.

Democracy may well be a weak institution; democratic governments may well be so constrained by large economic units beyond their control that even when they do not share an ideological perspective with capital, they are unable to seriously alter the social conditions of the population. But democratic governments none the less are much more able to respond to public pressures than dictatorships, much more accountable to ordinary citizens, and much less easily provoked into using force. Three centuries of struggles have been invested in the creation of democratic forms, and three centuries of talking about democracy have created a strong democratic ideology. One needs to beware of those who would dismiss that struggle and that ideology for any reason, least of all because it is imperfect.

6

Socialism implores us to create a more humane and egalitarian society. The fundamentalist religions cry out for a less permissive, more disciplined society. Liberalism speaks for the virtues of individual freedom tempered by compassion and the rule of law. These are ideologies of our time and place, and whether we agree with one or another of them, they all suggest that Canadians desire a well-ordered, kindly society. Perhaps, besieged on every hand by hucksters and sectarians, they wonder how that is ever to be achieved, but at this moment, in any event, they do not seem to be prepared to adopt perspectives that justify genocide, racism, extreme inequalities, harsh justice, or a completely free market economy.

The dilemmas are many. How do we create an industrial society, whether its productive mechanisms are publicly or privately owned, in which apparent opposites are combined in the perfect mixture? How, for example, can such a society motivate its most talented (in the broad, not the narrow sense of that term) to provide their gifts to the society at large without disproportionately enriching those blessed with talent? How is excellence to be posited as a goal unless excellence is especially rewarded? How would surplus be accumulated for the development of more humane technologies, if everyone were fully and equally paid for their labour? How would standards be established and achieved if there were no hierarchy of authority, no adjudication, no judges? How could we be both more equal and more disciplined, more compassionate and more rigorous? Are we prepared to lose equality in favour of discipline, or the reverse? How much equality are we willing to give up in order to maintain high degrees of individual freedom; or, conversely, how much freedom are we willing to forego in order to increase equality? How can everyone be employed, and if full employment is beyond possibility, how can everyone be assured of sufficient income to survive? How can the quality of life be improved by the new technologies?

These are questions that go beyond the problem of property rights. But all of them are also questions of property because the ownership of technology has profound implications for its uses, its direction, its benefits.

The traditional platform of the left has included public ownership of the major means of production. This has long been believed to be the only way of avoiding a situation where one small class controls the conditions of life for everyone else. The obvious objection to this proposal is that where one agency—the state—is both the only employer and the political decision-maker, too much power is concentrated in the hands of government officers. Another objection is that the state bureaucracy would become unwieldy, and, having no market accountability to rein it in, could become abusive. These are serious reservations, even where it is acknowledged that the present arrangement also concentrates too much power in the hands of corporate decision-makers. Is there another solution to private property rights?

Both right-wing and left-wing proposals for decentralization of economies have been advanced in Canada and elsewhere. Both object to the mass society, standardization, mega-projects, centralized governments, and the enormous control over people's lives held by a few corporate directors and/or political leaders. The right-wing version argues in favour of dismantling central institutions and letting individuals have the freedom to redesign small scale social institutions via the market-place. Left-wing versions are concerned with providing communities and worker co-operatives with decision-making rights over resources and industries in their regions. There are clearly very different forms of decentralization, but they are equally concerned with dismantling centralized governments and huge corporate empires.

Some arguments for devolution of political power and decentralization of economic power go beyond these in advocating the abandonment of industrial society altogether. Re-creation of simpler, rural societies operating with small technologies and regional rather than world markets is the objective of some groups. These alternative visions may grow through the final decade of the 20th century. They have not yet become embedded in widely adopted ideologies, though their proponents' concerns with the environment and conservation have already affected the values of Canadians with other ideological perspectives.

The new technologies themselves may create a post-industrial society as some prophets argue. Production of concrete goods may become a relatively small activity in the total world economy, while trade in information becomes the major activity. Possibly information-intensive societies would not need to "conquer" nature or destroy natural environments as industrial society has done for the past two centuries. Again, the question is, who would control the information flows, who would have access to them, who would make decisions about employment, leisure time, distribution of wealth, and uses of information? What would be the nature of a government if information industries remain in private hands subject to the market conditions for profitability?

To re-create a society in which all members have some decision-making capacity about the economy and social institutions which shape their lives; to redesign technology so that it serves people rather than corporate organizations; to redevelop regional societies so that they are neither so small that they lack internal capacities to maintain small industries and cultural institutions, nor so large that they destroy human aspirations and relationships; to conserve and live peaceably with the earth: these are goals worthy of our energies. In the end, it does not matter whether we label such goals liberalism, conservatism, socialism, or some new *ism* invented for such a purpose. What matters is that collectively human beings strive for goals more noble than the turning of all life into market commodities, and find means of living peaceably together. To do this, they need both a high measure of equality and the personal freedom to express their talents and wishes.

Ideologies are by their nature limited versions of complex realities. They take a single value or a few related values and posit the perfect society as the one which maximizes these: equality, individual freedom, the unhindered market-place, an end to class rule, or a legitimation of class rule. One begins to move beyond ideology by recognizing that societies cannot maximize one value without simultaneously decreasing many others. One cannot have perfect equality without loss of personal freedoms; nor absolute freedom without creating great poverty for much of the population. To recognize this is the beginning of a theory of society. To worry about it, recognizing that one has no perfect solutions, is the beginning of a voyage beyond ideology.

NOTES

CHAPTER 1: IDEOLOGY AND SOCIAL ORGANIZATION

1. Max Weber, *The Protestant Ethic and the Spirit of Capitalism* (New York: Charles Scribner's Sons, 1958, 1904).
2. Christopher Middleton, "The Sexual Division of Labour in Feudal England," *New Left Review*, Vol. 113–114 (January–April 1979) pp. 147–168.
3. Joseph Schumpeter, *Social Classes/Imperialism*, translated by Heinz Norden (Cleveland: World Publishing, 1965), p. 67.
4. Karl Marx, *Capital* (1867), translated by Samuel Moore and Edward Aveling (New York: International Publishers, 1967), Vol. 1, pp. 762–763.

CHAPTER 2: INDIVIDUALISM AND EQUALITY

1. At the level of sociological theory, the leading proponents of this perspective on industrial society are Talcott Parsons, Marion Levy, Kingsley Davis and Wilbert Moore. The most systematic attempt to apply this system to the Canadian social structure is that by Daniel W. Rossides, *Society as a Functional Process: An Introduction to Sociology* (Toronto: McGraw-Hill, 1968).
2. For a discussion of subjective class membership, see Peter C. Pineo and John C. Goyder, "Social Class Identification of National Sub-Groups," in J.E. Curtis and W.G. Scott (eds.), *Social Stratification in Canada* (Scarborough: Prentice-Hall, 1973), pp. 187–196.
3. For a critical perspective on this generalization and a more extended discussion, see J. Paul Grayson and L.M. Grayson, "Class and Ideologies of Class in the English-Canadian Novel," *The Canadian Review of Sociology and Anthropology*, 15:3 (August, 1978), pp. 265–283. A discussion of regional differences is provided in Patricia Marchak, "Given a Certain Latitude—a (Hinterland) Sociologist's View of Anglo-Canadian Literature," *In Our Own House: Social Perspectives on Canadian Literature*, edited by Paul Cappon (Toronto: McClelland and Stewart, 1978), pp. 178–205.
4. Lord Durham, *Report*, 1839. Selections are given in J.M. Bliss (ed.), *Canadian History in Documents* (Toronto: Ryerson Press, 1966), pp. 50–62. For a review of the historians' interpretations of Canada, see S.R. Mealing, "The Concept of Social Class," *The Canadian Historical Review*, 46:3 (September, 1965), pp. 201–218.
5. In the literature prior to the publication of the first edition of this book, there were some exceptions noted, including Gustavus Myers, *A History of Canadian Wealth*, reprinted by James Lewis and Samuel, 1972; and Stanley Ryerson, *Unequal Union* (New York: International Publishers, 1968). Since that time the

exceptional literature has greatly increased. A number of historians, together with other social scientists, have undertaken a "revision" of Canadian history. Their views are discussed further on in this text.

6. John Porter, *The Vertical Mosaic* (Toronto: University of Toronto Press, 1967), Chapter 9; Wallace Clement, *Canadian Corporate Elite, An Analysis of Economic Power* (Toronto: McClelland and Stewart, 1975).

7. Revenue Canada, *Taxation 1983, Taxation Statistics.* (Ottawa: Minister of Supply and Services, Canada, 1985), Summary Table 2, p. 32.

8. Senate, Special Committee on Poverty, *Poverty in Canada* (Ottawa: Information Canada, 1971), Table 2, p. 12.

9. Economic Council of Canada, *Fifth Annual Review* (Ottawa: Queen's Printer, 1968).

10. National Council of Welfare, *Bearing the Burden/Sharing the Benefits* (March, 1978); *The Working Poor* (June, 1977); *The Hidden Welfare System* (November, 1976); *Women and Poverty* (October, 1979); *Jobs and Poverty* (June, 1977); *Poverty Lines* (annual); *Poverty Profile, 1985* and others; all published in Ottawa by the Council.

11. National Council of Welfare, *The Working Poor.*

12. National Council of Welfare, *1986 Poverty Lines*, p. 5.

13. Porter, *The Vertical Mosaic*, p. 112.

14. National Council of Welfare, *Women and Poverty*, p. 20, and Table 3.

15. Statistics Canada, *Income Distributions by Size in Canada, 1984*, Table 21, (Ottawa 1984).

16. This appears to be the meaning of middle class which persons in this income bracket themselves adopt.

17. Dominion Bureau of Statistics, *University Student Expenditure and Income in Canada, 1961–62*, Part II, (Ottawa, 1963), Table 16. See also, Minister of Industry, Trade and Commerce, *Post-Secondary Student Population Survey, 1968–69* (Ottawa: Queen's Printer, March, 1970), Table 23.

18. Max von Zur-Muehlen, *The Educational Background of Parents of Post-Secondary Students in Canada* (Ottawa: Statistics Canada, March, 1978), Tables 16 and 22.

19. Leonard Marsh, *Canadians In and Out of Work, A Survey of Economic Classes and Their Relation to the Labour Market* (Toronto: Oxford University Press, 1940) p. 243. This remarkable study of the pre-war class structure in Canada has been largely overlooked by Canadian scholars.

20. Porter, *The Vertical Mosaic*, Chapters V and X–XVIII.

21. Canada, Department of Labour, *Women in the Labour Force*, annual (Ottawa: Information Canada).

22. Economic Council of Canada, *Towards Equity* (Ottawa: Minister of

Supply and Services, Canada) p. 2; and *Women in the Labour Force,* Part I (Canada: Dept. of Labour, 1983), p. 33.

23. National Council of Welfare, *Poverty Profile, 1985.*

24. W. Kalbach and W. McVey, *The Demographic Basis of Canadian Society* (Toronto: McGraw-Hill, 1971), Fig. 8:6, p. 209, and Table 10:8, p. 258.

25. Royal Commission on Bilingualism and Biculturalism, *Report,* Book III, Part I (Ottawa: Information Canada, 1969).

26. Jacques Brazeau, "Quebec's Emerging Middle Class," *Canadian Business* (March, 1963), pp. 30–34, 39, 40, provides an early analysis of these trends.

27. The changes are outlined in several essays in *Quebec. State and Society,* edited by Alain G. Gagnon (Toronto: Methuen, 1984). See especially, essays by Marc Renaud, Jorge Niosi, and Pierre Fournier.

28. For a long discussion of the differences in mental attitudes and life-styles between the industrial and pre-industrial people see Karl Polanyi, *The Great Transformation* (Boston: Beacon Press, 1944).

29. The phrase, now generally applied to any work ethic, derives from Max Weber, *The Protestant Ethic and the Spirit of Capitalism* (New York: Scribner and Sons, 1958).

30. National Council of Welfare, *Bearing the Burden/Sharing the Benefits,* and *The Hidden Welfare System.*

31. National Council of Welfare, *The Hidden Welfare System,* p. 17.

32. Revenue Canada, *Taxation 1983, Taxation Statistics* (Ottawa: Minister of Supply and Services, 1985), Table 2, p. 59.

33. See for detailed analysis, National Council of Welfare, *Bearing the Burden/Sharing the Benefits* (Ottawa: March, 1976), p. 11.

34. There is evidence that this is not due to the disinclination on the part of women to join unions, but is due, rather, to the failure of union organizers to adequately represent those women who are organized in unions that also represent men, and to the difficulty of organizing workers who are employed in small offices and shops. See, for studies of women in unions, P. Geoffroy and P. Sainte-Marie, *Attitude of Union Workers to Women in Industry,* Study No. 9, Royal Commission on Status of Women (Ottawa: Information Canada, 1971); and Patricia Marchak, "White Collar Workers and Unions," *Canadian Review of Anthropology and Sociology,* 10:2 (May, 1973), pp. 134–147; and Marchak, "Les femmes, le travail et le syndicalisme au Canada," *Sociologie et Sociétés,* Vol. 6, No. 1 (mai, 1974), republished as "Women, Work, and Unions in Canada," in *International Journal of Sociology* (Winter 1975–76), pp. 39–61.

CHAPTER 3: FREE ENTERPRISE IN (RELATIVELY MORAL) NATION STATES

1. For a long discussion of the theories of economic history in Canada

see Daniel Drache. "Rediscovering Canadian Political Economy," *Journal of Canadian Studies*, Vol. XI, No. 3 (August, 1976), pp. 3–18. One of the early proponents of this view was W.A. Mackintosh, see for example, "Economic Factors in Canadian History," in W.T. Easterbrook and M.H. Watkins, *Approaches to Canadian Economic History* (Toronto: McClelland and Stewart, 1967) (essay written in 1923), pp. 1–15. The Economic Council of Canada does not state this view explicitly, but implies it throughout many publications, including *Living Together, A Study of Regional Disparities* (Ottawa: Minister of Supply and Services, 1977).

2. Lester Pearson, *Canadian Liberal*, X:1 (September, 1958) p. 2.
3. John Stuart Mill, "On Liberty" (1849), in *The Utilitarians* (Garden City, N.Y.: Doubleday, 1961), pp. 479 and 484.
4. Lester Pearson, *Canadian Liberal*, X:1 (September, 1958) p. 2.
5. Edmund Burke, *Reflections on the Revolution in France* (1970) (Harmondsworth, England: Penguin Books, 1968).
6. Cited in Kenneth McNaught, *The Pelican History of Canada* (London: Penguin, 1968), p. 190.
7. Government of Canada, *Foreign Direct Investment in Canada* (Ottawa: Information Canada, 1972), Table 1, p. 15.
8. *Ibid.* The higher proportion of control as shown in Table 2, p. 16, indicates a more rapid growth in control than in ownership. American firms account for 80% of foreign control.
9. Corporations and Labour Returns Act, *Report 1983* (Ottawa: Statistics Canada, 1986), Part I, p. 44.
10. *Ibid*, p. 23 and text Table 1, p. 26.
11. *Ibid.*, Tables 9, 10 and text, p. 25.
12. *Ibid.*, Table 9, p. 25.
13. Kari Levitt, *Silent Surrender* (Toronto: Macmillan of Canada, 1970), p. 64.
14. Government of Canada, *Foreign Direct Investment in Canada*, p. 26. Reproduced by permission of Information Canada.
15. *Ibid.*, p. 52.
16. *Eighth Report of the Department of Defence Production, 1958* (Ottawa: Queen's Printer, 1959), p. 26. Reproduced by permission of Information Canada.
17. For an account of this see John W. Warnock, *Partner to Behemoth, The Military Policy of a Satellite Canada* (Toronto: New Press, 1970), Chapter 7; and Philip Resnick, "Canadian Defence Policy and the American Empire," in *Close the 49th Parallel*, edited by Ian Lumsden (Toronto: University of Toronto Press), pp. 94–115.
18. The Canadian government provided 48.5% of the financing between 1959 and 1967 of 306 projects under the Defence Production Sharing Agreement. Under the Defence Industrial Research Program government grants for 50% of the total costs are given to industries with no obligations for repayment and the industry retaining benefits. See Warnock, *Partner to Behemoth*, pp. 254–256, Tables from House of Commons Debates, January 15, 1969, p. 4316.

19. News Release, Department of Industry, Trade and Commerce, May 27, 1974.
20. Warnock, *Partner to Behemoth*, provides a detailed account of this episode.
21. *The Financial Post*, "Defence Sharing Deal is Truly Big Business," February 4, 1967. Estimates here are of $500 million in materials for American military use in the early 1960s, much of this in nickel, steel, copper, iron ore, and aluminium. The sale of these raw materials together with arms, planes, and component parts of American armaments is estimated by Warnock as in the neighbourhood of $900 million for the 1965–67 period. In addition to these, there are chemical warfare items such as defoliants, herbicides, and gases which were tested or manufactured in Canada for use in Vietnam.
22. For a brief but illuminating history, see H.C. Pentland, "A Capitalistic Labour Market," *Canadian Journal of Economics and Political Science*, XXV, No. 4 (November, 1959), pp. 450–461.
23. For a view of the differences between the American and Canadian developments, see Gad Horowitz, "Conservatism, Liberalism, and Socialism in Canada, An Interpretation," *Canadian Journal of Economics and Political Science*, Vol. 32, (1966).
24. From *The Liberal Party* by J.W. Pickersgill, reprinted by permission of The Canadian Publishers, McClelland and Stewart Limited, Toronto.
25. Corporations and Labour Returns Act, *Report 1983* (Ottawa: Statistics Canada, 1985), Part I, Text Table IX, pp. 48–49.
26. John Porter, *The Vertical Mosaic* (Toronto: University of Toronto Press, 1967), p. 234.
27. C.A. Ashley, "Concentration of Economic Power," *Canadian Journal of Economics and Political Science*, XXIII, No. 1, (February, 1957) as cited in Porter, *The Vertical Mosaic*, pp. 234–235.
28. Wallace Clement, *The Canadian Corporate Elite, An Analysis of Economic Power* (Toronto: McClelland and Stewart, 1975); and *Continental Corporate Power, Economic Linkages Between Canada and the United States* (Toronto: McClelland and Stewart, 1978). See especially, *Canadian Corporate Elite*, pp. 156–162.
29. Don Westell, *Globe and Mail*, August 25, 1984, B1; see also *Report on Business Magazine* (annual) and *The Financial Post 500* (annual) for detailed listings.
30. Westell, *op.cit.*
31. Government of Canada, *Foreign Direct Investment in Canada*, pp. 100–101; and Clement, *Continental Corporate Power*.
32. Lawrence Copithorne, "Natural Resources and Regional Disparities: A Skeptical View," *Canadian Public Policy*, Vol. V:2 (Spring 1979), pp. 181–194.
33. For discussions of Newfoundland's situation, see Ralph Matthews, "The Development of Underdevelopment in Newfoundland 1949–1972," *Journal of Canadian Studies*, Vol. 13.4 (Winter 1978–79),

pp. 89–108; David Alexander, *The Decay of Trade, An Economic History of the Newfoundland Saltfish Trade, 1935–1965* (St. John's: Institute of Social and Economic Research, Memorial University of Newfoundland, 1977); and other publications by the Institute.

34. Khayyam Z. Paltiel, *Political Party Financing in Canada* (Toronto: McGraw-Hill Ryerson, 1970).
35. Porter, *The Vertical Mosaic*, p. 137.
36. Dennis Olsen, "The State Elite," in Leo Panitch (ed.), *The Canadian State, Political Economy and Political Power* (Toronto: University of Toronto Press, 1977), p. 206.
37. For a detailed description of public corporations, see Hershel Hardin, *A Nation Unaware* (Vancouver: J.J. Douglas, 1974).
38. John Richards and Larry Pratt, *Prairie Capitalism: Power and Influence in the New West* (Toronto: McClelland and Stewart, 1979).
39. Daniel Bell, *The End of Ideology* (Glencoe, Illinois: Free Press, 1960).

CHAPTER 4: THE PREROGATIVES OF A RULING CLASS

1. Sir Francis Bond Head in J.M. Bliss (ed.), *Canadian History in Documents, 1763–1966* (Toronto: Ryerson, 1966), pp. 44–45.
2. *Ibid.*, p. 43.
3. For discussion of this see Fernand Dumont and Guy Rocher, "An Introduction to a Sociology of French Canada," in Marcel Rioux and Yves Martin, *French-Canadian Society* (Toronto: McClelland and Stewart, 1964), Vol. 1, pp. 178–200, especially pp. 188–197.
4. Marcel Rioux, *Quebec in Question* (Toronto: James Lewis and Samuel, 1971), p. 60. Quote from Thomas Chapais, *Discours et converences*, Quebec, 1908.
5. Herbert F. Quinn, *The Union Nationale Party: A Study of Nationalism and Industrialism in Quebec*, Ph.D. thesis, Columbia University, 1959. See also Rioux, *Quebec in Question*.
6. Gilles Laflamme, *L'Education Syndicale à la Confédération des Syndicats Nationaux*, M.A. thesis, Laval University, 1968, p. 30, as cited in translation by Henry Milner and Sheilagh Hodgins Milner, *The Decolonization of Quebec* (Toronto: McClelland and Stewart, 1973), p. 120.
7. *Ibid.*
8. Translation and synopsis of passages from Jean Hulliger, *L'Enseignement social d'eveques canadiens de 1891–1950* (Montreal: Editions Fides, 1958), in Milner and Milner, *The Decolonization of Quebec*, p. 109.
9. From *The Decolonization of Quebec* by Henry Milner and Sheilagh Milner reprinted by permission of the Canadian Publishers, McClelland and Stewart Limited, Toronto.
10. Quinn, *The Union Nationale Party*, pp. 80–81.
11. *Ibid.*, pp. 89–121.

12. Lita-Rose Betcherman, *The Swastika and the Maple Leaf, Fascist Movements in Canada in the Thirties* (Toronto: Fitzhenry and Whiteside, 1975).
13. *Ibid.*, p. 14.
14. *Ibid.*, p. 18.
15. *Ibid.*, p. 105.
16. Esther Einbinder, "Attitudes Toward Jews in Toronto," Unpublished M.A. thesis, University of Toronto, 1934, cited in Betcherman, *The Swastika and the Maple Leaf*, pp. 49–50.
17. Betcherman, *The Swastika and the Maple Leaf*, p. 107.
18. Reprinted from *French Canada in Transition*, pp. 217–218, by E.C. Hughes by permission of The University of Chicago Press. Copyright © 1943 The University of Chicago Press.
19. Betcherman, *The Swastika and the Maple Leaf*, p. 7.
20. L.G. Reynolds, *The Control of Competition in Canada* (Cambridge, Mass.: Cambridge University Press, 1940), p. 5.
21. Vernon C. Fowke, *The National Policy and the Wheat Economy* (Toronto: University of Toronto Press, 1957).
22. C.B. Macpherson, *Democracy in Alberta* (Toronto: University of Toronto Press, 1953), p. 153, citing Alberta Social Credit *Chronicle*, March 29, 1935.
23. *Ibid.*, p. 152, citing *Chronicle*, August 16, 1935.
24. Discussed in Macpherson, *Democracy in Alberta*, pp. 156–157. Quotations from Aberhart, *Social Credit Manual*, 1935, pp. 33–35 and 47.
25. *Ibid.*, p. 158; citing Alberta Social Credit *Chronicle*, April 12, 1935.
26. *Ibid.*, pp. 10–20.
27. Pierre Trudeau, "Some Obstacles to Democracy in Quebec," in *Federalism and the French Canadians* (Toronto: Macmillan, 1968), pp. 103–123; p. 110 quoting radio station CBF program, "Prières du Matin: élévations matutinales," June 20, 1956.
28. Albert Faucher and Maurice LaMontagne, "Economic Structure and Social Stratification," in Rioux and Martin, *French-Canadian Society*, p. 267.
29. Mason Wade, *The French Canadians 1760–1967* (Toronto: Macmillan of Canada, 1968), Vol. 2, pp. 1109, quoting *Le Devoir*, 2 mai 1949.
30. *Ibid.*, p. 1109. The document was *Le problème ouvrier en regard de la doctrine sociale de l'église* (Quebec: 1950).
31. Hubert Guindon, "Social Unrest, Social Class, and Quebec's Bureaucratic Revolution," *Queen's Quarterly*, LXXI (Summer 1964), pp. 150–162.
32. Charles Taylor, "Nationalism and the Political Intelligentsia," *Queen's Quarterly*, LXXII (Spring 1965), pp. 167–68.
33. Maurice Pinard, *The Rise of a Third Party* (Scarborough: Prentice-Hall, 1971).
34. Jane Jacobs, "The Question of Separatism, Part I: A Tale of Two

Cities," *The Canadian Forum*, Vol. 59, no. 696 (February, 1980), pp. 7–10. Two further parts are in subsequent editions.
35. *Ibid.*, p. 10.

CHAPTER 5: THE EXPOSURE OF A RULING CLASS

1. Karl Marx and Frederick Engels, *Manifesto of the Communist Party* (1848) (Peking: Foreign Languages Press, 1972), pp. 30–31.
2. Karl Marx, "Die moraliserinde Kritik und die kritische Moral," as quoted in translation by Ralf Dahrendorf, *Class and Class Conflict in Industrial Society* (Stanford: Stanford University Press, 1957), p. 11.
3. *Ibid.*, p. 34.
4. *Ibid.*, p. 35.
5. *Ibid.*, p. 36.
6. V.I. Lenin, *Imperialism, the Highest State of Capitalism* (Peking: Foreign Languages Press, 1970), pp. 93–94. Quote from *Die Neue Zeit* XVI, I, 1898, s. 304.
7. *Ibid.*, especially Part VII, pp. 104–118.
8. *Ibid.*, p. 119.
9. André Gunder Frank, *Capitalism and Underdevelopment in Latin America* (New York: Monthly Review Press, 1969).
10. This apt phrase was suggested by W.E. Willmott, University of British Columbia, in an exchange of memoranda regarding the crisis of employment for Canadians in Canadian universities, February, 1973.
11. For a sustained argument on the effects on culture of economic domination see Kari Levitt, *Silent Surrender* (Toronto: Macmillan of Canada, 1970). See also, articles in Ian Lumsden, *Close the 49th Parallel* (Toronto: University of Toronto Press, 1970). Several magazines regularly feature articles on this subject, including, particularly, *Canadian Forum* and *This Magazine*.
12. The Science Council of Canada has published a series of detailed studies of the technological process as it affects Canadian development. One of these is John N.H. Britton and James M. Gilmour, *The Weakest Link, A Technological Perspective on Canadian Industrial Underdevelopment*, Background Study 43 (Ottawa: Science Council of Canada, 1978).
13. W.W. Rostow, *The Stages of Economic Growth, A Non-Communist Manifesto* (Cambridge University Press, 1960).
14. Karl Marx, preface to the first German edition, *Capital*, edited by F. Engels, Vol. 1 (New York: International Publishers, 1967), p. 8.
15. Marx, "Feuerbachian Criticism of Hegel," in "Excerpt—Notes of 1844," *Writings of Young Marx on Philosophy and Society*, edited and translated by Lloyd D. Easton and Kurt H. Guddat (New York: Doubleday, 1967), p. 289.
16. Marx, "The German Ideology—Hegel and Feuerbach," *ibid.*, p. 424.

17. *Ibid.*, p. 414.
18. *Ibid.*, p. 415.
19. *Ibid.*, p. 433.
20. *Ibid.*, p. 438.
21. Guy Swanson, *Birth of the Gods* (Ann Arbor: University of Michigan Press, 1964).
22. Marx, "The German Ideology—Hegel and Feuerbach," p. 439.
23. Karl Marx, *Capital* (1887), edited by F. Engels, Vol. 1, *The Process of Capitalist Production* (New York: International Publishers, 1967), especially Chapter XV, "Machinery and Modern Industry."
24. Marx and Engels, *Manifesto of the Communist Party*, p. 33.
25. Leo Panitch (ed.), *The Canadian State: Political Economy and Political Power* (Toronto: University of Toronto Press, 1977).
26. James O'Connor, *The Fiscal Crisis of the State* (New York: St. Martin's Press, 1973).
27. Leo Panitch, "The Role and Nature of the Canadian State," in Panitch, *The Canadian State*, pp. 3–24, especially p. 7.
28. Ralph Miliband, *The State in Capitalist Society* (London: Quartet, 1973).
29. A joint federal–Ontario grant of $68 million was awarded to Ford Motor company in 1978 to induce the company to build a plant in Ontario. An expected 2500 jobs were involved. Two years later, Ford laid off several thousand workers in Canada. See James Laxer, *Canada's Economic Strategy* (Toronto: McClelland and Stewart, 1981) pp. 138–146; and Stephen Clarkson, *Canada and the Reagan Challenge* (Ottawa: Canadian Institute for Economic Policy, 1982) pp. 128–134.
30. Leo Panitch, "The Development of Corporatism in Liberal Democracies," *Comparative Political Studies*, Vol. 10, No. 1 (April, 1977), p. 66; also in "Corporatism in Canada," *Studies in Political Economy*, No. 1 (Spring 1979), p. 44.
31. Reginald Whitaker, "Images of the State in Canada," in Panitch, *The Canadian State*, p. 43.
32. Herschel Hardin, *A Nation Unaware* (Vancouver: J.J. Douglas, 1974).
33. Larry Pratt, *The Tar Sands, Syncrude and the Politics of Oil* (Edmonton: Hurtig, 1976).
34. See Chapter 4. Panitch, "Corporatism in Canada," discusses the difference between a corporatist ideology and a corporatist state.
35. Frank Parkin, *Marxism and Class Theory, A Bourgeois Critique* (New York: Columbia University Press, 1979).
36. See, for example, Marx and Engels, *Manifesto of the Communist Party*, p. 31.
37. Nicholas Abercrombie, Stephen Hill, and Bryan S. Turner, *The Dominant Ideology Thesis* (London: Allen and Unwin, 1980).
38. Frederik Engels, *The Origin of the Family, Private Property, and the State* (New York: International Publishers, 1968).
39. V.I. Lenin, *The State and Revolution* (Moscow: Foreign Languages Publishing House, 1917 nd).

40. Nicos Poulantzas, "The Problem of the Capitalist State," *New Left Review*, No. 58: 67–78, (1969); and *Political Power and Social Classes* (London: New Left Books, 1974).
41. Miliband, *The State in Capitalist Society*.
42. Antonio Gramsci, *Selections from Prison Notebooks* (New York: International Publishers, 1971).
43. O'Connor, *The Fiscal Crisis of the State*.
44. I have argued this position in "The New Right and the State in the New Economic Reality" paper presented to the XIth World Congress of Sociology, New Delhi, India, August, 1986.
45. Max Weber, *The Theory of Social and Economic Organization*, edited by Talcott Parsons (New York: Free Press, 1947).
46. Max Weber, *The Protestant Ethic and the Spirit of Capitalism* (New York: Charles Scribner's Sons, 1958).
47. Emile Durkheim, *Suicide*, translated by J.A. Spaulding and G. Simpson (New York: Free Press, 1951).

CHAPTER 6: CLASS AND CLASS PROTEST

1. Martin Robin, *Radical Politics and Canadian Labour, 1880–1930* (Kingston, Ont.: Industrial Relations Centre, Queen's University, 1968), p. 41, quoting *The Independent* (Nanaimo, B.C.), May 24, 1902.
2. *Loc. cit.*
3. *Ibid.*, quoting L.T. English, *Vancouver World*, Dec. 11, 1909.
4. Clark Kerr and Abraham Siegel, "The Inter-Industry Propensity to Strike," in A. Kornhauser *et al.* (eds.), *Industrial Conflict*, (New York: Prentice-Hall, 1954).
5. H.C. Pentland, "A Capitalistic Labour Market," *Canadian Journal of Economic and Political Science*, XXV, no. 4. (November, 1959) pp. 450–461 describes the development of a capitalist labour market in Canada. For accounts of the development of the trade-union movement see Charles Lipton, *The Trade Union Movement in Canada, 1827–1959* (Montreal: Canadian Social Publication, 1966), and Bernard Ostry, "Conservatives, Liberals, and Labour in the 1870's," *The Canadian Historical Review*, XLI, no. 2 (June, 1960), pp. 93–127.
6. Kenneth McNaught, *A Prophet in Politics* (Toronto: University of Toronto Press, 1959), p. 99.
7. This chronology is based on the account in Stuart Jamieson's history, *Times of Trouble: Labour Unrest and Industrial Conflict in Canada, 1900–66*, Task Force on Labour Relations Study No. 22 (Ottawa: Information Canada, 1971), Chapter III; and on A. Belawyder, *The Winnipeg General Strike* (Toronto: Copp Clark, 1967).
8. *La Presse*, Montreal, May 19, 1919, quoted in Belawyder, *The Winnipeg General Strike*, p. 16.

9. *The Globe,* Toronto, May 19, 1919, quoted *ibid.,* pp. 16–17
10. *The Morning Leader,* Regina, May 30, 1919, quoted *ibid.,* pp. 16–17.
11. K.J. Dixon's Address to the Jury, Winnipeg: Defence Committee, 1920, No. 6, quoted *ibid.,* pp. 17–18.
12. Charles Lipton, *The Trade Union Movement in Canada, 1827–1959* (Montreal: Canadian Social Publications, 1966), p. 170, quoting Alphonse Verville, June 28, 1917, and June 29, 1917, in speeches in the House of Commons.
13. *Western Labor News,* editorial, April 25, 1919, quoted in Belawyder, *The Winnipeg General Strike,* p. 13.
14. Jamieson, *Times of Trouble,* pp. 175–176.
15. D.C. Masters, *The Winnipeg General Strike* (Toronto: University of Toronto Press, 1950), p. 112.
16. For a general review of the population growth, see W. Kalbach and W. McVey, *The Demographic Basis of Canadian Society* (Toronto: McGraw-Hill, 1971).
17. Jamieson, *Times of Trouble,* describes these conditions in Chapter IV also with reference to the study of the United States' conditions during this period by Irving Bernstein, *The Lean Years: A History of the American Workers, 1920–1933* (Baltimore, Md.: Penguin Books, 1966).
18. *Ibid.,* p. 194. Reproduced by permission of Information Canada.
19. See *Liberal Speakers' Handbook,* No. 17 (Ottawa: National Liberal Committee, September, 1925), pp. 11–12. The legislation in question was actually an anti-narcotics bill.
20. *Ibid.,* No. 24 (September, 1925) p. 10.
21. *Ibid.,* No. 17 (September, 1925), Part I, p. 4.
22. Jamieson, *Times of Trouble,* p. 235, quoting *Debates,* House of Commons, 1934, II, 1523, and *Final Report on the Unemployment Relief Scheme for the Care of Single Homeless Men Administered by the Department of National Defence, 1932–1936,* Ottawa, 1937, Vol. I, p. 1. Other works on the relief camps and riots are few, and scholarly study of this period is not well advanced. Jamieson includes excerpts from R. Liversedge, *Reflections on the On-to-Ottawa Trek* (Vancouver: Broadway Printers, no date), for a participant's view. Another, journalistic account is given in W. Gray, *The Winter Years—the Depression on the Prairies* (Toronto: Macmillan, 1966).
23. Research Committee of the League for Social Reconstruction, *Social Planning for Canada* (Toronto: Thomas Nelson and Sons, 1935). The writers were Eugene Forsey, J. King Gordon, Leonard Marsh, J.F. Parkinson, F.R. Scott, Graham Spry, and Frank H. Underhill. The Methodist minister who wrote the foreword and played such a significant role in the early movement was J.S. Woodsworth.
24. Report of Executive to Ontario Provincial Convention, 1936, quoted in Leo Zakuta, *A Protest Movement Becalmed* (Toronto: University of Toronto Press, 1964), pp. 37–38 © University of Toronto Press, 1964.

25. *Ibid.*, p. 32.
26. Co-operative Commonwealth Federation Programme, adopted at First National Convention held at Regina, Saskatchewan, July, 1933, second paragraph.
27. *Winnipeg Declaration of Principles of the Co-operative Commonwealth Federation/Parti Social Démocratique du Canada,* 1956.
28. Zakuta, *A Protest Movement Becalmed,* Chapter 2 for a description.
29. *The Regina Manifesto,* section 10.
30. Zakuta, *A Protest Movement Becalmed.* Quotations from "Special Bulletin," September 12, 1939, issued by the National Secretary.
31. *Ibid.*, p. 55.
32. *Ibid.*, p. 60.
33. *Ibid.*, p. 61. Statement issued by 8th National Convention, 1944.
34. Section 98 of the Canadian *Criminal Code,* as amended by "An Act to Amend the Criminal Code," Statutes of Canada, 1919, c. 45, s. 1. Reproduced with permission of the Minister of Supply and Services Canada.
35. From *The Communist Party in Canada* (1975), p. 36 by Ivan Avakumovic reprinted by permission of The Canadian Publishers, McClelland and Stewart Limited, Toronto.
36. *Ibid.*, pp. 96–98. See Also Norman Penner, *The Canadian Left, A Critical Analysis* (Toronto: Prentice-Hall, 1977), p. 149.
37. Penner, *The Canadian Left,* pp. 148–150.
38. *Ibid.*
39. *Ibid.*, p. 158, citing Canadian Press dispatch, May 29, 1944.
40. Avakumovic, *The Communist Party In Canada,* p. 142.
41. *Ibid.*, pp. 148–150.
42. Wallace Clement, *The Canadian Corporate Elite, An Analysis of Economic Power* (Toronto: McClelland and Stewart, 1975); Tom Naylor, *The History of Canadian Business, 1867–1914,* 2 vols., (Toronto: James Lorimer, 1965).
43. Vernon C. Fowke, *The National Policy and the Wheat Economy* (Toronto: University of Toronto Press, 1957), "The National Policy 1879–1979," *Journal of Canadian Studies,* Vol. 14, No. 3 (Autumn, 1979); and Naylor, *The History of Canadian Business;* and Clement, *The Canadian Corporate Elite.*
44. John Richards and Larry Pratt, *Prairie Capitalism: Power and Influence in the New West* (Toronto: McClelland and Stewart, 1979).
45. Patricia Marchak, "Labour in a Staples Economy," *Studies in Political Economy,* No. 2 (Autumn 1967), pp. 7–35.
46. John Kenneth Galbraith, *The New Industrial State,* 2nd ed., (New York: New American Library, 1971).

CHAPTER 7: NATION AND NATIONAL PROTEST

1. *Maclean's*, editorial, January 1, 1949, p. 1.
2. Matthew Halton, "Will the Atlantic Pact Work?" *Maclean's*, January 15, 1949, p. 7.
3. F.H. Soward, "Canada in a Two Power World," *Behind the Headlines*, CII, No. 1, (Spring 1948), p. 3.
4. *Canadian House of Commons Debates*, III (April 29, 1949) pp. 2790–2795. This and other quotations are cited in John W. Warnock, *Partner to Behemoth, The Military Policy of a Satellite Canada* (Toronto: New Press, 1970), Chapter 2. This section owes much to his pioneering study.
5. Lester Pearson, "The Development of Canadian Foreign Policy," *Foreign Affairs*, An American Quarterly Review XXX, No. 1, p. 29. Reprinted by permission from *Foreign Affairs*, October 1951. Copright 1951 by Council on Foreign Relations, Inc.
6. Copyright © 1953 by Norman D. Palmer and Howard C. Perkins, *International Relations*, p. 333, (Boston: Houghton Mifflin Company). (This book has undergone revision since 1953, and the wording of some of the sections cited here have been changed in the 3rd ed., 1969.)
7. *Ibid.*, p. 861.
8. *Ibid.*, p. 866.
9. *Ibid.*, p. 866.
10. *Ibid.*, pp. 868–869.
11. *Ibid.*, p. 970.
12. *Ibid.*, p. 970.
13. *Maclean's*, interview, July 6, 1957, p. 52.
14. Willson Woodside, "Soviets Count on U.S. Collapse—How About Own Economy? *Saturday Night*, LXIII (February 14, 1948), cited by Warnock, *Partner to Behemoth*, p. 50.
15. *Ibid.*, speech by Dulles, March 10, 1949.
16. Max Werner, "Russia Won't Attack," *Maclean's*, January 1, 1949, pp. 5, 33–35.
17. John W. Holmes, "Is There a Future for Middlepowermanship?" in J. King Gordon (ed.), *Canada's Role As a Middle Power* (Toronto: Canadian Institute for International Affairs, 1966), pp. 101–102.
18. "With Us or Against Us," *Saturday Night*, LXIV (May 31, 1949), p. 5.
19. "The Waffle Resolution, October, 1969," in Dave Godfrey (ed.), *Gordon to Watkins to You* (Toronto: New Press, 1970), pp. 103–108.
20. *Ibid.*, debate at national convention, NDP, p. 114.
21. Léandré Bergeron, *The History of Quebec, A Patriot's Handbook* (Toronto: New Canada Publications, 1971).
22. *Ibid.*, p. 217.
23. *Ibid.*, p. 229.
24. *FLQ Manifesto*, as quoted in *Vancouver Province*, October 9, 1970, p. 2.

25. Gilles Bourque and Nicole Laurin-Frenette, "Social Classes and National Ideologies in Quebec, 1760–1970," translated by P. Resnick and P. Renyi from an original article published in *Socialisme Quebecois*, No. 20, 1970, in Gary Teeple (ed.), *Capitalism and the National Question in Canada* (Toronto: University of Toronto Press, 1973), pp. 186–210. © University of Toronto Press, 1973.

26. Various of these documents have been collected and published by Daniel Drache (ed.), in *Quebec—Only the Beginning, the Manifestoes of the Common Front* (Toronto: New Press, 1972).

27. Stanley B. Ryerson, "Quebec: Concepts of Class and Nation," in Teeple, *Capitalism and the National Question*, pp. 212–227, especially at p. 215.

28. Godfrey, *Gordon to Watkins to You*, Walter Gordon's statement at the University of Alberta, Edmonton, November 27–29, 1969, pp. 120–125. Mr. Gordon advocated a 30% take-over tax as a deterrent to foreign investors. When asked in the House of Commons by T. Douglas (NDP) whether the government was considering such an action, Mr. Benson (Liberal Minister of Finance) replied: "I will consider this to about the same degree as my hon. friend is considering the suggestions of Mr. Watkins."

29. Patrick McGeer, editorial, "The View from B.C.: The Great Columbia Giveaway," *Maclean's*, June, 1973, p. 12.

30. Leon Dion, "Quebec and the Future of Canada," in Dale C. Thomson (ed.), *Quebec Society and Politics: Views from the Inside* (Toronto: McClelland and Stewart, 1973), pp. 251–263, especially at p. 253. The original text was presented in French as a brief to the Special Joint Committee of the Senate and of the House of Commons on the Constitution of Canada, March 30, 1971.

31. Mr. Justice Thomas R. Berger, *Northern Frontier Northern Homeland, The Report of the Mackenzie Valley Pipeline Inquiry: Vol. 1* (Toronto: James Lorimer in association with Publishing Centre, Supply and Services, Canada, 1977).

32. *Ibid.*, p. vii.

33. *Ibid.*, p. 1.

34. Useful references on the "free trade debate" are: Fred Lazar, *The New Protectionism. Non-Tariff Barriers and Their Effects on Canada* (Ottawa: Canadian Institute for Economic Policy, 1981); Abraham Rotstein, *Rebuilding from Within. Remedies for Canada's Ailing Economy* (Ottawa: Canadian Institute for Economic Policy, 1984.); Canadian Institute for Economic Policy, Brief to the Macdonald Commission, "The Pitfalls of Free Trade," in Daniel Drache and Duncan Cameron (eds.), *The Other Macdonald Report* (Toronto: Lorimer, 1985) pp. 129–135.

CHAPTER 8: THE NEW RIGHT

1. For extended arguments on this see George Gilder, *Wealth and*

Poverty (New York: Basic Books, 1981); R. Nozick, *Anarchy, State and Utopia* (Oxford: Blackwell, 1974); F. Hayek, *The Constitution of Liberty* (London: Routledge and Kegan Paul, 1960).

2. William Cochrane (senior vice-president of corporate services at Guaranty Trust) *Globe and Mail*, November 3, 1986, p. A7.
3. Ayn Rand, *Atlas Shrugged* (New York: Random House, 1957) and other novels as well as essays.
4. Gilder, *Wealth and Poverty*, Chapter 4.
5. Milton Friedman, "Market Mechanisms and Central Economic Planning," *Warren Nutter Lecture in Political Economy to the Thomas Jefferson Center Foundation* (Washington, D.C.: The American Enterprise Institute, 1981) p. 9; and stated at greater length in Milton and Rose Friedman, *Free to Choose* (New York: Macmillan, 1980) and other books.
6. These statements are found in the popular works of Friedman, in many of Ronald Reagan's speeches, in (Fraser Institute Director) Michael Walker's columns in the *Financial Post* and the *Vancouver Province*, in radio talk shows by members of the Fraser Institute here and parallel institutes throughout the industrial countries.
7. As cited by Marian Sawer, "Political Manifestations of Australian Libertarianism," in *Australia and the New Right*, ed. by Sawer (Sydney: Allen and Unwin, 1982) p. 6. See for almost identical statement, Herbert Grubel, in CBC television interview on "Pacific Report," Sept. 29, 1983; and in Fraser Institute, *Focus on Friedman* (Vancouver, 1982).
8. Fraser Institute, *Focus on Friedman*.
9. *Rent Controls, Myths and Realities* (Vancouver: Fraser Institute, 1981). See also, *The Province*, July 12, 1983, B3 for Walker's response to the B.C. budget and removal of rent controls.
10. Nozick, *Anarchy, State and Utopia*, argues that taxation is a form of theft.
11. Irving Kristol, *Two Cheers for Capitalism* (New York: Basic Books, 1978) p. 16.
12. A detailed profile of the corporate supports is given in Cliff Stainsby and John Malcolmson, *The Fraser Institute, the Government and a Corporate Free Lunch* (Vancouver: Solidarity Coalition, October, 1983). See also, Fraser Institute, annual reports.
13. Most clearly stated in the foreword, explaining the origins of the Commission, in David Owen, Zbigniew Brzezinski, Saburo Okita, *Democracy Must Work. A Trilateral Agenda for the Decade.* The Triangle Papers: (New York: New York University Press, 1984).
14. Michel J. Crozier, Samuel P. Huntington, Joji Watanuki, *The Crisis of Democracy. Report on the Governability of Democracies to the Trilateral Commission.* (New York: New York University Press, 1975) p. 173.
15. *Ibid.*, p. 183.
16. *Ibid.*, p. 181.
17. *Ibid.*, p. 174.

18. *Ibid.*, p. 177.
19. Owen et al, 1984, p. 5.
20. Both Crozier et al and Owen et al argue this case.
21. Crozier et al., p. 177.
22. Owen et al., p. 4.
23. *The Plain Truth*, Vol. 50:8 (October, 1985) p. 22.
24. *Ibid.*, Vol. 51:6 (June, 1986) p. 16.
25. *Ibid.*, Vol. 51:5 (May, 1986).
26. *Ibid.*, Vol. 50:8 (October, 1985) p. 8.
27. *Ibid.*, Vol. 50:8 (October, 1985) p. 5.
28. *Ibid.*, Vol. 50:8 (October, 1985) p. 6.

CHAPTER 9: IDEOLOGY AND SOCIAL CHANGE

1. Samuel Bowles, D. Gordon, and T.G. Weisskopf, *Beyond the Wasteland* (New York: Anchor/Doubleday, 1983) provides statistical details and trend data.
2. *The Economist*, March 2, 1985; *Asahi Evening News*, May 6, 1985; *The Economist*, May 4, 1985: all provide statistics on the trade and credit balances at the time of writing. For overall patterns see also Barry Bluestone and Bennett Harrison, *The Deindustrialization of America* (New York: Basic Books, 1982); and Bowles et al. For an illuminating essay on Japanese growth see David Edgington, "Japanese Transnational Corporations and the Economic Integration of Australia in the Asia-Pacific Region," working paper no. 15, Transnational Corporations Research Project, Faculty of Economics, University of Sydney, Sydney, Australia, 1983; and for statistics on Canadian exports and imports see Peter Richards and Clyde Weaver, "Canada and the Changing Economy of the Pacific Basin, A Ten Year Prospect for Canadian Exports to Japan," working paper no. 16, Institute of Asian Research, University of British Columbia.
3. Geoffrey Hodgson, "State of the Nation," *Boston Globe Magazine*, January 18, 1981, p. 16, cited in Bluestone and Harrison, *The Deindustrialization of America*, p. 5.
4. Robert B. Reich, *The Next American Frontier* (New York: Penguin, 1984) pp. 121-22.
5. Bluestone and Harrison, *The Deindustrialization of America*, p. 140.
6. "Westinghouse and Toshiba plan venture," *Globe and Mail*, December 18, 1984, B3.
7. Bluestone and Harrison, *The Deindustrialization of America*, p. 143.
8. See for study of the garment industry, F. Froebel, J. Heinrichs, and O. Kreye, *The New International Division of Labour* (Cambridge: Cambridge University Press, 1980); on the electronics industry, see "Delicate Bonds: The Global Semiconductor Industry," special issue of *Pacific Research*, Vol. XI (1), (January, 1980); and June Nash and Maria Patricia Fernandez-Kelly (eds.), *Women, Men, and the*

International Division of Labor (New York: State University of New York Press, 1983) pp. 39-69.

9. F.E.I. Hamilton, and G.J.R. Linge (eds.), *Spatial Analysis, Industry and the Industrial Environment*, Vol. 2—*International Industrial Systems* (London: John Wiley, 1981) p. 65.

10. See, for case studies of impacts on women, Heather Menzies, *Women and the Chip* (Montreal: Institute for Research on Public Policy, 1981); and Joan Wallach Scott, "The Mechanization of Women's Work," in *The Mechanization of Work, Scientific American* (San Francisco: W.H. Freeman, 1982), pp. 89-98. For general descriptions of the changes in office work and commerce, see other chapters in *The Mechanization of Work*.

11. Patricia Marchak, *Green Gold: The Forest Industry in British Columbia* (Vancouver: UBC Press, 1983); and "Rise and Fall of the Peripheral State," in R.J. Brym (ed.), *Regionalism in Canada* (Toronto: Irwin, 1986), 123-160.

12. Accounts of the industry are given in: Ross Perry, *The Future of Canada's Auto Industry, the Big Three and the Japanese Challenge* (Ottawa: Canadian Institute for Economic Policy, 1982); Stephen Clarkson, *Canada and the Reagan Challenge, Crisis in the Canadian-American Relationship* (Ottawa: Canadian Institute for Economic Policy, 1982); James Laxer, *Canada's Economic Strategy* (Toronto: McClelland and Stewart, 1981); Canada, Reisman Commission, *Inquiry into the Automotive Industry, The Canadian Automotive Industry, Performance and Proposals for Progress* (Ottawa: 1978); and Canadian Automotive Consultative Sector Task Force, *A Report by the Sector Task Force on the Canadian Automotive Industry* (Ottawa, 1978).

13. These events have been documented in several collections of essays, notably: W. Magnusson et al., (eds.), *The New Reality* (Vancouver: New Star, 1984); Robert C. Allen and Gideon Rosenbluth, (eds.), *Restraining the Economy* (Vancouver: New Star, 1986). See also, separate essays published by The Pacific Group, Centre for Policy Alternatives (Vancouver); and British Columbia Economic Policy Institute (Department of Economics, UBC, Vancouver).

14. For descriptions of this and numerous other movements of the same type see R.D. Rosen, *Psychobabble* (New York: Avon, 1975); Christopher Lasch, *The Culture of Narcissism, American Life in an Age of Diminishing Expectations* (New York: W.W. Norton, 1978); Mark Brewer, "'We're Gonna Tear You Down and Put You Back Together," *Psychology Today* (August, 1975), pp. 35-36, 39-40, 82, 88-89.

15. *Bible*, King James Version, Matthew 16:26.

16. J.W. Younger, secretary of the Steel Company of Canada, Hamilton, Ont. reported in the *Globe and Mail*, Feb. 11, 1969, cited in Kari Levitt, *Silent Surrender* (Toronto: Macmillan of Canada, 1970), p. 37.

17. Sir Francis Bond Head in J.M. Bliss (ed.), *Canadian History in Documents, 1763-1966* (Toronto: Ryerson, 1966), pp. 44-45.
18. F. Engels, *Origins of the Family, Private Property, and the State* (1884) (New York: International Publishers, 1968) pp. 155-157.
19. James O'Connor, *The Fiscal Crisis of the State* (New York: St. Martin's Press, 1973), p. 6.
20. *Task Force on Canadian Unity, A Future Together, Observations and Recommendations* (Ottawa: Supply and Services, 1979), p. 16.
21. *Ibid.*, p. 125.

SELECTED REFERENCES FOR FURTHER READING ABOUT CANADA

Allen, Robert C. and Gideon Rosenbluth (eds.). *Restraining the Economy. Social Credit Economic Policies for B.C. in the Eighties* (Vancouver: New Star, 1986).

Abella, Irving. *Nationalism, Communism, and Canadian Labour* (Toronto: University of Toronto, 1973).

Alexander, David. *The Decay of Trade, An Economic History of the Newfoundland Saltfish Trade, 1935-1965* (St. John's: Institute of Social and Economic Research, Memorial University of Newfoundland, 1977).

Armstrong, Pat, and Hugh Armstrong. *The Double Ghetto: Canadian Women and Their Segregated Work* (Toronto: McClelland and Stewart, 1978).

Asch, Michael. *Home and Native Land. Aboriginal Rights and the Canadian Constitution* (Toronto: Methuen, 1984).

Avakumovic, Ivan. *The Communist Party in Canada, A History* (Toronto: McClelland and Stewart, 1975).

Berger, Mr. Justice Thomas R. *Northern Frontier Northern Homeland, The Report of the Mackenzie Valley Pipeline Inquiry: Vol. 1* (Toronto: James Lorimer in association with Minister of Supply and Services, 1977).

Betcherman, Lita-Rose. *The Swastika and the Maple Leaf, Fascist Movements in Canada in the Thirties* (Toronto: Fitzhenry and Whiteside, 1975).

Britton, John N.H., and James M. Gilmour. *The Weakest Link, A Technological Perspective on Canadian Industrial Underdevelopment*, Background Study 43, (Ottawa: Science Council of Canada, 1978).

Brym, Robert J. (ed.). *The Structure of the Canadian Capitalist Class* (Toronto: Garamond Press, 1985).

———. *Regionalism in Canada* (Toronto: Irwin, 1986).

Brym, Robert J. and R. James Sacouman (eds.). *Underdevelopment and Social Movements in Atlantic Canada* (Toronto: New Hogtown Press, 1979).

Calvert, John. *Government Limited. The Corporate Takeover of the Public Sector in Canada* (Ottawa: The Canadian Centre for Policy Alternatives, 1984).

Clement, Wallace. *Continental Corporate Power, Economic Linkages Between Canada and the United States* (Toronto: McClelland and Stewart, 1978).

———. *The Canadian Corporate Elite, An Analysis of Economic Power* (Toronto: McClelland and Stewart, 1975).

———. *The Struggle to Organize. Resistance in Canada's Fishery* (Toronto: McClelland and Stewart, 1986).

Connelly, Patricia. *Last Hired First Fired: Women and the Canadian Work Force* (Toronto: Women's Press, 1978).

Dacks, Gurston. *A Choice of Futures. Politics in the Canadian North* (Toronto: Methuen, 1981).

Drache, Daniel and Duncan Cameron (eds.). *The Other Macdonald Report* (Toronto: James Lorimer, 1985).

Economic Council of Canada, *Living Together, A Study of Regional Disparities* (Ottawa: Supply and Services, 1977).

Forcese, Dennis. *The Canadian Class Structure*, 2nd ed. (Toronto: McGraw-Hill Ryerson, 1980).

Fournier, Pierre. *The Quebec Establishment* (Montreal: Black Rose, 1976).

Fowke, Vernon, C. *The National Policy and the Wheat Economy* (Toronto: University of Toronto Press, 1957).

Frideres, James S. *Native People in Canada Contemporary Conflicts*, 2nd ed. (Scarborough, Prentice-Hall, 1983).

Government of Canada, *Foreign Direct Investment in Canada* (Ottawa: Information Canada, 1972).

Grant, George. *Technology and Empire: Perspectives on North America* (Toronto: Anansi, 1969).

Guindon, Hubert. "Social Unrest, Social Class, and Quebec's Bureaucratic Revolution," *Queen's Quarterly*, LXXI (Summer 1964), pp. 150-162.

Horowitz, Gad. *Canadian Labour in Politics* (Toronto: University of Toronto Press, 1968).

House, J.D. *The Last of the Free Enterprisers: The Oilmen of Calgary* (Toronto: Macmillan of Canada, 1980).

Hughes, Everett C. *French Canada in Transition* (Chicago: University of Chicago Press, 1943).

Inglis, Gordon. *More Than Just a Union. The Story of the NFFAWU* (St. John's: Jesperson Press, 1985).

Innis, Harold A. *The Fur Trade in Canada: An Introduction to Canadian Economic History* (Toronto: University of Toronto Press, revised edition 1956) (original: 1930).

Jamieson, Stuart. *Times of Trouble: Labour Unrest and Industrial Conflict in Canada, 1900–66*, Task Force on Labour Relations Study No. 22 (Ottawa: Information Canada, 1971).

Kealey, Gregory S., and Peter Warrian (eds.). *Essays in Canadian Working Class History* (Toronto: McClelland and Stewart, 1976).

Layton, Elliott. *Dying Hard, The Ravages of Industrial Carnage* (Toronto: McClelland and Stewart, 1975).

Levitt, Kari. *Silent Surrender* (Toronto: Macmillan of Canada, 1970).

Lipsett, Seymour Martin. *Agrarian Socialism, The Cooperative Commonwealth Federation in Saskatchewan*, 2nd ed. (Berkeley: University of California Press, 1971).

Luxton, Meg. *More Than a Labour of Love. Three Generations of Women's Work in the Home*. (Toronto: The Woman's Press, 1980).

Macpherson, C.B. *Democracy in Alberta* (Toronto: University of Toronto Press, 1953).

———. *The Real World of Democracy, Massey Lectures* (Toronto: Canadian Broadcasting Corporation, 1965).

Mahon, Rianne. *The Politics of Industrial Restructuring. Canadian Textiles* (Toronto: University of Toronto Press, 1984).

Marchak, M. Patricia. *In Whose Interests, An Essay on Multinational Corporations in a Canadian Context* (Toronto: McClelland and Stewart, 1979).

———. *Green Gold. The Forest Industry in British Columbia.* (Vancouver: UBC Press, 1983).

Marsden, Lorna, and E. Harvey. *Fragile Federation: Social Change in Canada* (Toronto: McGraw-Hill Ryerson, 1979).

Marsh, Leonard. *Canadians In and Out of Work, A Survey of Economic Classes and Their Relation to the Labour Market* (Toronto: Oxford University Press, 1940).

Maslove, Allan M. (ed.). *How Ottawa Spends* (Toronto: Methuen, annual).

Matthews, Ralph. *"There's No Better Place Than Here," Social Change in Three Newfoundland Communities* (Toronto: Peter Martin, 1976).

———. *The Creation of Regional Dependency* (Toronto: University of Toronto Press, 1983).

McNaught, Kenneth. *The Pelican History of Canada.* (London: Penguin, 1969).

Milner, Henry. *Politics in the New Quebec* (Toronto: McClelland and Stewart, 1978).

Myers, Gustavus. *A History of Canadian Wealth* (Toronto: James Lewis and Samuel, 1972), (original: 1913).

Naylor, Tom. *The History of Canadian Business 1867–1914*, 2 vols. (Toronto: James Lorimer, 1975).

Nelles, H.V. *The Politics of Development: Forests, Mines and Hydro-Electric Power in Ontario 1849–1941* (Toronto: Macmillan of Canada, 1974).

Noisi, Jorge. *Canadian Capitalism* (trans. Robert Chodos) (Toronto: Lorimer, 1980).

———. *Canadian Multinationals* (trans. Robert Chodes) (Toronto: Garamond Press, 1985).

Olsen, Dennis. *The State Elite* (Toronto: McClelland and Stewart, 1980).

Page, Robert. *Northern Development. The Canadian Dilemma* (Toronto: McClelland and Stewart, 1986).

Panitch, Leo (ed.). *The Canadian State: Political Economy and Political Power* (Toronto: University of Toronto Press, 1977).

Penner, Norman. *Winnipeg 1919 (Second Edition) The Strikers' Own History of the Winnipeg General Strike* (Toronto: James Lorimer, 1975).

———. *The Canadian Left, A Critical Analysis* (Toronto: Prentice-Hall, 1977).

Perry, Thomas L. and James G. Foulks. *End the Arms Race: Fund Human Needs.* Proceedings of the 1986 Vancouver Centennial Peace and Disarmament Symposium (Gordon Soules, 1986).

Ponting, J. Rick (ed.). *Arduous Journey. Canadian Indians and Decolonization* (Toronto: McClelland and Stewart, 1986).

Porter, John. *The Vertical Mosaic* (Toronto: University of Toronto Press, 1967).

———. *The Measure of Canadian Society: Education, Equality, and Opportunity* (Toronto: Gage, 1980).

Quinn, Herbert F. *The Union Nationale, Quebec Nationalism from Duplessis to Levesque,* 2nd ed. (Toronto: University of Toronto Press, 1979).

Resnick, Philip. *The Land of Cain: Class and Nationalism in English Canada 1945–1975* (Vancouver: New Star, 1977).

———. *Parliament vs. People, an Essay on Democracy and Canadian Political Culture* (Vancouver: New Star, 1984).

Richards, John, and Larry Pratt. *Prairie Capitalism: Power and Influence in the New West* (Toronto: McClelland and Stewart, 1979).

Rioux, Marcel. *Quebec in Question* (Toronto: James Lewis and Samuel, 1971).

Rioux, Marcel and Yves Martin. *French-Canadian Society,* 2 vols. (Toronto: McClelland and Stewart, 1964).

Ryerson, Stanley. *Unequal Union: Roots of Crisis in the Canadas, 1815–1873* (Toronto: Progress, 1973).

Scott, Jack. *Canadian Workers, American Unions: How the American Federation of Labour Took Over Canada's Unions* (Vancouver: New Star, 1978).

Smucker, Joseph. *Industrialization in Canada* (Toronto: Prentice-Hall, 1980).

Wade, Mason. *The French Canadians 1760–1967,* 2 vols. (Toronto: Macmillan of Canada, 1967).

Warnock, John W. *Partner to Behemoth, The Military Policy of a Satellite Canada* (Toronto: New Press, 1970).

———. *Profit Hungry. The Food Industry in Canada* (Vancouver: New Star, 1978).

Watkins, Mel. (ed.). *Dene Nation. The Colony Within* (Toronto: University of Toronto Press, 1977).

Whitaker, Reginald. *The Government Party: Organizing and Financing the Liberal Party of Canada 1930–58* (Toronto: University of Toronto Press, 1977).

Williams, Glen. *Not for Export: Toward a Political Economy of Canada's Arrested Industrialization* (Toronto: McClelland and Stewart, 1986).

Zakuta, Leo. *A Protest Movement Becalmed* (Toronto: University of Toronto Press, 1964).

EVENTS IN CANADIAN HISTORY: A REFERENCE CHRONOLOGY

THE 17TH CENTURY

Development of the fur trade along the St. Lawrence; Iroquois-Huron/Algonquin conflicts involving alliances with Europeans (Europeans provide weapons); Huron/Algonquin driven out of the St. Lawrence Valley; rapid growth of New England colonies and trading arrangements between these colonies and the West Indies; slow growth of French colony.

1663   New France becomes a royal province (population approximately 2000)

1670   Charles II of England grants a monopoly trading charter to the Hudson's Bay Company, headed by Prince Rupert.

THE 18TH CENTURY

Expansion of the fur trade and continuing conflicts between English and French trading interests, culminating in conquest of New France by Britain.

1713   *Treaty of Utrecht* grants sovereignty of Hudson's Bay, Newfoundland, and Nova Scotia (Acadia) to the English.

1720s   Fur trade extends to the Prairies.

1749   British establish a base in Halifax, Nova Scotia, with 2500 settlers. French establish a fortress in the Annapolis Valley (Acadia).

1755   Expulsion of the Acadians from Nova Scotia. (*Note:* By this time there were approximately two million settlers in New England and 70 000 settlers in New France.)

1755-60 Series of military clashes between France and England along the St. Lawrence, culminating in the surrender of Quebec after the defeat of Montcalm and the capture of the Louisbourg fortress.

1763   *Treaty of Paris* marks the end of the European Seven Years' War and Britain's acquisition of New France (except St. Pierre and Miquelon). *Royal Proclamation* outlines intention to introduce English laws and representative assembly.

1774   *Quebec Act* guarantees religious and legal rights for French in Quebec.

1779-83 Formation of the North West Company by Montreal fur traders and financiers.

1780s   Influx of Loyalists from the United States.

1789-93 Exploration of the Mackenzie and Peace Rivers, expansion of the fur trade in British Columbia.

1790s   Growth of ship-building industry in the Maritimes, and further development of fishing and forestry industries.

1791   *Constitutional Act* (also called the *Canada Act*) amends the
        Quebec Act to provide British government for the Loyalists.

THE 19TH CENTURY

1800-1867

European immigration; slow development of an urban labour force; conflict
with the United States and internal debates over future relationships with
the U.S.; reduction of imperial preference benefits and move toward Confederation; beginning of the "railway era."

1812-14 "War of 1812" (invasion of British North America by U.S.
         forces repelled); war concluded by *Treaty of Ghent*. (*Note*: U.S.
         population at this time was about seven and a half million; the
         British North American population was about one-half million.)

1817   Establishment of the Bank of Montreal by the North West
         Company interests.

1817   *Selkirk Treaty* between British Crown and Chippeway and Cree
         Nations provides land adjacent to the Red River to Britain in
         exchange for "quit rent" of annual present of tobacco.

1818   Convention between U.S. and Britain establishes 49th parallel
         as boundary between Canada and the United States from Lake
         of the Woods to the Rocky Mountains.

1821   Merger of the North West Company and the Hudson's Bay
         Company.

1836   Publication of *The Backwoods of Canada* by Catherine Parr
         Trail.

1837   Rebellions in Upper and Lower Canada led by William Lyon
         Mackenzie and Louis Joseph Papineau.

1839   Lord Durham's *Report on the Affairs of British North America*.

1840   *Act of Union* creates the United Province of Canada (pro-
         claimed in force 1841).

1846   "Responsible government" granted to Nova Scotia (imple-
         mented in 1848).

1848-49 British Government establishes free trade, abolishes the
         Navigation Acts through various legislative Acts which reduce
         Canada's benefits from Imperial preference laws.

1849   Publication of the *Annexation Manifesto*, signed by 300 Anglo-
         phone Montrealers, calling for separation from Britain and
         political union with U.S.

1852   Publication of *Roughing It in the Bush* by Susanna Moodie.

1854   *Treaty of Reciprocity* removes tariffs between the United
         Province of Canada and the U.S.

1858   Fraser River Gold Rush begins and the colony of British
         Columbia established.

1859   Completion of the Grand Trunk Railway (Sarnia to Montreal;
         extensions to U.S.).

1867-1900

Confederation; continuing European immigration but also continuing emigration from Canada to U.S.; entry of Manitoba and B.C. to Confederation; construction of a transcontinental railway; beginnings of the trade union movement; introduction of "the National Policy"; and continuing debate on Canada's relationship with Britain and U.S.

1867   Confederation between Ontario, Quebec, New Brunswick and Nova Scotia; *British North America Act, 1867 (BNA Act)* grants control of trade and commerce, taxation, currency, banking, public credit financing, navigation, sea and inland fisheries, Indian lands and Indian governance, immigration, and the criminal law powers to the Federal Government (s. 91); grants direct taxation for provincial purposes, municipal institutions, property and civil rights, and "the Management and Sale of Public Lands Belonging to the Province" to Provincial Governments (s. 92); education to be under provincial jurisdiction, and protection guaranteed for both Roman Catholic schools outside of Quebec and Protestant schools within Quebec (s. 93); English and French to be equal in the Federal Parliament and Quebec Legislature (s. 133).

1867   American Congress expresses deep concern at the founding of a British monarchical state in the north; U.S. purchases Alaska.

1867-72   Conservative government headed by John A. Macdonald; development of policies to consolidate control of the West, settle the Prairies, establish tariff policies and construct railways.

1869-70   The Hudson's Bay Company relinquishes Rupert's Land. Charter and trading monopoly in the Northwest Territories in return for cash and land compensations; territory becomes part of Canada.

1869-70   Red River Rebellion led by Louis Riel.

1870   *Manitoba Act* establishes new province with guarantees for French and English as equal official languages and for denominational schools; Crown lands to be administered by the Federal Government.

1871   B.C. enters Confederation.

1871   *Treaty of Washington* between Britain and U.S. establishes West Coast territorial boundary and agreements regarding fisheries.

1873   Pacific Scandal (over railway contracts) forces resignation of the Conservative government.

1873-78   Liberal government led by Alexander Mackenzie; economy in depression; failure of attempts to re-negotiate *Treaty of Reciprocity* with U.S.

1874-76   Canada First movement (established in 1868) publishes *The Nation*; Goldwin Smith and Edward Blake support the nationalist position; Blake subsequently takes an annexationist (continentalist) position in *Canada and the Canadian Question* (1881).

1876   *Indian Act* enacted (amendments and consolidation of previous Acts respecting Indians).

1878-96 Conservative government led by John A. Macdonald followed by John Abbott, John Thompson, Mackenzie Bowell, and Charles Tupper; formal introduction of the "National Policy"; imposition of tariffs.

1880-81 Contract granted to the Canadian Pacific syndicate for the building of a transcontinental railway; line officially completed in 1885.

1885   Northwest Rebellion (also referred to as the Second Red River Rebellion and the Riel Rebellion).

1886   Founding of the Trades and Labour Congress of Canada (TLC).

1889   Manitoba School Question: issues of separate schools, bilingualism and the teaching of French arise; legislation restricting the use of French in schools later upheld by the Judicial Committee of the Privy Council.

1896-   Liberal government led by Wilfrid Laurier reaches a compro-
1911   mise solution on bilingualism in Manitoba; introduces higher Canadian tariffs in response to rise in U.S. tariffs.

1898-   Yukon Gold Rush.
1903

THE 20TH CENTURY

1900-1939

"Second Industrial Revolution" in Europe and North America involving the development of oil and electricity as industrial fuels, mechanized transport and farm machinery, mass production technologies, rapid urbanization and growth of the urban, industrial labour force; growth of large, international corporations and increasing concentration of industrial wealth; influx of American-owned industries into Canada; organization of agrarian political parties and several socialist parties; rapid growth of trade unions and development of "international" unions with head offices in the U.S., branches in Canada; First World War; economic depression.

1900-12 Economic "boom" and rapid growth of the wheat economy on the Prairies.

1903   Formation of the Socialist Party of Canada (SPC) (merger of earlier groups).

1905   Alberta and Saskatchewan become provinces; Federal Government retains control of resources until 1930.

1908   Publication of *Anne of Green Gables* by Lucy Maud Montgomery.

1911   Founding of the Social-Democratic Party of Canada (SDPC).

1911-17 Conservative government led by Robert Borden.

1912   Publication of *Sunshine Sketches of a Little Town* by Stephen Leacock.

1914-18   First World War.

1916   Manitoba eliminates bilingual schools; Ontario restricts use of French in schools.

1916   Manitoba gives the right to vote to women.

1916-18   "Farmer's Platform" advanced by the Canadian Council of Agriculture (platform includes the right to vote for women, direct democracy, public ownership of utilities and natural resource development, progressive income tax).

1917   Conscription introduced despite resistance in Quebec.

1917-21   Unionist government representing coalition of Conservative and Liberal parties led by Robert Borden and Arthur Meighen.

1917-23   Legislation and arbitration regarding Federal Government takeover of several near-bankrupt railway companies and formation of the publicly owned Canadian National Railway (formally established 1919).

1918   Western affiliates of TLC defeated at National Convention when they oppose conscription and advance the cause of industrial unionism contrary to prevailing principles of "craft" and international unionism; growing conflict within the TLC between western and central Canadian representatives; formation of the "Western Labour Conference."

1918   Quebec legislature debates separation from Canada (no vote recorded).

1918   *Election Act* enfranchises women (becomes law in 1919).

1918   Imposition by Federal Orders-in-Council of compulsory arbitration for industrial disputes; bans on strikes; the Social Democratic Party and the Industrial Workers of the World (and other associations) declared illegal; public use of Russian, Ukrainian and Finnish and several other languages prohibited; penalties established for possession of radical literature.

1918-28   "Social Gospel" movement receives strong support in Prairies from Methodist and other Protestant churches (the movement emerged in Canada during the 1880s and continued throughout the 1930s).

1919   United Farmers of Ontario elected as Provincial Government.

1919   Organization of the "One Big Union" movement by labour representatives in the western provinces.

1919   The Winnipeg General Strike.

1921   Last of the Indian Treaties signed (Treaty II).

1921   Founding of the Communist Party of Canada (re-grouping of socialist parties).

1921   United Farmers of Alberta (founded in 1909) elected as Provincial Government (in power until 1935).

1921   Formation of the Catholic Confederation of Labour in Quebec.

1921-26   Liberal government led by Mackenzie King; Parliament includes 64 members of the Progressive Party (a federation of farmers' unions in the western provinces and Ontario), and first socialist member of the House (J.S. Woodsworth, Winnipeg).

1922 United Farmers of Manitoba elected as Provincial Government.

1923 Imperial Conference establishes principle of independent foreign policy for members of British Empire.

1925 Publication of *Settlers of the Marsh* by Frederick Philip Grove.

1925 Formation of the United Church of Canada.

1926 Balfour Declaration at Imperial Conference describes British Empire as an association of "autonomous communities" equal in status.

1926 Constitutional crisis re: Governor-General's right to refuse dissolution of Parliament; brief government under Arthur Meighen (Conservative).

1926-30 Liberal government led by Mackenzie King.

1927 *Old Age Pensions Act* enacted.

1927 Federal Farm Loan Board established.

1927 Publication of *Jalna* by Mazo de la Roche.

1927 Dominion-Provincial Conference with provinces demanding greater control over resources and trade.

1929 Crash of New York stock market.

1929-39 Economic depression; conditions particularly severe on Prairies and in Atlantic regions (by 1933, the official unemployment rate was 23%).

1930 Publication of *The Fur Trade in Canada: An Introduction to Canadian Economic History* by Harold Adams Innis.

1930-35 Conservative government led by R.B. Bennett.

1931 *Statute of Westminster* gives effect to Balfour resolutions providing for independence of Dominion governments. *BNA Act* to be patriated pending amending formula agreed upon by provinces and Federal Government.

1932 Establishment of work relief camps for single unemployed males under administration of the Department of National Defence.

1932 First of several Acts to establish the Canadian Broadcasting Corporation (completed 1936).

1933 Founding of the Co-operative Commonwealth Federation and publication of the *Regina Manifesto*.

1934 CCF becomes official opposition in Saskatchewan and B.C. provincial legislatures.

1934 Organization of Le Parti National Social Chretien led by Adrien Arcand; development of Swastika Clubs in Ontario; establishment of Canadian Nationalist Party in Manitoba.

1934 First of several Acts to establish the Bank of Canada (completed 1938).

1935 Canadian Wheat Board established.

1935 Election of Social Credit Party in Alberta led by William Aberhart (continues in power until 1971).

1935 R.B. Bennett proclaims "New Deal" reform policies including unemployment insurance, farm credits, minimum hours of work legislation (following the Stevens Commission on Price Spreads recommendation that the Federal Government increase its control of the economy).

1935 Publication of *They Shall Inherit the Earth* by Morley Callaghan.

1935 Regina Riot terminates the "Trek to Ottawa" by unemployed workers from relief camps.

1935-40 Liberal government led by Mackenzie King; Social Credit party takes all Alberta seats; CCF takes 7 seats.

1936 National Harbours Board established.

1936 Supreme Court of Canada rules that much of "New Deal" legislation is unconstitutional, infringing on provincial rights under s. 92 of the *BNA Act*.

1936 Union Nationale Government elected in Quebec (in power until 1939; regained power in 1944 and remained in office until 1960).

1937 Rowell-Sirois Commission appointed to investigate federal-provincial relations and make recommendations.

1937 Quebec government enacts "An Act Respecting Communistic Propaganda" (better known as the "Padlock Law"); this was declared unconstitutional by the Supreme Court of Canada in 1957.

1937-38 Trade agreements between U.S. and Canada; reduction of tariffs.

1938 TLC expels Canadian branches of Committee for Industrial Organization (CIO) unions; split in the labour federation; CIO unions join All Canadian Congress of Labour to form Canadian Congress of Labour (parallel occurrences in U.S.).

1939 Canada declares war on Germany and enters Second World War as an independent nation allied to Britain.

1940-1980

Second World War followed in Canada by economic prosperity; introduction of social welfare legislation; rapid growth of foreign ownership of Canadian industry; rapid technological change including extensive development of computer technology; continental integration of defence establishments; "Quiet Revolution" in Quebec, and growth of separatist movements; development of oil industry in Alberta and Saskatchewan; continuing debate over provincial-federal relations; proportion of women employed for income increases; feminist movement demands reforms; population doubles between 1945 and 1975.

1939-45 Canada engaged in Second World War.

1940 *Unemployment Insurance Act* enacted (requires amendment to *BNA Act*).

1940 Rowell-Sirois Commission Report recommends more federal control of economy and co-responsibility for social welfare measures.

1940	Communist and Fascist parties banned.
1940-57	Liberal government, led by Mackenzie King, then Louis St. Laurent.
1941	*Hyde Park Declaration* provides for increase in U.S. purchases of Canadian war materials and moves toward common defence arrangements.
1941	Publication of *As For Me and My House*, by Sinclair Ross.
1941	Dominion-Provincial Conference at which Rowell-Sirois recommendations are opposed by provinces (led by Ontario).
1942	Plebiscite to free government from pledge not to impose conscription indicates continuing opposition to conscription in Quebec.
1942-45	Eviction of Japanese Canadians from B.C.
1943	Canadian Congress of Labour endorses CCF as "political arm of labour" and CCF becomes the official opposition in Ontario.
1944	CCF government elected in Saskatchewan (in power until 1964).
1944	Limited conscription imposed.
1945	Publication of *Two Solitudes* by Hugh MacLennan.
1946	*Citizenship Act* creates Canadian citizenship; Canadians continue as British subjects but British subjects no longer have automatic citizenship.
1947	Abolition of appeals in civil cases to the Judicial Committee of the Privy Council (appeals in criminal cases had been abolished in 1931); Supreme Court of Canada becomes the Court of final appeal for Canadians.
1947	Publication of *Who Has Seen the Wind* by W.O. Mitchell.
1947	Discovery of oil at Leduc in Alberta.
1949	North Atlantic Treaty Organization (NATO) established.
1949	Asbestos Strike in Quebec.
1949	Newfoundland enters Confederation.
1950-53	Canadian participation in Korean War as member of United Nations force.
1951	Massey Report (Royal Commission on National Development in the Arts, Letters, and Sciences, established in 1949) recommends policies to reduce U.S. cultural influence.
1951	*Old Age Security Act* enacted.
1952	B.C. elects Social Credit government (in power until 1972 and again from 1975-).
1952	Establishment of Atomic Energy Commission of Canada as Crown corporation.
1952	Establishment of St. Lawrence Seaway Authority (Treaty for Joint Development of the Seaway with the United States signed in 1954; earlier agreements had established precedents for joint control).
1953	Opening of Shakespearean Festival at Stratford, Ontario.
1954	Canada becomes member of International Control Commission in Vietnam by decision of the Geneva Conference.

254 IDEOLOGICAL PERSPECTIVES ON CANADA

1956	Pipeline Debate regarding Liberal government financing of U.S.-controlled company to build Trans-Canada pipeline.
1956	Ousting of Communist unions from TLC; merger of union federations to form Canadian Labour Congress (CLC).
1957	North American Air Defence (NORAD) agreements signed.
1957	Establishment of Canada Council to aid universities and the arts.
1957	Royal Commission on Canada's Economic Prospects (better known as "the Gordon Commission") publishes a critique of foreign ownership of Canadian industry.
1957-61	Economic recession accompanied by inflation and rising unemployment rates.
1957-63	Conservative government led by John Diefenbaker.
1958	CCF publishes the *Winnipeg Declaration*.
1959	Publication of *The Apprenticeship of Duddy Kravitz* by Mordecai Richler.
1960s	Sharp decline in the birth rate in Quebec.
1960	Election of Liberal government in Quebec led by Jean Lesage; beginning of "Quiet Revolution" with educational reforms, limitations on influence of the clergy, nationalization of hydro-electric power.
1960	Founding of Rassemblement pour l'independence national (RIN) in Quebec; publication of *Parti pris*.
1960	James M. Minnifee publishes *Peacemaker or Powder-Monkey* (critique of Canadian dependence on the U.S. for defence).
1961	CCF and CLC jointly found New Democratic Party.
1962	Introduction of Medicare in Saskatchewan.
1963	Appointment of Royal Commission on Bilingualism and Biculturalism; first Report published in 1965; recommendations for increased use of French and employment opportunities for French-Canadians.
1963-79	Liberal government led by Lester B. Pearson, then by Pierre E. Trudeau.
1964	Publication of *The Stone Angel* by Margaret Laurence.
1964	Columbia River Agreement signed by Canada and U.S.
1965	Heeney-Merchant Report, *Canada and the United States, Principles for Partnership* (joint report by two federal governments).
1965	*Canada Pensions Act* enacted.
1966	Publication of *A Choice for Canada* by Walter Gordon.
1966-70	Union Nationale government in Quebec.
1968	Publication of the Report of the Task Force on the Structure of Canadian Industry, *Foreign Ownership and the Structure of Canadian Industry*.
1968	Establishment of National Museum of Canada.
1968	St. Leonard school crisis in Quebec over Bill 63 (language rights).
1969	"Waffle Manifesto" debate at National Convention of NDP.
1969	Establishment of Canadian Film Development Corporation.

1969	Formation of Parti Quebecois in Quebec.
1970	"FLQ Crisis" in Quebec; imposition of *War Measures Act* by Federal Government.
1970	Publication of the *Report of the Royal Commission on the Status of Women* recommending extensive economic and social reforms. (*Note:* By 1970, women comprised over 33% of the labour force and 50% of all adult women were employed for income.)
1970	Publication of *The Edible Woman* by Margaret Atwood; and *Fifth Business* by Robertson Davies.
1970-76	Liberal government in Quebec; new language bill (Bill 22).
1971	Conservative government elected in Alberta led by Peter Lougheed.
1973	Canada recognizes China and begins to develop new foreign policies.
1974	"Oil Crisis": cost of oil imports rises, and conflict increases between oil-producing regions of Canada and Federal Government over prices and royalties.
1976	Parti Quebecois elected in Quebec.
1977	*Charter of the French Language Bill* passed in Quebec.
1979	Conservative government led by Joe Clark.
1980	Liberal government led by Pierre Trudeau.
1980	Defeat of the Referendum on Sovereignty Association in Quebec.
1980	Federal-Provincial Premiers Conference concludes with no agreement on amending formula for *BNA Act*; continuing conflict over division of powers and other constitutional proposals by Federal Government.
1983	Social Credit government re-elected in British Columbia on a "restraint" platform; Solidarity Coalition sponsors public demonstrations in Vancouver.
1984	Conservative government elected federally, under Brian Mulroney. Government initiates bilateral trade negotiations with the United States government.

INDEX